THE RISE
OF THE GUARDIANS

THE RISE OF THE GUARDIANS

A CLARION CALL TO THE CHURCH IN GREAT BRITAIN

JOHN MASTERS

tell the truth publishing

First published in Great Britain
In 2012 by TTT Publishing

Tell The Truth Publishing
www.tttp.co.uk

A CIP catalogue record of this book
is available from the British Library

ISBN 978-0-9571561-0-4

Printed in Great Britain by
CPI Group (UK) Ltd, Croydon, CRO 4YY

The Rise of the Guardians

'So rise my brother, Rise with me,
And today we shall change the course and path,
Not just for ourselves,
But for many more, And many yet to come.
And shake the earth,
And strike the ground with ensign in our hands,
And send a tremor to the enemy camp,
And tell them we shall come,
And with sword and blood,
And heavenly fire,
Shall drive them into Hell itself.'

CONTENTS

Foreword

Man in the 21st Century has declared himself enlightened and no longer in need of God. His agenda is the satisfaction of self at whatever cost. But this so-called enlightened man, enlightened through education and science is no different from his forebears.

We have abandoned the gold standard of the King James Bible which underpinned the Judeo-Christian heritage of this once Great Britain, and replaced it with a secular emptiness which satisfies only those who are looking for favour from man and who suffer from consciences so seared they think they can offend God with impunity.

John Masters, my dear friend and brother in the Lord, has written a book for our time. This call to action is made with passion and anointing. While it would be wrong to call the book inspired in the same way the Holy Scriptures are inspired, I have little doubt it was written under the anointing of God.

My brothers and sisters I commend this book to you. Its message is challenging and timely. Be honest with yourselves before the Throne of Grace for you cannot hide the truth from God. Is this book speaking to you as it speaks to me? Are you willing to pay the price?

The heart of God calling us to return as a nation to righteousness in Christ, to a fear of the Lord, and to godly living and legislation can be seen on every page. This is not a book to condemn but to inspire the Children of God to action. Judgment has to begin at the House of God; it cannot begin anywhere else. The Church must come under judgment. However the purpose is not to condemn but to bring repentance and a return to full fellowship with our Lord and Creator.

Child of God stand up for Truth and for Righteousness. May God bless you and lead you all by His Spirit into all Truth. May he urge you and encourage you to stand firm as a Guardian of Truth in these times.

Col. John Campbell
Hythe, Kent

Introduction

I wish to say at the beginning of this book that although I have written this volume especially to my own beloved nation of England and indeed the whole of Great Britain, I hope very much that wherever you are in the world and whatever your race and family, that you will take the message to heart for your own people, and you will respond to the call of God upon your life for your own country and its future.

I would hope that you will take the time and be diligent enough to look up all of the Bible references and underline them, especially when they speak to you. I use the King James Authorized Version and therefore it would be wise to use the same when checking as other versions may not say the same thing.

Above all it is my prayer that the message of this book will go forth as a trumpet call to arouse both the sleeping Warriors and the true Guardians in every nation upon earth.

> "Down the centuries the Church has had to endure many steep and rugged pathways. But the promise is that with God as our guide we may have the strength to live our lives courageously. May The Lord's blessing be with you as you embark on the deliberations before you."
>
> Her Majesty Queen Elizabeth II

From Her Majesty's speech to the General Synod 2009

TROUBLE IN THE KINGDOM

Chapter One

Trouble In The Kingdom

OUR LAND IS FULL OF ENEMIES. That is, enemies of the Gospel and the kingdom of light, because we have forsaken God and his holy Word. Anarchy and rebellion lie just around the corner and a disgruntled unrest is stirring throughout the country.

Foreign religions march in our streets of liberty demanding that their cruel and outrageous laws become the rule of this nation. It feels like our cities have become cauldrons of conspiracy and hatred toward the indigenous Anglo-Saxon race that dwell within these shores. We are no longer allowed to express our own views or personal faith for fear of being arrested and charged with being intolerant or 'likely to cause an offence'.

We see the numbers of foreigners from all over the world crossing our borders growing by the day and more concerning than that is the number of children being born to those already here. Is it a crime to speak the truth? Do I not say just what the great majority actually think?

It is a despicable lie to suggest that we are a prejudiced people. We have extended the arm of friendship to folk from all over the world and offered shelter and sanctuary to multitudes of oppressed and persecuted families from every kingdom on the planet. The Christian ethos of this nation is both welcoming, generous, kind and benevolent, and extends friendship and compassion to those in need. It is this essence of the Gospel that has woven such unique and kind expressions of acceptance within our country.

As the Queen said to her bishops just a few years ago *"When so much is in flux... there is a renewed hunger for that which endures and gives meaning. The Christian Church can speak uniquely to that need for at the heart of our faith stands the conviction that all people irrespective of race background or circumstances can find lasting significance and purpose in the Gospel of Jesus Christ."*

I do wish she would speak more often of her convictions and faith in Christ.

Too many of us who have been silent for so long. The only real prejudice we can see is that which is vented towards us from some of the very people we granted consolation and safety to. Every day we as a people are spat upon and despised by the marauding antagonists and we in our sometimes stupid excess of tolerance and kindness walk on the other side of the road and let them mock at us. The English have always said 'sorry' when somebody else trod on their toes or knocked into them in the supermarket. This cultural attitude of decency has been taken advantage of and it is this type of generosity of spirit that allows the bullies to behave as they do. Perhaps it is time to take stock of where we are and time to begin to stand up to the belligerent protester's demands.

Schools are forced to teach our children what Christians would call false religions and many teachers are obliged to keep their mouths shut about their own faith or face losing their jobs and even going to prison. Religious bigots from other nations are on our streets trumping their cruel beliefs in many of our towns and cities but it seems that Christians are forbidden to publicly declare their faith for fear of upsetting anyone of a different mindset.

We as a nation offered a welcome to all those who wished to come and abide under our umbrella of prosperity, free education, free healthcare and freedom of speech. That covering was a canopy of grace and kindness; of mercy and compassion. It was also the sanctuary of our national faith **Protestant Christianity**.

The history and Constitution of this country is Christian through and through and it is the reflection of the teaching of this great faith that makes us the over tolerant and welcoming people we are. It is indeed this glorious faith that is the real 'great' in Great Britain.

The Queen as Head of State is Defender of the Faith.
What faith? *The historical and 'cultural' faith of this nation*: the Protestant Reformed Christian faith as taught in the Bible. *Fact.*
We are a Christian nation by Law. *Fact.*

Look at the solemn words from the Coronation Oath sworn by the Monarch:

Archbishop to the Queen:

"Will you to the utmost of your power maintain the Laws of God and the true profession of the Gospel? Will you to the utmost of your power maintain in the United Kingdom the Protestant Reformed Religion established by law? Will you maintain and preserve inviolably the settlement of the Church of England and the doctrine,

worship, discipline and government thereof as by law established in England? And will you preserve unto the Bishops and Clergy of England and to the Churches there committed to their charge all such rights and privileges as by law do or shall appertain to them or any of them?"

The Queen responds: "All this I promise to do."

But now we are abused beyond all measure and our freedoms and benefits are being trampled on as though they were nothing. Aliens (that is aliens to this nation historically) living amongst us now vent their hatred at all the things that made us and this country what it is today. They complain about everything that does not fit in with their own devious aims. They wish to destroy our culture our history and our future freedoms all in the name of their 'gods' and personal ambitions.

Every Englishman knows that what I am saying here is true but he may fear to say it lest somebody report him and land him in trouble. But why is this? Others can march in our capital with placards telling the British police to 'Go to Hell' whilst even more threaten on their homemade banners to 'Kill all the enemies' of their brand of religion.

There are actually many people from other nations with their own personal beliefs dwelling here who love this country and who also would concur strongly with what I am saying. They cannot understand why the Anglo-Saxons do not fight back for what is truly their history and their dignity. They came here to get away from the troubles in their own countries only to find that the mobs of religious extremists, drug-dealers, terrorists, prostitution racketeers, thieves, murderers, scammers and tyrants all followed them to the same town and even to the same street.

Our voices are being stifled and silenced by the ever increasing demons of *'multiculturalism' 'political correctness'* and *'human rights'*. This triangulation of wickedness seeks to suppress and eventually extinguish the voice of reason and common-sense.

Have you not noticed how we have become less and less able to make our voices heard in our own country? This is more than a coincidence. This is the nature of the war that is within our borders. The devil wants us silenced once and forever.

It appears that 'Freedom of Speech' is no longer a right for those who name the name of Christ in this place. However it is a liberty that was once ours many years ago and should be so today.

Alien religions now demand that their voice and theirs alone be heard whilst the Christians are forced to sit back silently doing little more than nothing. It is time to take back what the devil has stolen from us, to set the matter right, and bring equality and fairness back to our people.

I might point out that whenever there is personal or national opposition and trouble, it usually comes in a group of three. A trinity of evil seeks to use this Biblical principle of strength ('a threefold cord is not quickly broken', Ecclesiastes 4:12) in its efforts to secure dominance.

For instance the spirit of 'self-pity' (victimisation) will usually show itself strong by uniting with 'self-righteousness' ("I've done nothing wrong") and the spirit of 'accusation'. These are common bed-fellows and can be observed together more often than any other combination of evil powers. They are particularly vile once working in agreement as they offer no hope or place of reconciliation for estranged parties. You can observe this phenomenon in personal and domestic conflict as well as in national opposition. They say that trouble always comes in threes and I believe there is indeed a deep spiritual significance behind this. I will mention some of these evil triplets further on in this book.

Throughout this great country, principalities and powers and the rulers of the darkness of this world are waging a battle twenty-four hours a day against the people of God and against the freedoms that Christianity brought to this little Island.

Our own young people are out drinking every night ending up senseless and often violent because they have no cause to fight and have no real freedom anymore which rightly belongs to them long before it does to any outsider.

We are a fighting people and we need a good quarrel sometimes to get rid of the frustration of being locked up and imprisoned in our own homes and country by our own government and its ridiculous habit of bowing to alien demands. We are a warrior people and that is why we are known today for our 'football hooligans'.

You can only suppress and antagonise such a people so far before they will rise up and begin to rebel. Foreigners seem to get all the privileges long before we are ever awarded them and this naturally provokes a huge sense of injustice and resentment amongst the indigenous population. Why the government cannot see and recognise this frustration is enough to baffle any sensible person. It is almost like the leaders themselves wish for our demise.

100,000 children go missing every year in the UK; our young women are targeted by foreigners seeking to lure them into the sex-trade and abuse them until they die. The cess-pit of pornography and perversion seems to grow deeper by the day and there seems to be less and less moral restraint and protection afforded to our children and teenagers.

The media mesmerize the masses with whatever they see fit or whatever the government sees fit and our young people are issued plastic controllers for their pretend gaming lives to make sure they never use their creativity and amazing abilities to become 'great' themselves again.

The church seems quite irrelevant and is so involved in itself, its own avarice and greed and plans to get a better house or better job that it has lost sight of its real objective. It has lost the whole 'art' of communication and knows neither how to speak with God nor how to talk with men. It would rather go swanning off to some stupid conference at the cost of thousands of pounds than spend the same money on helping a lonely or poor neighbour out of their debt. Now which of these two alternatives do you suppose that God would prefer?

In fact it would be true to say that the church (and I mean the people and the 'performers') is so wrapped up in its own selfish ambitions and pride that it does not even hear the crying and pleading needs of society all around it. Nearly every conference is about 'increase', personal blessing, extra wealth, ambition and success.

When did you last go to a conference that spoke of giving to the poor (as opposed to giving to the preacher) or of personal evangelism, opening our homes to the less fortunate, reaching our children for Christ, spending on our young people to win their hearts? If there was such a meeting then I can virtually guarantee that there were less than thirty people in attendance. Many 'Christians' live in a false pretentious environment. They actually believe that they are alright, that nothing bad will happen to them and they are going to Heaven when they die. They do not however have any appetite for the place just now but would rather enjoy everything they can squeeze out of this world whilst they are alive. Their eyes are on what they can achieve buy, sell, and entertain themselves with.

When did your church last address the needs of the poor in their town? When did your fellowship last make a plan to reach the thousands of young people sprawling around the pubs (bars) and clubs of your city? When did you all sit down and talk about how we can help those around us who are lonely, in debt, homeless, jobless, without support? I know you are happy to talk about those in your own circle within the church but what about those that are outside?

One thing that I have noticed on my travels in India is that the poor help the poor but the rich generally do not. They help only themselves. It is just the same here.

When did your church last have a giving day for the struggling mums and dads who live next door to them? I know you had a collection for the new building, the new seats, or the new PA system but these things do not mean anything to those outside and that is where the good news should first of all go. Perhaps if we did those things that were more needful then the other things would come along in their appropriate time if at all necessary.

The pastor does not need a brand-new Mercedes. Driving a nice expensive car does not make you any better than the shop-thief or the delinquent. Anyway it will probably swell your head and make you think that you are more important than anybody else on the road. The building is not as important as the lives around you. A building can save nobody. Millions spent on bricks and mortar would be better invested in the propagation of evangelistic materials or the distribution of the Bible or just helping the poor and the underprivileged. The Gospel will save the worst and transform them into a saint but the Gospel is not your church and not your denomination. Both of those are man-made. The Gospel is the power of God and belongs to no-one. It is free to whoever believes and it is free to give away.

There is a growing unrest and tension in this country that cannot be ignored or settled. There are confrontations that are getting bolder and more aggressive in their nature. To many it feels like Eastern Europe has flooded our towns and centres of employment and the rest of the world seem to be creating no-go ghettos in our cities. Everyone but our leaders can see it and it will not be long before the seething pot boils and overflows. Then they will say, "Oh dear how could this have happened? Please be calm everyone."

It is a bit like the 'binge' drinking that has become a plague amongst the young adults of this land (particularly the whites). Government officials now moan and groan about this huge and destructive problem that afflicts the youth but fail to acknowledge that it was them who opened the drinking houses for 24 hour drunkenness. They were the ones who gave the licence and then complained when it got out of hand and went wrong. The same thing is happening with immigration and their pandering to the noisy European 'human rights' activists and the radical extremists of unfamiliar religions.

'Charity begins at home' is a well known saying that is actually a truth that the Bible teaches.

'Is not this the fast that I have chosen? to loose the bands of wickedness, to undo the heavy burdens, and to let the oppressed go free and that ye break every yoke? Is it not to deal thy bread to the hungry and that thou bring the poor that are cast out to thy house? When thou seest the naked that thou cover him; and that thou hide not thyself from thine own flesh *[you do not ignore the needs of your own people]*?' Isaiah 58:6-7.

These verses from Isaiah speak to the Jewish nation about their responsibility to their own people. It is alright sending money abroad and giving billions of pounds to help out ailing countries but if we neglect the care and support of our own people then we are worse than uncivilized savages. Even animals know to look after their own before running around for everyone else. **It is time for this government to put the needs of the indigenous people and their historic faith back at the top of the list in this nation.**

We are quite happy to help and support and feed those who come here legitimately for their good and safety but if we crush our own people at the expense of 'political correctness' (which is hardly ever correct) then we do ourselves much mischief and harm. Our poor are always among us.

'For the poor shall never cease out of the land: therefore I command thee saying, Thou shalt open thine hand wide unto thy brother [speaking of a race] to thy poor and to thy needy in thy land.' Deuteronomy 15:11. That is *Thy* brother, *Thy* poor, *Thy* needy, in *Thy* land. We should all help all the poor but make sure that we take care of our own poor first. It is downright hypocrisy to go flying off round the world helping every Tom Dick and Harry with their distresses when we utterly disregard the pain and trouble our own family is suffering at home.

It is immoral to give hand-outs and preferential treatment to those from other countries living here and treat our own people with contempt or as second-class citizens. All these other races stand by their own and would sooner let a hundred of us die than see their own kin short of bread. Why? Because they are 'family' and as a family they will look after their own before attending anyone else. So why do we not look after our own people in such a way? There is always enough kindness and charity to go round everyone so why despise our own family?

"One ought to be just [do what is right] before one is generous." (Winston Churchill) British Christians sending their millions of pounds every year to American 'televangelists' might consider that their own country needs Christ first and needs to hear the Gospel.

There are enough good men here to preach the word and win this nation but they cannot afford to go because they get no financial support.

All the money is flying off to buy some new jet-plane or television station or silk suit for the 'name it-claim-it' preacher. It is exactly the same now in India. It is time for the believers in this country to get some concern for the dying of their own land and stop paying for the silicon implants to make their television 'heroes' or 'heroines' look younger than they really are.

Keep your tithes and gifts in a special account somewhere and ask God for wisdom to put it to 'New Testament' use. You will be blessed and so will the people whom you give it to and the difference is this: **you will see where it goes and what it accomplishes** and that will bring joy to your life and a desire to do even more.

You can plan your own evangelistic 'outreach' or perhaps sponsor some evangelists here or in India to become full-time preachers. I would rather invest in a man than a building. The New Testament does not teach that you should bring ten percent of your income and dump it in an offering dustbin on Sunday. It teaches that we should give liberally out of the great love we have for Jesus Christ and make sure that it is doing the work of God and not being buried where no-one can see it anymore.

Giving in the New Testament is not limited to the 10% that the preacher screams for. There is no account or level of giving imposed or enforced on anyone. It just says 'Give, and it shall be given unto you; good measure, pressed down and shaken together and running over, shall men give into your bosom. For with the same measure that ye mete [in the same way you give] withal it shall be measured to you again.' Luke 6:38

All the hocus-pocus nonsense of preachers lying to you that you will go to Hell if you do not give your tithe to them needs to come to an end and those rogue preachers brought to justice. It is right to support your local church and make sure that your senior leader and his family are secure financially but to keep on throwing money at something just because you are in fear of a curse or damnation is absolutely wrong. There is no fear in love. (1John 4:18) Giving is a 'free-will' thing. To what or who we give is a 'moral' decision. When someone tells you that you will suffer or come to poverty if you do not send money to their 'ministry' then be certain that is the place never to send anything. God does not put a gun to your head. Neither does he tell you to keep feeding the greedy selfish and over-fed preacher with your hard-earned cash.

You will understand that I am speaking more about the begging television evangelists and the charismatic and African churches than I am the Church of England. I think that the latter would be hard pressed to keep a new coat of paint on their front doors at present and they need all the help they can get.

But look sensibly for the areas of need (make sure that the men who teach sound doctrine are fed and blessed: 1Timothy 5:17), and purchase some Gospel seed and go plant some heavenly harvest. You will come rejoicing bringing in the sheaves. 'He that goeth forth and weepeth bearing precious seed, shall doubtless come again with rejoicing, bringing his sheaves with him.' Psalm 126:6

'For as many as were possessors of lands or houses sold them and brought the prices of the things that were sold and laid them down at the apostles' feet: and distribution was made unto every man according as he had need.' Acts 4:34-35.

Notice that it was not buried in secretive bank accounts or placed in building funds nor turned into luxury items and houses for the platform speaker. It was distributed amongst the needy 'family'. The apostles did not open savings accounts nor send it to their home countries for their next personal investment or building another mansion. It was completely transparent and the account was visible to absolutely everyone.

The apostles were not in love with money. They worked with their own hands for their requirements. They would sooner give than receive. What a difference to the financial dealings of 'ministries' today! Who on the television could you possibly trust to do right with your money in a New Testament context? We are not told to bring our assets and wealth and lay them at the feet of the self-titled, self-elevated, so-called 'apostles' for their new jet or limousine or unnecessary 'head-office'.

By every means support your local church especially where the vision and goal is to reach the area with the Gospel but if the money is just to be lost in a bag which never opens to the poor and needy in the family then think again.

England needs Christ!

So why are we not doing something about it? Get your money back, think long and hard before you go bury your fortune in some denominational bottomless bucket and make sure that you know where every penny goes after handing it over. You have a responsibility to invest wisely and with all due diligence. (Matthew 25:14-28)

Alternatively begin your own mission; get a plan and do something with your life, your talents and your increase which can change lives and maybe even change a nation.

Perhaps if you give a small fortune to the 'big-name' evangelist they may just welcome you into their special 'family' or invite you to sit on the stage with the other very important guests (and I have seen plenty of that going on) but this means nothing. It is just pride. If you do it for that reason then your giving is corrupt and unacceptable by God. If the 'preacher' shows you respect and an audience only because you gave so well then he is wrong and his heart is wicked before God (James 2:1-5).

In some churches the congregation superstitiously obey every word of the platform 'performer' and re-mortgage their homes, give up their savings, and may even be persuaded to sell their souls to get a better chance at becoming successful and rich. And they do this simply because the preacher orders them to because they need to buy a bigger building.

The famous C.T. Studd inherited a family fortune after his father died and he was actually serving God as a missionary in China at that time. He had very little funding, was without any savings and was supporting a number of other missionaries and their families out in the field. Read his story if you can be bothered and see what sort of heart the 'real' missionaries had. He did not put a penny or pound of it into his own account but immediately gave it all away to various evangelistic agencies including George Muller for his work amongst Bristol's orphans and The Salvation Army for their pioneering work in India.

Can you imagine one of our silk-suited preachers doing something like that today? Fame fortune and fantasy (a cocky evil trio) are the driving forces behind so many men and women in 'ministry' today. A new car or house might be the first item on the agenda for many of them if they were to receive such a benefit.

You do not need a fortune however to do something worthwhile and of eternal value. A bit of love and care for your neighbour, a helping hand, an electricity bill paid or some groceries bought might be the very bridge that you can build to win the poor family to Christ (oh but of course there is not much enthusiasm to win the poor as we would rather go for the middle-class and keep the church's appearances 'respectable' and the income level good). Actually from my many years of observation I have noticed that the poor are far more likely to be generous and faithful than the rich.

It is no wonder that among our own people there is a huge resentment and antagonism towards the church. They see the nicely dressed folk going and singing their little songs whilst the population around them are battling with mounting troubles and trials but with no one to help.

The anarchists scream their hatred at anything authoritative and the general population dismiss the church as being of no relevance and no earthly good to anybody except the old and infirm. We as a nation have rejected God's ways and sought to live without him trying to fill the vacuum with materialism, secularism and intellectualism. This artificial 'trinity' of deceit has built a stronghold of unbelief and defiance within the heart of the nation and magnetized the population into its empty lie.

Such a tower of rebellion against God can only be brought down when the Guardians arise and fulfil their Heaven-ordained commission.

If you are rich then why not come and build or rent for us a 'real' Bible College (or two) for raising a new generation of preachers and evangelists either here in England or over in India where there is a ripe harvest-field waiting for labourers to be trained? If we teach them truth and sound doctrine then they will be able to teach others also.

'And the things that thou hast heard of me among many witnesses, the same commit thou to faithful men, who shall be able to teach others also.' 2Timothy 2:2

Lamentations speaks so clearly into our situation at this current time: 'Our inheritance is turned to [handed to, taken by] strangers [other nations], our houses to aliens [foreigners]. We are orphans and fatherless [without those strong, wise, and caring enough to guide and protect us], our mothers are as widows [defenceless and subject to the marauding cruel enemies of unrighteousness amongst us]. We have drunken our water for money [even that which should be simple and free to us as a people we have to pay for now]; our wood is sold unto us [that which we once had by right, our freedoms and liberties are now only available to those who marched in and never earned them]. Our necks are under persecution [we are a people pressed and crushed by others who sneer and snort at us]: we labour [work every hour, day and night just to pay the bills], and have no rest. We have given the hand to the Egyptians and to the Assyrians [we find ourselves bowing and scraping to foreigners and their wretched demands] to be satisfied [just to feed ourselves] with bread. Our fathers have sinned and are not [are dead]; and we have borne [carried the consequences of] their iniquities. Servants [those who had no right, or authority, or licence here] have ruled over us: there is none that doth deliver us out of their hand.'

So let us pray with all our hearts just as Jeremiah prayed, **'Turn thou us unto thee, O LORD, and we shall be turned; renew our days as of old.'** Lamentations 5:1-21

THE STRANGE WONDER

Chapter Two

The Strange Wonder

'Behold [look and deeply consider] ye despisers and wonder [be astonished, amazed] and perish [clear-off, go away, vanish]: for I work a work in your days, a work which ye shall in no wise believe, though a man declare [tell] it unto you.' Acts 13:41

Here is a strange wonder, that a soul such as I can still hold distinct favour with the Most High. I say *strange* because those who cannot perceive the love of God in its breadth and length and cannot comprehend with all the saints just how awesome and unfathomable that love is will find it hard to understand how one who was an apparent failure now seems to bask in the sunshine of God's favour. It angers my enemies, frustrates those who hate me, puzzles the 'religious' and pretenders and confuses those that can do no more than point the finger in accusation.

God is the God of the impossible. When men say it cannot be done, when logic declares it inconceivable, when the devil and his minions write it off, then the Almighty God of mercy and grace delivers a flood of miraculous goodness and loving-kindness. He laughs at the frustration of those who cannot figure out or perceive his eternal love towards this treasure of his. He bought this object of his desire with an inconceivable and incomprehensible price and he is not for letting it go or allowing his enemy the joy of rejoicing over what men see as a defeat.

'Many there be which say of my soul, 'There is no help for him in God.'

'But Thou, O LORD, art a shield [defence] for me: my glory [honour that makes honourable] and the lifter up [the exalter] of mine head.' Psalm 3:2-3

'Surely, shall one say, in the LORD have I righteousness and strength: even to him shall men come; and all that are incensed against him shall be ashamed.' Isaiah 45:24

Surely, shall I say, 'In the LORD have I righteousness and strength: even to me shall men come; and all that are incensed [furious, angry, displeased and making accusations] *against me shall be ashamed* [confounded and confused].' (Isaiah 54:17; Isaiah 61:10; 2Corinthians 5:21)

Furthermore God is going to restore the foundations of many generations in this great country of ours. He is going to restore the 'walls of Jerusalem' here and establish his chosen ones back to favour and righteousness. 'Christians' from all over the world have written us off as though we were beyond recovery but just watch and see what God is going to do! (Isaiah 58:12; Psalm 51:18; Joel 2:32).

'And I will strengthen them in the LORD; *and they shall walk up and down in his name,* saith the LORD.' Zechariah 10:12

'And they shall build the old wastes, they shall raise up the former desolations, and they shall repair the waste cities, the desolations of many generations.' Isaiah 61:4

'And they shall be as though I had not cast them off: for I am the LORD their God, and will hear them.' Zechariah 10:6

We have a great English anthem that says:

And did those feet in ancient time
Walk upon England's mountain green?
And was the holy Lamb of God
On England's pleasant pastures seen?

And did the countenance divine
Shine forth upon our clouded hills?
And was Jerusalem builded here
Among those dark satanic mills?

Bring me my bow of burning gold!
Bring me my arrows of desire!
Bring me my spear! O clouds, unfold!
Bring me my chariot of fire!

I will not cease from mental fight,
Nor shall my sword sleep in my hand,
Till we have built Jerusalem
In England's green and pleasant land.

Who else has such a magnificent hymn with such deep implications?

And before anyone suggests that there was no 'spiritual' interpretation intended in these words just consider what the poet Blake inscribed beneath these words he penned: 'Would to God that all the Lord's people were Prophets.' Numbers 11:29. I love this nation and so does God. He has not given up on us!

Another strange wonder: **He entrusted us with the Divine Oracle, his Holy Word, to take it to the entire world,**

and subsequently thousands of missionaries left their homes and their loved ones for the sake of the 'lost' in distant lands. Some returned and some did not but all of them threw worldly care to the wind and went and stormed the powers of darkness with the Gospel of light. How amazing is that?

This sheds a whole new understanding on the verse that follows: 'Open ye the gates, [so] that the righteous nation [people, guardians] which keepeth [who have the solemn charge to guard, protect and keep] the truth may enter in.' Isaiah 26:2. That objective 'pioneering' spirit that so identified the believers in days gone-by has been forgotten and replaced by a subjective spirit of self-gratification and self-absorption (bless me, make me rich, make me successful, heal me, help me, forgive me).

It is time for the pioneer spirit to be resurrected once again. It is time for the gates to be opened once more which have been shut in our faces for far too long. It is time for those who know the truth and are given the task of holding the truth in its purity, doctrine, and honour, to come again with the word of power to this nation.

The Bible is the most feared of all things upon earth by our enemies. It is the Sword of the Spirit and when wielded in the hands of God's people who understand doctrine it has the power to break every threat against us and chase out every evil principality and power from our coasts. The expertise of wielding the Sword is not in how loudly or dramatically you can swing it but in the knowledge of **sound doctrine** (something these days which is dismissed or belittled by the 'stars' of 'Christian' television).

'For the time will come [**has come**] when they will not endure [not accept] sound doctrine; but after their own lusts shall they heap to themselves teachers [who will tell them sweet things to please their carnal natures], having itching ears.' 2Timothy 4:3 (Titus 1:9; Titus 2:1; 1Timothy 4:16)

'If any man will do his will, he shall know of the doctrine, whether it be of God, or whether I speak of myself.' John 7:17

It is because of this Sword that God has blessed us like no other nation upon earth.

Just take the time to research our long and glorious history and see the marvelous hand of God keeping protecting and increasing us. We have been a blessing throughout the whole earth and in spite of all the haters and loathers of our blood this nation is a great nation.

To cite an example: When the pope paid the king of Spain with bags of gold to invade our nation with his Inquisitors (torturers and murderers] and soldiers in 1588 to murder Queen Elizabeth I and place a Roman Catholic tyrant upon the throne of England, Queen Elizabeth (a great Christian believer) called the whole country to pray for God's help.

God answered their prayer and sent an extraordinarily strong wind (recorded as a hurricane) and blew the Spanish Armada completely off course allowing us to overcome them and scuttle them. The Queen, in thanks to God minted a medal immediately afterwards (one of which is in the National Maritime Museum) and had these words inscribed upon it: 'He (יהוה) blew with his winds and they were scattered'. Another coin showed the English on their knees praying for God's intervention.

In April 2011 the Deputy Prime Minister Nick Clegg (leader of the Liberal Democrats) did his utmost to try and overthrow the law that forbids our monarch from marrying a Roman Catholic. Our freedom from Rome was bought at a dreadful price in previous centuries (you can learn the history in Foxes Book of Martyrs) and here is a man who would eagerly have undone all that was achieved and turn this nation from Protestant Christian to Roman Catholic if he could. His wife is Spanish and a practising Roman Catholic. He claims to be an atheist but he has vowed to bring his children up as Catholics.

It is amazing really that at a time of severe economic decline and unemployment and other serious social challenges, several wars in which the country finds itself involved that this man would make such a concentrated effort during his first months in office to undo a law dating back to 1701 that protects us from Rome. I sense that there were very dark and sinister powers behind him encouraging him in his most privileged position.

We do not fight against flesh and blood. If you have no idea why this is such an important issue then research our history a little and you might be surprised at what has been covered up and forgotten. '**My people are destroyed** [silenced, perishing] for lack of knowledge [because they do not know the truth].' Hosea 4:6b

When we found ourselves in dire conflict with Germany and Hitler's Nazis our Prime Minister Winston Churchill again and again sought urgent and desperately needed help from America (our daughter nation). The USA was quite unwilling to come to our aid (unless it was to supply us with bank loans and equipment on lease) even though our situation was dreadfully hopeless. That is, until the Japanese suddenly and without provocation attacked Pearl Harbour. America immediately declared themselves at war alongside us and came to the fight. God knows how to answer our prayers.

We are still a threat to all those who hate peace and justice and still a main target of all those who despise the Son of God. To this day we are a prime objective of the RC Church and oh, how the pontificator in the Vatican would just love to rule Great Britain if he could.

The blood spilt by countless Christian martyrs stain the earth throughout this land and the prayers of multitudes of saints from former generations still plead before God's throne on our behalf.

We do not need to argue with other religions whatever they may be but simply and 'earnestly contend for the faith which was once delivered to the saints' (Jude 1:3), and spread the Word of God throughout the land.

'For I am not ashamed of the gospel of Christ: **for it is the power of God unto salvation** to every one that believeth; to the Jew first, and also to the Greek [all those outside of Israel].' Romans 1:16

The Bible was never meant to be kept locked up in the church or kept on the bookshelf in the believer's houses. It is to be set free and sown liberally as the seed of life in every town and city and wherever men may live. The printed page is still the most powerful means of communication that we have at our disposal. Never despise the value of a simple Gospel tract which preaches the truth of the Word.

This country is built upon the Word of God, both our Constitution, our laws, our welfare state, our education system and the crowning and Coronation of every King or Queen over the centuries who sat upon the throne of England.

I was delighted to read of our Prime Minister's words this week when he stated that Britain should be "proud to be a Christian country". (Daily Telegraph)

Every monarch is anointed with holy oil at their Coronation upon the very same ancient stone that Jacob rested his head on when he saw the angels ascending and descending from Heaven and upon which King David of the Bible himself was anointed. It is a most solemn and holy gathering before God.

Look up on Google and see the old footage of the Queen's Coronation in 1953 and take good note of the words, the reverence and the symbolism of every part of the ceremony. Listen to the awesome and moving Coronation anthem 'Zadok the Priest', written by Handel at the request of King George 1 for his son's ascension to the throne.

> *'Zadok the priest and Nathan the Prophet,*
> *Anointed Solomon, King.*
> *And all the people rejoiced.*
> *And all the people (Alleluia) rejoiced, and said*
> *God save the King!*
> *Long Live the King!*
> *God Save the King!*
> *May the king live forever,*
> *Alleluia, Alleluia, Amen.*
> *Amen, Amen, Amen, Alleluia Amen.'*

It is time to revive our history and re-discover who we are in God. We are a people who need to find our identity again. There is more to us than meets the eye.

The devil has lied to us and through the satanic media and ungodly Members of Parliament (including some recent Prime Ministers) he has buried our true identity under the demonic deception of 'political correctness'.

May the scales fall from our eyes so that we may see again what it is that God has called us to be. Let us dig the old wells and bring the water of truth and enlightenment to our people once more. Let our enemies be very scared as light and the truth are sent from Heaven to earth. (Psalm 43:3). Let the name of Jesus Christ God's only Begotten Son be exalted throughout this great nation!

I visited the home of a Muslim yesterday and noticed that there was a sticker over the door saying: 'The name of Allah be praised'. Inside his house was no end of pictures of Mecca, Mosques and Arabic writings praising their prophet.

When calling on 'Christian' homes the first thing one might notice is the television, the worldly music, or just the absence of anything that might suggest that they have any faith whatsoever. Surely we should not be embarrassed of the name of our Redeemer and Saviour? Should we not take every opportunity and occasion to lift his name up before everyone who enters our house? We ought to carry His name wherever we go and be seeking to promote his praise throughout our society.

It is time for the Word of God which he has magnified, made great above all his name, to be exalted throughout our borders once again. If anyone hears what God is saying then let them join hands to do something that will bring about a new Reformation throughout this land and leave an eternal inheritance that we are not ashamed of.

Two things of significance happened around the time of the last Reformation. In God's perfect timing the printing press was invented and the Bible was translated into English, thus allowing the multiplication of the Word and its wide-scale distribution. It was also the period when we broke free of Roman Catholicism and dumped all of the idol worship, 'Mary' worship and priest worship. It broke the chains which the priests and bishops used to hold the people captive, steal their money and keep them obedient through fear of being cast out of the church. It revealed a way to know God directly without the need of a priest or pastor or pontiff.

The Reformation was the most significant time in all of our history and changed the entire world in due course. It brought us freedom from the slavery of false religion and has subsequently transformed millions of lives in every country ever since then.

Most denominations today have reverted to the old Roman Catholic practises of honouring the pastor (priest) more than God. The congregation are led to believe that the minister is always teaching truth because he claims to know more than they do and so they slavishly bring their money and above all, fear in case they get thrown out or just ignored ('excommunicated'). Many ministers behave more like 'popes' and cardinals lording it over the congregation, than they do the humble servants of Christ. 'I wrote unto the church: but Diotrephes who loveth to have the pre-eminence among them, receiveth us not.' 3 John 1:9

But 'whosoever of you will be the chiefest, shall be servant of all. For even the Son of man came not to be ministered unto, but to minister, and to give his life a ransom for many.' Mark 10:44-45

It is time to turn the tables over and start again. It is time for an 'Awakening' in the land.

If however you are one of those who think that things are just going to get worse and worse then surely the best thing is to sell everything you have and use every effort and means to bring the Word of God to this country once more. If you are more of an optimist and feel that things will actually get better then you should be even more constrained to spend your time and money in propagating the Word of God.

God keeps for himself a remnant (a few left behind, survivors, loyalists) and here in this country there is still a remnant who are waiting his 'time'. Right now they are being prepared and positioned for the coming of his glory. It is in this respect that I believe there will be an amazing move of God in 'backsliders' who are grieved in spirit and outside of the churches, but not outside of the everlasting grace and covenant of God.

It is time for such to come back to God, renew their vows, cast off their sins, and prepare for battle. He has not given up on you! Grace is bigger than your sin and misery. Mercy is greater than your failure and personal devastation. The Bible is louder and stronger than all the heresies of the church and the false prophets of religion.

Grace is going to raise up and exalt many who the church despised, who were cast out, ignored, hated and ridiculed.

God will take the broken pieces of humanity that the religious leaders put out from their assemblies and exalt them to places of dignity and nobility.

Read Zechariah, chapter 3 and diligently consider: 'Thus saith the LORD of hosts; If thou wilt **walk in my ways** and if thou wilt **keep my charge**, then thou shalt also judge [govern, direct, execute justice and rightness in] my house, and shalt also keep [be a watchman, sit within] my courts, and I will give thee places to walk among these that stand by [the angels and ambassadors of Heaven].' (v.7)

It is time to stand in heavenly places to receive instruction, to stand in the gap to defend our nation and to stand before God for our youth, (Jeremiah 21-22).

God loves our young people and our children. There are evil plotting enemies dwelling within these shores that hate them and wish them all dead or abused and desecrated; but let God arise and let his enemies be scattered.

'Let God arise, let his enemies be scattered: let them also that hate him flee before him. As smoke is driven away, so drive them away: as wax melteth before the fire, so let the wicked perish at the presence of God. But let the righteous be glad; let them rejoice before God: yea, let them exceedingly rejoice. Sing unto God, sing praises to his name: extol [lift up] him that rideth upon the heavens by his name JAH [God, the God of my salvation], and rejoice before him.' Psalm 68:1-4

It is time to fight for our nation and for our people.

'Be not ye afraid of them: remember the Lord, which is

great and terrible, and fight for your brethren, your sons, and your daughters, your wives, and your houses.' Nehemiah 4:14

When the Jews were threatened with destruction from their enemies around them (read the Book of Esther, and note 4:14), they were told to fight for their lives and their rights as the people of the one true God. When those that they lived among and even their close neighbours sought their annihilation and the dismissal of their faith they did not just lie down and let the enemy have his way. They stood their ground and defied every opposition to his face and got their voice and presence known.

It is surely time for the believers in this country to make their stand and dare to defy the intimidating hosts of hatred that have set their aims and plans to see Christianity abolished from this wonderful land of ours.

'The Jews had light and gladness and joy and honour. And in every province and in every city whithersoever the king's commandment and his decree came, the Jews had joy and gladness, a feast and a good day. **And many of the people of the land became Jews** [believers] for the fear of the Jews fell upon them.' Esther 8:16-17

A strange wonder indeed to those who know not the Lord.

I have spoken about our country being 'at war' and indeed we might extend this matter to all 'Christian' countries at this time. However this is not a war of bombs and guns and swords (although we see these things in abundance from those who seek to force their wills upon others) but this is essentially a 'spiritual battle and it can only be fought and won using 'spiritual' weaponry and tactics. We do not need to start a riot, a demonstration, throw stones, or stand in the street shouting back at the raging extremists. We simply have to do what the Bible says and 'stand in the gap', use our God-given authority and faith to break every opposition, tear down the strongholds of screaming defiance, capture and liquidate the hostile imaginations and plans for our destruction and send confusion and blindness into the enemy camp.

We just need to learn how to pray effectually and fervently out of living righteous lives (James 5:16), and nothing shall be impossible to us. We need to bring the Word of God sharply into focus and get the Gospel of truth out of the church and back into the community. Let us rise up to the position that God has called us and pray passionately until righteousness rain down on this great land.

'Sow to yourselves in righteousness, reap in mercy; break up your fallow ground: for it is time to seek the LORD, till he come and rain righteousness upon you.' Hosea 10:12

God save the Queen and all of the Royal household. God raise up righteous men and women in our government and remove all who are the enemies of the kingdom of God. God confuse all of our adversaries and their secret plotting against us. God save our children and young people. God save our nation.

A CRY
TO
THE SLEEPERS

Chapter Three

A Cry To The Sleepers

Somewhere hidden away, unknown unrecognized, perhaps completely unaware of who they really are, are God's 'Sleepers'. These are mighty and powerful warriors who are called from before the foundation of the earth to rise in these last days. From time to time in their lives they have felt a great sense that they were on this planet for some profound reason, but never quite figured out what that was. During the more 'spiritual' moments of their lives, they have felt an urgency, and a 'call' to something higher and more important than the everyday business and tasks that they are currently engaged in. There is a sense of 'destiny' upon them, and no matter what they do, or what they may achieve in life, there is still this 'vacancy', this 'emptiness' within them seeking fulfilment.

God always has a remnant, even when a nation turns its back on all that is right and good; they are still there, in place, awaiting the stirring of the Holy Spirit. These warriors are his secret agents and they are so secret that they do not even realize who they are themselves or what they are called to do. When a country is under threat, when God's people are being crushed, when it seems that all hope is gone and we have gone too far to get things back together again, then these chosen vessels of God will begin to awake from their sleep and hear the voice of the Lord. They are the reserve army of God (the remnant, Isaiah 10:21; Joel 2:32) and will be equipped and marshalled in the greatest hour of need that a people may face. This army is not drawn from the 'super-pseudo-spiritual', the rich and mighty, the influential and titled, or the platform players and performers. There may indeed be one or two chosen from the well-to-do and noble but the great majority will come from the unseen, the poor, the troubled, the discontent and often the rejects of church and society.

'For ye see your calling, brethren, how that not many wise men after the flesh, not many mighty, not many noble, are called [but thank God it says 'not many', and not, 'not any']: But God hath chosen the foolish things of the world to confound the wise; and God hath chosen the weak things of the world to confound the things which are mighty; And base things of the world, and things which are despised, hath God chosen, yea, and things which are not, to bring to nought things that are: [so] that no flesh should glory [steal the praise] in his presence.' 1Corinthians 1:26-28

Neither is age an issue. Every generation will be represented in this coming conflict and each of them will know God for themselves. They will learn to be masters in the use of the spiritual weapons that God gives them and will be expert in strategy and breakthrough. They will tear down the citadels of wickedness and defiance and utterly spoil the plans of the enemies of the Gospel in this land.

The antagonists will not even see them and the religious will look on in puzzlement as changes begin to happen all around them. They will not be showing off on platforms or stages and will not seek to have their names up in lights but they will cause the ground to shake under their feet.

Wherever they tread they will bring authority, judgment and deliverance. They will strike fear into their opposition and adversaries without ever necessarily being identified themselves. They are the glorious 'Resistance' movement that derail the plotting of the enemy, that expose their secret terror cells, that bring confusion upon their leaders, and instil 'mental-ness' into the heads of their advisors, (2Samuel 15:31; 2Samuel 16:23; 2Samuel 17:14-23).

You may see some of these as people going about their daily routines, working in a shop or office, looking just like anybody else, but once their duties are done they become like shadows in the night. Where they go and what they do only God really knows, but be certain that they are not sat in front of the television throwing their lives away. They are out there somewhere tearing down the towers of evil, wielding the Sword of the Spirit against the powers of darkness bringing deliverance and light into situations for which they will never get any recognition in this world. They are targeting the destructive plans of our antagonists and standing in the gap to defend their people.

They may not be heard for their shouting and screaming but they know who they are in God and they know the power of their words spoken out-loud or whispered articulately in the dark of the night.

Perhaps the man stood on the side of the road with his mobile phone to his ear is speaking to nobody but God, declaring things over his town that will halt the progress of our enemies. In the loneliness of night, across the soggy fields in the driving rain and storm another figure raises high a standard against all of the defiant works of darkness. Nobody knows he is there but he fights not against flesh and blood. He wrestles with the rulers of the darkness in this nation and contends with evil principalities and powers unseen by the physical eye.

Yet another stands unobserved beneath his umbrella outside strategic centres of government or the citadels of evil and rebellion within our capital and claims the ground beneath his feet as the place where he will turn the tide of wickedness and cause righteousness to exalt this nation once again.

Their voice and magnificent authority will bring down the man-made citadels of the apostate churches, run by the deceitful and crafty millionaire 'apostles' selling their magic healing water and offering false healings and lying prophecies to their silly flocks of utterly insensible sheep.

Their faith will drive the armies of the false gods of religion (whatever religion it might be) down into the depths of the sea just like the Egyptian armies at the Red Sea. (Exodus 15:4)

Some of them stand alone whilst others join secretly together to lay siege against the violent determinations of those who plot against us as a people. They are like the wind; you can not identify where they are coming from or where they are going next but you can feel the turbulence in their wake and might even hear the results of their influence.

'The wind bloweth where it listeth [desires, determines], and thou hearest the sound thereof, but canst not tell whence it cometh [from where it came], and whither it goeth [where it will go next]: so is every one that is born of the Spirit.' John 3:8

They will not go round boasting to anyone about what they do and will not tell another soul of the battles in which they engage, for few would understand and more would ridicule. Even their families might think them 'touched' or mentally unstable; but their orders come from Christ Jesus himself and their rewards and medals will only get pinned on them in Heaven. Whilst many considered them fools upon earth the whole of the Redeemed of God will one day see who they truly were and be amazed and humbled at the position of honour granted to them by the King of Kings.

This is God's mighty army that are privileged to know him, to sit in his council chambers and execute his commands throughout the earth. They will be a scourge to the hypocrites and the false prophets and will expose the lies and pretence of the greedy charlatans of religion.

You may not recognise them when they attend the church assembly or stand in the queue at the shop but their presence will affect everything around them and will cause destinies and plans to be changed by nature of the position they hold in God. When they walk down your street households will be touched, secret wickedness will be exposed, light will come into the darkness and spiritual dimensional 'shifts' will occur. Let me explain before you suddenly think that I have gone 'weird'. When a car moves along the motorway it has an effect on the air around it, creating a change in its pattern and behaviour. You have probably noticed this when overtaking a huge lorry and your little car gets buffeted by the turbulence as you try to get past. The same goes for any vehicle whether that be a plane or a ship or a train. Their physical movement alters the dimension of the air or the water around them. We may not necessarily see the change but we can most certainly feel it and see the results. When there is an earthquake at sea the effect and resulting dimensional changes are seen some time after as can be recognised in the powerfully destructive nature of recent tsunamis. When we speak or create any type of sound it creates a sound wave which disrupts the regular flow of air. A loudspeaker, a band, a foghorn or a rocket taking off into space all cause changes and ripples in the airspace around them.

In the Spirit there are also mighty and powerful effects created when someone is moving in the plan and purpose of God. When they speak and pray there will be disturbances and effects that might be invisible to the naked eye but are mighty in God to the pulling down of strongholds. 'For the weapons of our warfare are not carnal [physical], but mighty through God to the pulling down of strongholds.' 2Corinthians 10:4

The Kingdom of Heaven travels with these warriors and whether people hear them or refuse them nonetheless they shall know of a certainty that the kingdom of God has visited that place through their simply being there. 'And say unto them, The kingdom of God is come nigh unto you.' Luke 10:9 'Be ye sure of this, that the kingdom of God is come nigh unto you.' Luke 10:11 'No doubt the kingdom of God is come upon you.' Luke 11:20 'For, behold, the kingdom of God is within you.' Luke 17:21

These will walk on a different level to most believers and will have a confidence and certainty about them which baffles the average church-goer. These agents do not talk about what they may have accomplished and indeed do not even discuss the mission that they are on. They are a wonder to others (Psalm 71:7) who just look on trying to 'suss' them out or 'discern' them.

But you cannot discern or figure out these servants of the Most High. 'He that is spiritual judgeth [examines, discerns] all things, yet he himself is judged [discerned] of [by] no man.' 1Corinthians 2:14-15. They do not need to prove their spirituality or divine call to anybody. They rest in the knowledge that God is with them and they do not need the approval of pastor or priest.

They are not infallible by any means whatsoever and it is their weakness that actually contributes to their strength. 'For when I am weak, then am I strong.' 2 Corinthians 12:10 'And he said unto me, My grace is sufficient for thee: for my strength is made perfect in weakness. Most gladly therefore will I rather glory [boast] in my infirmities [weaknesses of body, failure to reach the mark], [so] that the power of Christ may rest upon me. Therefore I take pleasure in infirmities, in reproaches, in necessities, in persecutions, in distresses for Christ's sake: for when I am weak, then am I strong.' 2Corinthians 12:9-10

'But we have this treasure [this knowledge of God] in earthen vessels [weak, fragile, even damaged clay jars], [so] that the excellency of the power may be [seen to be] of God, and not of us.' 2Corinthians 4:7

They may seem to own nothing and be struggling to survive at times, yet they walk as though they own the whole world.

'As sorrowful, yet alway rejoicing; as poor, yet making many rich; as having nothing, and yet possessing all things.' 2Corinthians 6:10

The 'religious' will always look for the faults or shortcomings of the 'spiritual' and no doubt will find many a thing to pick on to dismiss them as being servants of God. But as I have said, God's secret agents do not need anyone's approval neither the confirmation of self-elevated and argumentative church people. Let those that be ignorant be ignorant still (Revelation 22:11).

If you however believe that you are one of those ordained to such a glorious calling (1Kings 19:18) then all you need to do is hide yourself in Christ and do what the Lord tells you to do. Your orders will come from above as you wait before God and search out the truth of the Scriptures.

If you are a 'Sleeper' then this word comes to you to wake you up and rouse you to the urgent and majestic call of God upon your life.

It is time for the sleeping warriors to awake

'Awake, awake; put on thy strength, O Zion; put on thy beautiful garments, O Jerusalem, the holy city: for henceforth there shall no more come into thee the uncircumcised and the unclean. Shake thyself from the dust; arise, and sit down, O Jerusalem: loose thyself from the bands [chains, shackles] of thy neck, O captive daughter of Zion. For thus saith the LORD, Ye have sold yourselves for nought; and ye shall be redeemed without money.' Isaiah 52:1-3

Wake up, you warriors of God!

Wake up, you who are called and chosen to stand in these desperate days. Awake out of your slumber and senseless dreaming. Come to the light and prepare for battle. Here in this passage of Isaiah we find two callers seeking to awake the slothful warriors of God. Mr. Urgency is banging on your door and would all but kick it open if he could.

You lie down in your comfortable quilt of indifference, too lazy to get up and answer, yet pretending to yourself that all is fine and there is nothing that you can do to change the situation. The world is getting worse, and that is how it must be, but you will be saved because Christ will snatch you away before things get too difficult.

That is a lie! A fire is coming and it will burn the houses of the false professors of Christianity first.

Urgency is rattling your door because firstly, you are in danger and secondly, you have been summoned to attend the court of the Lord for a special hearing. There are no valid excuses for absenting yourself and there are penalties for refusing the command of the King. Heaven is waiting for your attendance and you had better get yourself ready to meet with the council and make sure that your attire is suitable and worthy.

And now, not only is the door being knocked, but the bell is being rung. Surely this is more than an irritation to you! You can bury your head under the covers and like the ostrich with his head in the sand believe that if you stay still, all this distraction will go away. However, the ostrich is going to get a solid kick from a steel toe-capped boot up its backside and you also will find the same coming your way if you refuse the call of God upon your life any longer.

There is a second caller at your door and his name is Mr. Insistence. He will shove a stick in the bell-button and if that does not work, he will throw bricks through every window of your house.

There will come such troubles in every room of your existence that will drive you crazy unless you respond to God's personal messengers. If you still refuse to heed the summons, then your house shall be burned to the ground and everything you took comfort in will be destroyed.

God commanded the light to shine and it shone. He commanded the ground to bring forth fruit and it brought forth. He commands us to hear his voice, yet we have the audacity to ignore him? He summons us to a meeting before his throne and we sit there playing on the computer? We think that we can mock God?

'Be not deceived; God is not mocked.' Galatians 6:7

'I also will choose their delusions and will bring their fears upon them; because when I called, none did answer; when I spake, they did not hear.' Isaiah 66:4

'And now, because ye have done all these works, saith the LORD and I spake unto you, rising up early and speaking, but ye heard not; and I called you, but ye answered not; Therefore will I do unto this house, which is called by my name, wherein ye trust and unto the place which I gave to you and to your fathers, as I have done to Shiloh. And I will cast you out of my sight,' Jeremiah 7:13-15

'Therefore will I number you to the sword and ye shall all bow down to the slaughter: because when I called, ye did not answer; when I spake, ye did not hear; but did evil before mine eyes and did choose that wherein I delighted not.' Isaiah 65:12

If Mr. Urgency and Mr. Insistence are at your door, you would do well to answer their requests and you would do yourself good to hear what their Master is saying. You may like to imagine that you are under the 'New Testament' now and therefore this sort of language is inappropriate, but listen to what the new Testament says:

'Wherefore (as the Holy Ghost saith, **To day if ye will hear his voice, Harden not your hearts** as in the provocation, in the day of temptation in the wilderness: When your fathers tempted me, proved me and saw my works forty years. Wherefore I was grieved with that generation and said, They do alway err in their heart; and they have not known my ways. So I sware in my wrath, They shall not enter into my rest.)' Hebrews 3:7-11

'**See that ye refuse not him that speaketh**. For if they escaped not who refused him that spake on earth, much more shall not we escape, if we turn away from him that speaketh from heaven: Wherefore we receiving a kingdom which cannot be moved, let us have grace, whereby we may serve God acceptably with reverence and godly fear: **For our God is a consuming fire**.' Hebrews 12:25,28 and 29

'For the time is come that judgment must begin at the house of God.' 1Peter 4:17

So, wake up; get up; and answer the call of God today. Your country needs you. The world needs you. The kingdom of God needs you. There is a gathering in Heaven and you have been called to attend and this is the Summons and you have been served this day.

It is time to give account of what you have been doing with your life and chose whose side you will be on in the battle for truth and liberty that we must all now face.

The nature of the Summons

'A sound of battle is in the land!'

A war is raging throughout the country, a battle between good and evil, between the forces of darkness and the force of light.

The future of this nation hangs perilously in the balances and you sit at home complaining about the weather and idly watching the world go by.

Antagonistic forces scream and shout in the streets of our cities, demanding the subservience of our people and the implementation of foreign laws and customs to supersede the freedoms of this great nation. A quick search on the internet will soon reveal the facts.

You sit there thinking that it will probably fizzle out in time or it will not affect you as you will be long gone before anything takes effect. Perhaps you stoically imagine that nobody can do anything about it because it has all gone too far already.

Do you not care for this nation? Do you not care for the people of this land? Are the children and is their future of no concern whatsoever to you? Are you of such a selfish and stubborn nature that the cry or generations to come has no effect upon you?

It is this very attitude that has brought about our current situation, where the world (particularly the EU) and false religions can barge into this nation and think to destroy our liberties, our culture and our history. If they had more licence then we would all most likely be put to the sword and our fantastic Christian heritage obliterated. Have no doubt; we are in a war that seeks to wipe out the Bible and our Christian faith once and for all. You may indeed think that I am an alarmist, but actually I am an alarm sounder.

You can go along to your local church and sing all the choruses you like, dance in the isles, fall on your back with your legs wiggling in the air, but it means nothing, does nothing and the enemy just derides and laughs even more.

You have been called to a fight, to engage in a battle, to stand in the gap for your people and your nation; but you would rather watch television, go to the shops, go for a meal and pretend that all is fine and there are plenty of others to go and do the fighting.

But now you have been 'called up' to defend your country and become a soldier of Jesus Christ.

'Thou therefore endure hardness, as a good soldier of Jesus Christ.' 2Timothy 2:3

'This charge I commit unto thee, son Timothy, according to the prophecies which went before on thee, that thou by them mightest war a good warfare.' 1Timothy 1:18

The First and Second World Wars saw countless ordinary men rise from their workplaces, their comfortable homes, their families and loved ones and leaving all behind, obey the call of the King, sign up to their duty and go fight for their future and their children's future. They kissed their families goodbye and headed off into the unknown, not knowing whether they would ever return to the peaceful shores of this island. They were not experts, not even experienced soldiers, but they obeyed the command went urgently to get trained and equipped and then faced the horrors of a wretched enemy who wished only for their complete annihilation.

A sound of battle is in this land right now. It has been steadily marching through our towns and villages; it has crept into our government, deceived our leaders, stamped its way into our schools and colleges and now is surely rising to become a tumult within our borders. It cannot be stopped by the House of Windsor, neither the politicians, nor the marching English protesters.

This great alien army amongst us can only be halted and brought to disarray and confusion by the Lord's own people daring to defy these enemies of the Gospel and of the wonderful heritage of this country. If you just stay at home amusing yourself with whatever the 'god' channel tickles you with, then you side with the enemy and give him the licence to walk up and down in this land doing whatever he wants. He is not phased or even bothered by 'Christian' television programmes.

This is not a war against people, not a fight against flesh and blood, but a mighty battle against the spiritual powers of darkness that hide behind the mob, the false religions, the anarchists and the deceiving politicians.

'**A sound of battle is in the land, and of great destruction.**' Jeremiah 50:20

You are called to come and fight, because, 'The time is fulfilled and the kingdom of God is at hand'. Matthew 1:15

The time is 'Now'. It is the right time, the only time; and this is the moment for the Sleepers to arise and the Warriors of God to come together and take on the opposition and deal with them properly.

Some have said and perhaps we all have thought from time to time that we are beyond hope now, that it might be impossible for things to change and for our land to be restored. But our God is the God of the impossible, the God who rules over all, the God who is the only true God throughout the entire universe. He is the Lord and he can turn things around even when all seems lost and futile.

As I quote at the beginning of *The Dignity of Righteousness:* **"There is no situation so chaotic that God cannot, from that situation, create something that is surpassingly good. He did it at the creation. He did it at the cross. He is doing it today**." - *Bishop H. C. G. Moule (1841-1920)*

In the Book of Judges, chapters six and seven, Gideon discovered that God was bigger than the most hopeless of situations and it was never a matter of how small and insignificant the resources and people may appear, but it was about how great and mighty their God was.

Against overwhelming odds, a hostile and hateful army that had outgrown his people numerically, a spirit of fear and disillusionment that possessed his own countrymen, Gideon was soon to see God's mighty hand at work in delivering the children of Israel.

This oppressed and silenced race was too afraid to speak out against the belligerent Midianites and dare not lift themselves up to oppose them. Everything that they did to promote their own welfare was crushed time and time again by the foreign army of scorners. The Israelites hid themselves in caves and away in the mountains of the countryside, whilst the antagonists sprawled throughout the towns and cities doing whatever they wanted. Eventually, even out in the farmlands, the enemy sought to thwart and destroy everything that the Israelites attempted for their own preservation. It seemed that any demands that Israel made were swiftly crushed, but whatever the Midianites demanded was granted them any day of the week. (Sound familiar?)

They cried to God for help (Judges 6:7-8) and God sent a messenger to them who told them that it was their own sin and rebellion against the Lord that had brought about this terrible situation.

When a people begin to pray for mercy, then it will not be long before the Father of all mercies attends to their cry. And if indeed he send a messenger, a prophet to expose their folly and draw them back to himself, it is because he ultimately intends to do good unto them, in spite of the destruction and havoc that sin has wreaked.

He raises up a man named Gideon and calls him to prepare an army to take on the enemy. He ends up with 32,000 untrained 'have-a-go' soldiers to stand up against the enemy's 135,000 battle-experienced troops.

That may sound pretty daunting under any conditions, but then God orders Gideon to whittle his own army down. He tells the men that if any of them are afraid or nervous, then they should go home to their wives immediately. Twenty two thousand of them ran home for tea and sentimental comfort, without a blink! This is exactly what will happen in the church today when this call to battle goes out.

So now he faces this huge and defiant oppressor with just ten thousand of his own men. However, even this reduced number is unfit for the fight ahead and must be sifted further. Through a simple test of fortitude and focus, another 9,700 are also sent back home. All that is left of the thirty two thousand men is three hundred ill-equipped and untrained would-be heroes. This basic exercise eliminated all those who were unwilling to lose their lives for the cause, who were still too attached to the world and its empty charms and who would prove reluctant to take any risks.

But with this little band God would show himself mighty and powerful in the face of the screaming and hollering hoards. Through faith they would 'put to flight the armies of the aliens'. Hebrews 11:34

These three hundred men were of a different nature to the tens of thousands who went back home. These are they who might be spoken of in Revelation 12:11, 'And they loved not their lives unto the death.' Or the type who Jesus spake of when he said, 'If any man come to me and hate not his father and mother and wife and children and brethren and sisters, yea and his own life also, he cannot be my disciple.' Luke 14:26

They were the men who would live with a higher focus and determination, who knew the 'call' of God in a way others did not: 'But this I say, brethren, the time is short: it remaineth, that both they that have wives be as though they had none; And they that weep, as though they wept not; and they that rejoice, as though they rejoiced not; and they that buy, as though they possessed not.' 1Corinthians 7:29-30

These were men divorced from the cares and affairs of this world and who were sold out to victory, no matter what that victory might cost. 'No man that warreth [goes to battle] entangleth himself with the affairs of this life; [so] that he may please him who hath chosen him to be a soldier.' 2Timothy 2:4

It is hard enough these days to get a man to come along to a regular prayer meeting, let alone set aside several days to wait on God and work some powerful deliverance in the nation. 'We have not wrought any deliverance in the earth; neither have the inhabitants of the world fallen.' Isaiah 26:18

We have made much noise in church and shown some effort to prove that we are as 'spiritual' as the one next to us. We may have moaned and groaned as one giving birth, but nothing significant or real actually happened. 'We have been with child, we have been in pain, we have as it were brought forth wind!' Isaiah 26:18.

Hmmm, that does not sound very pleasant, but half-heartedness and hypocrisy never produce anything sweet or glamorous.

This fight is not a half-hour screaming session aimed at Satan and all his hoards. This battle is long-term. If you are going to be part of the Engaging Force that will turn matters around and bring defeat to the enemy's camp, then you had better get yourself the right mindset. We are going to war, not with 'sword or spear' made by man: and this war may be the longest and hardest this nation has ever fought. It is not a war that will be staged in a stadium full of local church-goers for an evening prayer-gathering, but this battle will rage throughout every day and every night until victory is secured and the standard of the kingdom of God flies once more over our towns and cities.

God will take a few hopeless lepers, a handful of troubled outcasts, a small group of financially broke and desperate failures and turn them into the hand of deliverance for his people.

2Kings 7: Four dying lepers in desperation and abandonment, walk and stumble into the enemy camp, discover God's miracle and bring salvation and deliverance to the entire starving nation that was being held under siege. They walked away from their naturally stoical mindsets and took a chance on hope and faith.

1Samuel 22: Four hundred men, depressed, disillusioned and up to their necks in debt went down to David's hideout in the caves and there they were transformed into one of the most fearsome armies the world has ever seen. They became known as the 'valiant' men of David the king.

Acts 17:6: Twelve ordinary men from all sorts of backgrounds, along with a small band of their own disciples turned the world upside down through their faith and allegiance to Christ. Like the men who kissed their children goodnight, whispered a fond farewell to their wives before leaving England to fight Hitler's wretched armies in Europe, so these men forsook all that they had to save a dying world from the triumphing of Satan.

Do you want to play little church games and silly church politics, or do you want to be a real soldier of Jesus Christ?

Have no doubt, in opening this book and reading these chapters, you have now been 'served' your call-up papers and the King awaits your attendance on the parade ground.

STOP PLAYING SOLDIERS

Chapter Four

Stop Playing Soldiers

Everybody, it seems, wants to be in God's army, but only the desperate, the focused, the souls who are distressed at their circumstances and that of their nation will have the passion and stamina to see the fight through to the end.

These are they who are not afraid to lose their reputations (and probably have already lost them anyway) and indeed have nothing to lose by serving God.

As an old proverb says, 'Beware the man who has nothing to lose'. The most dangerous man is the one who has no reputation to defend, no home or treasure in this world which he is forever grasping and nobody to have to prove himself to except God.

Here is a man focused, envisioned, clear-headed and unafraid. He is not seeking to make anyone happy, to get himself a stage, or to make himself a name. He simply serves the King and carries out his orders. The secret to his success is unquestioning and prompt obedience. Here indeed is the finest of all soldiers.

Most men these days are tip-toeing around trying to keep the equilibrium and the peace and not cause offence to anyone. They are experts at dodging out of 'tricky' situations and have gotten used to hiding when trouble is in the air; no different to Gideon really. If it is not the wife they are hiding from, then it is the challenge to come out of the shadows and be bold and dare to contend for the truth instead of just trying to 'blend in' and look the same as everyone else.

We have become so versed in 'tolerance' and political correctness that we have forgotten that the Gospel and work of God is an offence to those who do not believe and wherever truth comes it causes people to become offended. (Isaiah 8:14; 1Peter 2:8)

Gideon's call of God would lead him to destroy his father's idol and devilish place of worship. It would antagonise his own people against him and place his life in peril. Before he could raise an army, he must first of all destroy the false beliefs and wicked practises of his own family and if they chose not to side with him, then let it be so, but he can only do what God tells him to do. If they will not join with him or follow him, then let them stay where they are, but he is going on a mission; there is no turning back and no sentimental or 'slushy' talk will divert him from his path.

So walk with me if you will,
And if not, then not;
But now I must be going
To be about the Master's work.
Engage myself completely,
And fasten heart to all that He compels me so to do.
So, go away if all you wish
Is to draw me back to that which holds no value,
No purpose, nor destiny, nor promise for eternity.
For I am His and He is mine,
From now and evermore to be.

Obedience is better than sacrifice

When we 'put up with things' just to keep someone else happy, when we know it is not the best or right thing for us, then we end up sacrificing our true calling for something less than God's purpose for our lives.

Often it is the 'fear of offending' that keeps us from doing what we know to be right. Our dread of the other person's reactions to our personal choices leaves us unable to perform our duty in the way we know we should.

We spend all of our efforts subsequently trying to maintain a 'balance' on things, juggling with our conscience, but compromising our deepest convictions.

To obey is a far better solution and in our obedience we need to exercise trust in God that he will undertake for us in all things, even the 'fall-out' that may occur when we choose to follow his directives.

Surely if God tells us to do something or to stop something then we simply have to obey and not question his wisdom. If we spend more time worrying about the side-effects of such actions we will end up disobeying God and fearing a person more than honouring the Lord. If this is where you find yourself today, then you have not come to a place of fully trusting God with everything and still think that you can work it out better than he can.

'To obey [God] is better than sacrifice.' 2Samuel 15:22

If we find ourselves failing God because we feel obliged to please another party, then we have become the servant of another mortal and the Bible says: 'Ye are bought with a price; be not ye the servants [slaves] of men [or women].' 1Corinthians 7:23

If you are a slave of another, if you do not have the freedom to do the things that God calls you to, then you are not able to come to war and fight 'the battles of the Lord', (1Samuel 25:28).

Get Free!

'Loose thyself from the bands of thy neck', (Isaiah 52:2)

Get a file and begin to cut off the chains of slavery and manipulation that have held you back from your priestly and kingly office for all these lost years (Revelation 1:6). Your time for rising has come. The chains of opposition and persecution, the shackles of being somebody else's servant and slave must be forced apart and opened so that you might enter into the promises and walk the corridors of spiritual government that oversees this nation.

Breaking off the ball and chain that the devil attached to your life, however many years ago, will possibly take a little more effort than just shouting, 'In the name of Jesus'. It may need planning, strategizing and a big spiritual angle grinder to cut through it and snap its hold. It will definitely take a momentous personal decision and some gritty determination to break free and stay free.

Loose yourself from the chains that you are wearing. You do not need a 'Christian counsellor', or a psychiatrist to help you with this. They never put the chains on you and they cannot take them off you. It was your decision to live as you do and to submit to someone else's dictates over your life. It was your will that succumbed to the enemy and accepted the spiritual handcuffs that would keep your hands bound from serving God to your fullest.

If you want to be free, then break off the things that drag you around, which steal all of your time, that intimidate you and hold you fast to a powerless and ineffective existence, rather than running hard and fast after God. There are no short cuts to liberty. If you want freedom, then get rid of the things that make you a slave and stop wearing the garments of a prisoner.

Choose this day who you will serve.

You may be a slave to your possessions. If so, then get rid of them all and prove that you are free from such shackles. Maybe you live in fear of losing your job or your house or your car. Get liberated from these worries and anxieties. You said that you trusted Christ to keep you every day of your life and yet you walk around in a constant state of concern and doubt for all these temporary comforts and necessities. He promised that he would never leave you or forsake you and he knows what you have need of. All you have to do is, 'Seek ye first the kingdom of God and his righteousness; and all these things shall be added unto you.' Matthew 6:33

You may be a 'slave' to another person, perhaps a partner, a girlfriend, a child, a church leader, a domineering mother, or a friend. You were never meant to be their servant and you do not need to be so any longer.

If you truly want to do something in God's kingdom, then it is time to set yourself free. You have asked God to break the chains, to release you, to sort out the situation more times than you can remember, but nothing ever seems to happen.

The Scripture tells us to loose the shackles from round our own necks, to free ourselves from the heavy burdens, to dismantle the chains of control and manipulation that others have placed upon us and to claim our life and freedom back. The men in this country need to hear this word in particular, for the future of our children may indeed depend upon your response to this challenge.

'The Spirit of the Lord GOD is upon me; because the LORD hath anointed me to preach good tidings unto the meek; he hath sent me to bind up the brokenhearted, **to proclaim liberty to the captives** and the opening of the prison to them that are bound.' Isaiah 61:1

Notice the phrase, 'to proclaim liberty to the captives'. The preacher simply declares that you are free, that you no longer need to live in your cell and you can loose the chains from off your neck. It is sufficient for me to tell you that God has made you free and granted you your full liberty to come and serve him.

This document proclaims your freedom by the word of God and tells you that you no longer need to be a slave to anybody or any thing. It is this message of good news that will give you the unction to change your life, for it comes from the awesome anointing of Isaiah 61.

There is no point in keep on asking God to do what we are commanded to do ourselves. He has won the victory for us at the cross in his Son Jesus Christ. All that we need do is obey him and enter into his conquering power.

It is not 'deliverance' that we need but obedience to God's word. 'For this commandment which I command thee this day, it is not hidden from thee [beyond your power or ability to perform], neither is it far off [somewhere in the distant future]. It is not in heaven, that thou shouldest say, Who shall go up for us to heaven and bring it unto us, that we may hear it and do it? Neither is it beyond the sea [at some super-spiritual 'revival' conference across the world], that thou shouldest say, Who shall go over the sea for us and bring it unto us, that we may hear it and do it?

But the word is very nigh unto thee, in thy mouth and in thy heart, [so] that thou mayest do it [you can do it].' Deuteronomy 30:11-14

If you put yourself in the situation you are now in, or allowed others to take advantage of you, then you can also take yourself out of the situation and stop others running your life according to their dictates. Christ made you free (John 8:36); free to choose, free to live the life he planned for you and free to hold your head up and be everything that you are inspired of God to be. He called you to liberty and joy in the Holy Ghost, (2Corinthians 3:7; Romans 14:17).

'Lift up your heads, O ye gates; and be ye lift up, ye everlasting doors; and the King of glory shall come in. Who is this King of glory? The LORD strong and mighty, the LORD mighty in battle.' Psalm 24:7-8

Lift up your head and lift up your heart to God and he shall give you the strength to walk away from the things that are wrong and enable you to cast off the chains of control and addictive behaviour.'Deliver [escape] thyself, O Zion, that dwellest with the daughter of Babylon ['confusion']... for he that toucheth [strikes, hurts] you toucheth the apple of his eye.' Zechariah 2:7-8

Note also this particular description of what God's people are to escape from. It is from the daughter of 'confusion' (which is what 'Babylon' means). Confusion is the child of 'envy and strife': 'For where envying and strife [contention] is, there is confusion and every evil work.' James 3:16

(Here again we see a 'trinity' of evil: the spirits of Envy, Strife and Confusion).

I do not pretend that there will not be a price to pay, or consequences to your actions, but if you are 'Looking unto Jesus, the author [beginner and captain] and the finisher [completer, perfector] of your faith' (Hebrews 12:1-2), then he will undertake for you and give you strength to meet the task. You can never over-estimate the value of liberty

We must learn to start saying: 'No!' to those who demand of us, who believe their will is more important than God's will for our lives.

At the end of the day, we shall either live for them, or live for God. You only have one life. Don't throw it away on something less than the outstanding and all-fulfilling plan of God. He has called us to rise to the challenge in these desperate days, to come to the battlefield and leaving everything behind, follow him with all of our hearts, souls and minds into destroying the enemy's positions, freeing the captives and delivering them from Satan's grip.

This world is not our home. This is a battlefield and the church upon earth is the church 'Militant'. The church 'Triumphant' is with Christ waiting for us to complete our tour of duty and win the day gloriously.

Forget praying the prayer of the conference thousands, 'Bless me and meet my needs, O Lord and then I will serve thee'. That prayer will never be answered. Serve Jesus

Christ now and he will bless you and meet all of your needs.

I met an old Indian man in London who told me that when God brings him loads of money from a new house he was building, he would then serve God in the Gospel. He will not and never shall, but if he does get lots of cash from his project he will just selfishly hoard it up, or find another project to make himself a bit richer. He already owns four other houses in one of the more affluent parts of the capital but continually moans about how poor he is whilst his daughter uses every trick in the book to claim any government benefits she can get. The rich are never satisfied. He is a sick and dying man but would rather have his wealth than his health.

You can run to church and 'play' at being a soldier and you can even dress up and look like a soldier, but it does not make you a soldier. Running around declaring that you are God's hero does not make you a hero and telling everyone that you are an apostle, a prophet or hold the 'end-time mandate' for the world's salvation is definitely a delusion and just another 'religious' game.

It is all a farce and nobody is really fooled except the gullible and the 'cheer-leaders' in the not-so-heavenly choirs and worship groups.

It is time to grow up and become men and throw away all the kindergarten nonsense of contemporary Christianity. The martyrs of old were true heroes who fought valiantly and died magnificently for King and kingdom. A brief record of a few of those wonderful martyrs is to be found at the back of this volume.

Get Strong!

The word that comes to your door is first, 'Awake!' and then, 'Put on your strength'.

This is not an instant job. People running to conferences singing, 'I am a winner' and other such choruses, does not make them strong. When they get back home they find themselves just the same as they were before they spent thousands of pounds or dollars on the glossy-advertised programme. The preacher 'peps' them all up, in the heat of the moment makes them 'feel' strong and then takes up an offering.

Strength is not a feeling, neither an atmosphere, neither some momentary 'experience'. **True strength is God in me, the muscles and sinews of his consistent faith working in me, the hardened steel and toughened cable of my knowledge of the Word and the tightly-twisted fibres and unbreakable nylon of my habitual prayer-life**.

Strength comes from waiting on God, diligently searching the Scriptures and discovering the real joy of the Lord and not just engaging in wall-to-wall chorus singing as is the manner in many of the charismatic churches these days. (One or two songs are quite sufficient and then give some practical teaching on how to prepare ourselves to meet with God, followed by the Word being preached and taught. You can sing as long as you like afterwards.)

Muscles need training and exercising, especially when they have been dormant or idle for years. Strength does not come all of a sudden but increases through activity, discipline and commitment. To 'put on thy strength' is to start somewhere to become strong again for God and learn how to be the overcoming warrior you are called to be. It means getting up in the morning and setting aside time in the Bible. It means feeding on God's Word until it becomes our life and substance. It is an ongoing process. It means going to God's 'gym' every day and working out, until we are fit for active service.

What we eat will contribute highly to how strong we really are. 'Man shall not live by bread alone, but by every word that proceedeth out of the mouth of God.' Matthew 4:4 (Underline this verse in your Bible)

'Put on thy strength', add some muscle to the feeble spiritual skeleton that you drag around with you.

Strengthen the muscle of your heart:

'Wait on the LORD: be of good courage and he shall strengthen thine heart: wait, I say, on the LORD. Psalm 27:14 'Be of good courage and he shall strengthen your heart, all ye that hope in the LORD.' Psalm 31:24 'But they that wait upon the LORD shall renew their strength; they shall mount up with wings as eagles; they shall run and not be weary; and they shall walk and not faint.' Isaiah 40:31

'Finally, my brethren, be strong in the Lord and in the power of his might.' Ephesians 6:10

Spiritual anorexia sent all but the three hundred soldiers in Gideon's army back home.

Exercise the muscle of your tongue: What you speak is what you are.

'I can do all things through Christ which strengtheneth me.' Philippians 4:13

'**Surely, shall one say**, in the LORD have I righteousness and strength: even to him shall men come; and all that are incensed against him shall be ashamed.' Isaiah 45:24

'No weapon that is formed against thee shall prosper; and every tongue that shall rise against thee in judgment thou shalt condemn [that is, you shall answer with your voice], for your righteousness is of God.' Isaiah 54:17

'The word is nigh [close to, next to, within] thy mouth and in thy heart: that is, the word of faith, which we preach; That if thou shalt **confess with thy mouth** the Lord Jesus and shalt believe in thine heart that God hath raised him from the dead, thou shalt be saved. For with the heart man believeth unto righteousness; and **with the mouth** confession is made unto salvation [deliverance, safety, healing and eternal security].' Romans 10:8-10

The word is more powerful than the sword or gun. The spoken word changes the world and alters the spiritual atmosphere. One word from a politician can send the price of shares tumbling, or make an entire nation feel good about itself. 'Where the word of a king [ruler] is, there is power.' Ecclesiastes 8:4

What you speak over yourself will ultimately be what you become. It is time to start to speak the word of God into your life and over your family. For the last ten years I have spoken a word over my nation every day in the firm belief that God will bring it to pass.

Singing the well-known and popular chorus, 'Let the weak say, I am strong', is not necessarily a good formula for being strong. The words quoted in this modern song are actually out of context entirely with what the singer is trying to imply. They are taken from Joel 3, where God is calling the heathen, his enemies, to the great end-time battle of the Lord! Like Elijah mocked the false prophets (1Kings 18), so God calls the heathen to get themselves strong to come and fight him! 'Beat your plowshares into swords and your pruninghooks into spears: let the weak say, I am strong. Assemble yourselves and come, all ye heathen and gather yourselves together round about.' Joel 3:10-11

Their hatred and defiance of God will be their utter defeat and destruction.

True strength will be added to you daily as you dig deep into God's word, seek him earnestly in prayer and begin to run after him with all of your heart, soul and mind. You do not become an Olympic champion after running for just one hour, but in the practise and perseverance of your dream the muscles get exercised that were never used before and day by day your strength will increase and make you into a winner.

It is time to get started. Do not put it off for another day, for that 'other' day may never come. Go now, pledge yourself to the Lord and to his call and enlist in his army.

DOES ANYONE CARE?

Chapter Five

Does Anyone Care?

First of all, let me say a few things that need to be said. To many simple folk they will think me strange to be writing about a war or conflict in this nation as though it were fact. It is only those with some wisdom who will understand and recognise that the things I speak of are real and frighteningly disturbing.

There is a war taking place right now in front of our eyes for the destruction of a race of people, their culture, their history and their future. Moreover, this battle is set for the extinguishing of the light of the Gospel and burying the Word of God.

We are told that our population is getting older and declining. I wonder if that also goes for the multitudes of foreigners that have crossed our borders over the last twenty years or so. I do not think so, for some have other plans which are long-term rather than just 'living for the moment'.

And anyway, why is our population apparently declining? Well, there is a very simple answer to this. We encourage and propagate abortion amongst our own people (following the wicked introduction of the Abortion Act in 1967 by David Steel of the Liberal Party). Furthermore, we have been encouraged not to have too many children and to use contraceptives as much as possible.

Russia has woken up to this simple fact in the light of its declining birth-rate, but how long before we do? It seems, apparently, that having children just complicates life and adds burdens to what is a very difficult period in this economic climate. How many millions of little lives have been killed in the womb over the last forty-five years? What might that generation have been doing today if they had been allowed to live? How many women are now on anti-depressants and suffering deeply because of their actions toward the unborn child?

We complain at how many children the immigrants have, but we 'terminate' (a politically correct word for kill) over 200,000 children every year! Why is our indigenous population getting older? This is part of the answer. In just thirty years we may have systematically wiped out approximately six million lives at the hands of our doctors and gynaecologists.

The other reason is the widespread practise of contraception that prevents our race from re-populating itself. Just think of the word 'contra-conception'. It is against conception, against continuation, against common sense, against 'normality'. It is the abandoning of the future survival of our race, especially when we are all getting older. Sex is not designed simply for pleasure, but for the proliferation and guarantee of future generations.

'I will therefore that the younger women marry, bear children, guide [manage] the house....' 1Timothy 5:14

Bringing children into the world is often considered as something of a 'handicap' and an undesired burden of responsibility. They are viewed as 'obstacles' to our personal prospects for success, our careers and self-achievement. Actually, the Bible says that children are the gift of God and are the fulfilment and delight of both mother and father.

We have simply been spun a lie.

Take the time to read the quotes below:

'Lo, children are an heritage [inheritance, gift] of the LORD: and the fruit of the womb is his reward.' Psalm 127:3

'Children's children [grandchildren] are the crown of old men; and the glory [excellence, boasting] of children are their fathers.' Proverbs 17:6

'Thy wife shall be as a fruitful vine by the sides of thine house: thy children like olive plants round about thy table. Behold, that thus shall the man [this is how the man shall] be blessed that feareth the LORD.' Psalm 128:3-4

'The just man walketh in his integrity: his children are blessed after him.' Proverbs 20:7

'And God blessed them and God said unto them: Be fruitful and multiply and replenish the earth [ie: **have loads of babies**] and subdue it: and have dominion over the fish of the sea and over the fowl of the air and over every living thing that moveth upon the earth.' Genesis 1:28

'And they blessed Rebekah and said unto her, Thou art our sister, be thou the mother of thousands of millions and let thy seed [children] possess the gate of those which hate them.' Genesis 24:60

'And he lifted up his eyes and saw the women and the children; and said, Who are those with thee? And he said, The children which God hath graciously given thy servant.'

Genesis 33:5 (Children are for loving, not despising).

'And Joseph called the name of the firstborn Manasseh: For God, said he, hath made me forget all my toil and all my father's house.' Genesis 41:51 (The joy of the birth of his son made him forget the hard work of previous years).

'And the name of the second called he Ephraim: For God hath caused me to be fruitful in the land of my affliction.' Genesis 41:52 (Again, he only found happiness in the birth of another child).

'And [God] said unto me, Behold, I will make thee fruitful and multiply thee and I will make of thee a multitude of people; and will give this land to thy seed [children] after thee for an everlasting possession.' Genesis 48:4

'Wherefore it came to pass, when the time was come about after Hannah had conceived, that she bare a son and called his name Samuel, saying, Because I have asked him of the LORD.' 1Samuel 1:20 (Children of the believer are truly the gift of God). 'Behold, I and the children whom the LORD hath given me are for signs and for wonders in Israel from the LORD of hosts, which dwelleth in mount Zion.' Isaiah 8:18 (Our children have a destiny that is linked to us as believing parents).

Children are our future!

I come from a family of thirteen and all of us are alive at this day including my mother who worked right up to the age of 80 years old.

So why are we told that it is better to kill the unborn, or just not get pregnant at all? Where does this lie come from and what could be the reason behind it?

It may indeed come from a government and other influential bodies both in our country and further abroad, but its roots are far more sinister and evil.

This is part of a demonic plot to eradicate our lineage and replace it with the confusion of a 'mixed multitude' (Nehemiah 13:3) that disdains our history, mocks us as a people and robs us of our freedoms and liberties. Moreover, its chief aim is to obliterate the Bible and the message of the Gospel from this nation that brought the Good News of Christ to the entire world. The devil, knowing that his time is short, is very afraid in case the sleeping Warriors ever wake up and he is even more anxious lest the Guardians arise from their slumber and dare to defy the rulers of darkness.

I was delighted to see that Melvyn Bragg has recently written a book *The Book of Books* showing the need to restore the King James Bible to its rightful place and recognise its powerful influence and the impact it has had in the history of our nation. If the baby William Tyndale had not been born we may never have had the Bible printed in English for all to read. If the baby Jesus had never been born we could never have been given eternal life.

Over the last thirty five years a dense spiritual darkness has crept over this land and engulfed everything that stood for righteousness, morality and truth. In 1976, I laughed when I read a book called, 'The Vision', by David Wilkerson. He claimed to have had a dream in which he saw the day coming when women would appear 'topless' on British television and where homosexuals would vaunt themselves publicly in the streets. I could never believe that we would ever allow such immorality on our televisions and the very suggestion that our streets might witness such behaviour was even more outrageous.

That was in 1976. Can you imagine a young man being shocked by such statements? Just three decades later our televisions and computers are soaked with the foulest of filth and degradation any mind could possibly conceive. There are now no restraints to the evil that has flooded this nation and desecrated everything noble and decent and good that was once the preservation and dignity of a great country.

In India you will get seven years in prison if you dare to produce pornographic literature and distribute it. All nudity and foul language is dubbed out of every film or television show from the West before it is ever aired. Just a few years ago nearly all the networks in Bombay were shut down because one of the American channels had failed to dub out a scene where a woman was shown topless. The police raided the offices and seized all of the decoders and took them to the High Court. It was some considerable time before things were restored. Sadly, as the West and its influence move into India, so these moral stands and defences will be broken down, not in a night, but slowly and stealthily.

The breakdown of all restraints in our country has allowed the despots and obnoxious criminals from other countries to invade these shores and open up their 'flesh-trades', their drug running and their kidnapping of children and young people into prostitution and other gross forms of slavery. The Times reported just recently that 'out of 56 men found guilty of child-sex offences linked to 'street grooming', only three of the convicted men where white.

The massive issue of 'child sex-grooming', with Pakistani men suggesting that white girls are 'easy meat' for sexual abuse has been highlighted by a former Home Secretary just recently.' He (Jack Straw) got slapped for saying so but at least he told the truth.

I am not suggesting in the slightest that these men are any more evil than some of our own similarly depraved countrymen, but when you open the front-door to the unknown you give licence to the devil to hurt your family.

Do you ever stop to consider why it is that over 100,000 children in this country go missing every year and nobody blinks an eye?

Can you believe that this statistic is factual and yet there seems no voice to cry out against it or even show any concern? Do you even care? And if you do not, then who will? Every five minutes a child (a precious life), goes missing.

In many of our cities the foreigners have taken over the 'care' industry. Do they really care for our old and sick? Do they really have compassion for our mentally disturbed? Do they do their job to their best because they have a natural concern for the thousands of poor traumatized children who are now without parents?

I dare to say that the answer to all these questions is a resounding 'No' for the great majority of these workers, (there will always be a very small handful that actually do have some human compassion). They have jumped into all these opportunities to fleece as much money from our welfare society as they can and not in any way because they love our poor and dying. I have watched the disgraceful way that our sick and elderly people have been abused and despised by the uncaring 'carers'. I have seen the poor little children being 'dragged' around by these so-called care workers.

I love my country and I love my people and it is high time that we woke up to where we are and the dreadful plight of our nation.

Why are our streets filled with young people drowning themselves in alcohol? Is it because nobody really cares for them and they are left to find reason and purpose for their own lives, but seeing no future of great significance, they 'eat drink and make merry, for tomorrow they die'? The government gives them the licence to drink at all hours and then condemns them for being drunk.

Dirty-minded, gross low-life perverts prey on the girls, seeking only to abuse them and humiliate them. The young men drown themselves in drink to find solace and comfort in a country that is now one of the loneliest in the world. The night sucks the victims deep into its evil arms and there is not a soul who seems to be concerned enough to do anything about it.

Prayer could change things but the Warriors are asleep in the night.

Our schools have been forced to abandon the Bible and any teaching on Creationism. Our children are now taught a bucketful of false and alien religions just to pacify the demands of the screaming immigrants. The God of love who I was taught about in the Bible as a child has now been cast indifferently to one side allowing the preachers of hate and intolerance to rant and rave their vile judgements against our race.

Our true indigenous history has been contorted and

twisted, or just completely bypassed in the curriculum so as not to cause any 'offence' to the foreign 'British' now living here. We are told that we have to keep saying 'sorry' for our past 'offences' during the time that we ruled a quarter of the world. What nonsense! The whole world speaks our language because we dared to do something and through that, delivered the Christian message to every country on the planet. On top of that we brought outstanding inventions, medical advances and discoveries, technology and infrastructure and education to country after country.

The African director (Trevor Phillips) who headed up the Equalities Commission recently stated that 'Muslims integrate into British society better than Christians do'! What ignorance! We are a 'Christian' nation, if not in practice, certainly historically. How or why do we need to 'integrate' into anything? This is our country. What an unlearned twit! We did not move into this place, it is our cultural Anglo-Saxon home.

But is this not just another way of undermining who we are as a people? And who is going to say or do anything about it? Do you actually care?

The Warriors are still asleep. Wake up!

Our prisons are full and overflowing, crime rages throughout the towns and cities; corruption and vice are on the increase. Our country is taken up with national lotteries and gambling. Our people have never heard the Gospel, (the true Gospel that is and not the 'god-tv' money-begging, bizarre-ministry programming that is often both hateful and embarrassing). Church is becoming less and less relevant as it continues to lose its ability to communicate in any sensible way to a society that needs loving more than it needs professional and slick hypocritical preachers.

Christians are barred from preaching in the streets in case we cause an offence, whilst the Muslim extremists abuse all of those restrictions without any regard to our law or equality, screaming and 'preaching' their archaic beliefs and demanding their primitive and uncivilised laws replace our democratic and rational constitution.

If a Muslim's ranting and raving about his foreign god offends me, can I, or will I get the same rights as them to complain to the police that they are offending me and propagating religious intolerance and see them shut up?

The problem however, is not the people you see in front of you, but the hidden enemies who lurk like shadows behind their flesh and blood. They are the real enemy; they are 'spiritual' beings not seen with the physical eye and unless we recognise them, identify them and know how to deal with them, we shall fail to change anything. They manipulate, deceive, delude and destroy individuals and entire communities and unless we tear down those strongholds and imaginations, they will sorely oppress everything that is good and right.

'We wrestle not against flesh and blood, but against principalities, against powers, against the rulers of the darkness of this world, against spiritual wickedness in high places.' Ephesians 6:12

We have the power to overturn all these things, if only the Warriors would wake up and start doing what they were meant to do. Our fight is not with sticks and stones against the trouble-makers, but we take the two-edged sword of God's Word and the power of all-prayer against the rulers of the darkness of this age and show this world the glory of our God. Nothing can withstand such an offensive.

'For the weapons of our warfare are not carnal [physical] but mighty [powerful, of a spiritual nature] through God to the pulling down [the demolition] of strong holds [the fortresses of our enemies].' 2Corinthians 10:4

'The night is far spent, the day is at hand: let us therefore cast off the works of darkness and let us put on the armour of light.' Romans 13:12

God is bigger than religion, no matter what that religion may be.

THE TIME
IS
NOW

Chapter Six

The Time Is Now

Many years ago I remember reading an article in the Daily Telegraph about a rather special magnolia tree.

A young couple were given the sapling twenty five years before on their wedding day and had planted it in the garden of their new house. Every year it grew a little more and like most plants, it shed its leaves in the autumn and then in spring it burst into fresh green foliage, delighting its owners once again.

However, on this particular spring day, something rather marvellous happened. Before the leaves could even get to the light, the whole tree produced flower buds for the first time in its life. One by one they opened out into the most glorious display that you could imagine.

Word got out to the horticulturists and garden centres around the nation and eventually Kew Gardens (one of the most famous centres in the country), also got wind of it and sent their senior staff up to the couple's house. They were green with envy because this magnolia was of a very unique variety which they also had been growing, but as of yet not one of theirs had ever produced a single flower in thirty years. Bus-loads of photographers and journalists invaded the garden and ordinary gardeners from all over the place came in the hope of catching a glimpse.

This particular strain could take up to thirty or more years to flower. There is a moment in its life when the beauty and majesty of the plant's glory is shown to the whole of the garden round about it and it is for that moment that it lives and breathes. And just to add to the wonder of the moment, this extraordinary event happened on the couple's twenty fifth wedding anniversary.

For a quarter of a century nobody took any notice of this tree, passing it by without even a glance. It was just another bush in somebody's garden, a bit boring and perhaps somewhat insignificant. Other gardeners might well have cut it down as it took up too much room and never seemed to do anything special. Who could have imagined what a transformation would take place all these years later?

Perhaps you have felt the same way about your life. You have sought for reason and purpose, been assured that there is some 'destiny' on you, but never finding what that was. Others have smirked when you mention that you know God has a 'calling' on your life and then sneeringly asked you to prove it. For many years you have lived and gone through the varied mundane experiences of life, but never really discovered what it is. You always had that sense of knowing there is something out there for you, but were never able to identify what exactly it was.

Others have looked at you and seen nothing of great value and yet you know inwardly that there is something special about your life.

I picked a bunch of wild poppies a few days back. They were growing in a huge field of rapeseed amongst millions of white daisies. They were of such a fantastic shade of red that they blazed their beauty across the landscape. I decided to only pick the ones which were not open yet, as I could then have the pleasure of watching them flower in front of me.

The poppy, before it opens and reveals its splendour, hangs its head down, drooping toward the ground as one asleep, encased in its own protective covering, not giving any hint as to its real glory and distinctiveness.

I woke this morning, looked across the room and saw that the heads were now turned upwards on their stems, stretching up toward the light. I knew that something was about to happen! Within an hour the shells that had concealed them and disguised their true identity fell off to the floor and the delicate and exquisite petals began to uncrumple from their confinement. My room is ablaze with their magnificence!

You may think that life has passed you by and the opportunities that you always longed for are now distant reflections. Maybe you always hoped that God would use you somehow to bring change to your nation, or influence to your own people, but life has taken its toll on you and you have all but given up.

Maybe you always knew deep inside that you should be engaged in prayer and evangelism, in the work of God's kingdom, but every time you tried to open a door, somebody would shut it in your face. You lost faith, gave up on hope and surrendered to complacency and just living as everyone else does.

I want to tell you that God still has a plan and a purpose for your life. Your best and finest hour is yet to come!

You may be a sleeping Warrior, a Guardian of the truth and you do not even know it yourself. Others have dismissed you, written you off, cast you aside, but God has not. Sin may have spoiled you, backsliding smashed your dreams, the devil persecuted you to death, but God has never given up on you!

Your time is yet to come. Satan will not have the last laugh on your life, but God will reveal his glory and his presence in you and show the world that you are loved by him.

'Behold, I will make them of the synagogue of Satan, which say they are Jews [pretending to be Believers] and are not, but do lie; behold, I will make them to come and worship before thy feet and to know that I have loved thee.' Revelation 3:9

'Behold, all they that were incensed [displeased, angry] against thee shall be ashamed and confounded: they shall be as nothing; and they that strive with thee shall perish.' Isaiah 41:4

Just like the magnolia or the poppy your true beauty is yet to be revealed.

If you are called to be a Warrior, then God is going to put upon you a spirit of prayer and intercession such as you have never known before. (Zechariah 12:10)

Television and all the distractions of this age will lose their hold over you and your heart will be changed by the wonderful power of God. You will have a new heart that bursts with the sunshine of the goodness of God and your mouth will speak a language of praise and thankfulness, instead of despair and doubt and worldly considerations. (Ezekiel 36:26)

Your tongue will be like the pen of one who can write with passion and style of the goodness and wonder of your God. It will tell the old story of the cross of Christ with conviction and compulsion to those who are lost in sin. You will shock yourself at the emotion and power of your own words.

I remember well my father-in-law shedding tears as he would share the Gospel of Jesus with an individual. I believe that Heaven wept at the sight of the crucified Saviour and should we not also be moved with compassion when preaching such a wonderful message?

'My heart is inditing [moving, stirring in] a good matter: I speak of the things which I have made [achieved, designed] touching [regarding] the king: my tongue is the pen of a ready [skilled] writer.' Psalm 45:1

Those around you will be astounded, especially the ones who despised you or considered themselves above you. Your head will now be lifted up above your antagonists and enemies.

'And now shall mine head be lifted up above mine enemies round about me: therefore will I offer in his tabernacle sacrifices of joy; I will sing, yea, I will sing praises unto the LORD.' Psalm 27:6

You are here for a reason, a grand purpose, 'for such a time as this'. What has gone on before has gone. What lies in front of you is now. It is time to forget the past, the good, the bad and the ugly and reach out to take what is placed in front of you right now.

'Forgetting those things which are behind and reaching forth unto those things which are before, I press toward the mark for the prize of the high calling of God in Christ

Jesus.' Philippians 3:13-14

The young orphan girl Esther, subjugated by a foreign power, lived inconspicuously in Jerusalem with her cousin Mordecai. He had taken her as his own daughter after her parents died. She was insignificant as far as her own people were concerned and even less important to the Persian invaders who now ruled over them. A small incident in Mordecai's life led to him informing the king of an assassination attempt. Much later this would lead to a situation that would ultimately revolutionise Esther's life and save the lives of hundreds of thousands of her own people.

The story is a most beautiful and profound illustration of God's divine intervention in the affairs of a nation. It wonderfully details all of the little 'insignificant' or 'chance' happenings that would lead to God's own people being delivered from certain death further down the line. (The Book of Esther is around halfway through the Old Testament).

God is in the small things as well as the great things and the small things are vital to the bigger things coming to pass. A seed falls into the ground, dropped from the beak of a solitary bird flying overhead. Many years later a fruit-bearing tree supplies the local village with the food it desperately needs before winter comes. What was more important, the seed, or the bird?

God is in the seed and in the bird that picked it up. He knows the future as though it were the past.

Never give up. Who knows whether you have come all this way for just this moment in the history of the world? There are no accidents with God. His 'Sleepers' may not have done much up until now, but they are being woken up at this time for the salvation and deliverance of his people.

Esther was enjoying the palace and all of the comfort of being the Queen, but she was God's 'Sleeper' for the children of Israel. If she ignored the call of God, then she would perish along with everyone else. She had to get up, take a risk, put her life on the line and stand in the gap to save her nation.

You are a vital piece of God's jigsaw for these days that we live in and it is time to put aside all the earthly plans that you may have made for the rest of your life and discover the high calling of God that he has for you.

Your country needs you!

Wherefore he saith, **Awake thou that sleepest**, and arise from the dead and Christ shall give thee light.' Ephesians 5:14

'Therefore **let us not sleep**, as do others; but let us watch and be sober.' 1Thessalonians 5:6

'It is high time to **awake out of sleep**: for now is our salvation nearer than when we believed.' Romans 13:11

The magnolia bloomed in its season of glory and it has fulfilled its destiny. There is a special moment for God's people to excel and show the glory of God in a way that they have never done before.

I remember the Colonel telling me of a preacher who was rather enthusiastic, even radical and ahead of his time. It was said that when he was younger, the people used to park their carriages and other means of transport a few blocks from his church, so as not to be recognised. When he was eighty years old you could not get near to the church for vehicles.

'Arise, shine; for thy light is come and the glory of the LORD is risen upon thee. For, behold, the darkness shall cover the earth and gross [dense] darkness the people: but the LORD shall arise upon thee and his glory shall be seen upon thee. And the Gentiles shall come to thy light and kings to the brightness of thy rising.' Isaiah 60:1-3

'Arise, shine!' It is a command not an invitation. It is not about singing stupid songs like, 'Shine, Jesus shine'. Jesus is not a light bulb and he does not need to be told to 'shine'. He is the eternal light of life, the glory of Heaven and the sunshine of the universe. The Scripture tells us to shine, not Christ.

'Thy light is come'. No more night, no more waiting for the break of day, for the sun has already risen upon thee and it is simply time to get up and put on your best clothes for God.

'The glory of the LORD is risen upon thee'. His glory is going to be seen all over you. You do not need to 'work it up', or make pretence at being anointed. As surely as the radiance of the early morning sun falls upon the tallest of trees and the highest of hills first, so those who will rise up to his call will know and experience the sunshine of his glorious brightness as they stretch themselves to his command.

The night of weeping is over; the tears are wiped away, for joy comes with the morning light. 'Weeping may endure for a night, but joy cometh in the morning.' Psalm 30:5

Darkness is covering the earth right now as never before and the threatening clouds of approaching storms are always there in the headlines for all to see. Gross darkness is consuming the nations and the world is filling with violence day by day.

But in the midst of such blackness, the light of God is going to rise upon the lives of those who hear his voice and all will see that the glory, blessing and goodness of God is resting upon them, (and I am not referring to the self-appointed 'apostles' who fly around in their private jets claiming that they need such luxuries to save the world! Nobody except beguiled and deluded 'Christians' are fooled by such titles and possessions.)

God's own glory will be seen upon the true Warriors of Christ. They do not need an expensive car, or flash clothes to try and convince others that they are blessed. The presence of God all over them will be the proof of God's divine favour and is far more valuable and attractive than mountains of wealth and material assets.

God is not going to share his glory with the proud and presumptive, nor with the silly flock that run around after them.

'Wherefore come out from among them and be ye separate, saith the Lord and touch not the unclean thing; and I will receive you.' 2Corinthians 6:17

And the Gentiles, the unconverted, will come to thy light. When God's light is upon us, when his glory rests on us and when his anointing covers us, then the unsaved will be drawn to him. They will see Christ more than they see us. Who needs a huge conference when God is amongst his people? Where two or three are gathered together in his name there is a 'conference' second to none. Who needs a glitzy 'Christian' music show when all of Heaven sings over you when you lift your voice to God? If the angels sing around you in the fields, then why do you need to worship the performing 'artists' of the travelling 'musical circus'?

Who needs to pay the glamour-preachers their tithing demands when Christ is walking with his children? He who has Christ has everything and does not need to try and 'bribe' God for extra blessings.

Who needs to travel halfway round the world for some dubious 'revival' led by even more-dubious preachers, when the glory of God sits on us right where we are? We shall have our own revival where the only 'personality' needed is that of Jesus Christ.

'Behold, the days come, saith the Lord GOD, that I will send a famine in the land, not a famine of bread, nor a thirst for water, but of hearing the words of the LORD: And they shall wander from sea to sea and from the north even to the east, they shall run [even fly] to and fro to seek the word of the LORD and shall not find it.' Amos 8:11-12

This is what has been happening for the last thirty years or so. The multitude of 'believers' have been running around the world chasing every 'prophet', 'apostle', 'revival' and 'experience' that has been on offer, in an attempt to discover the true words of the Lord. They are still running. It is laughable, yet sad.

You can go to America on a special package to chase tornadoes. If you are fortunate enough you may get to experience one first-hand but you cannot bring it back with you. At the end of the day, all you felt was the wind and now it is gone. You may come back with a photograph, but that is all you have.

The people run around trying to catch the wind, but God is not in the commotion, the noise, or the confusion. But he is found to be very near to them who seek him with a perfect heart (1Kings 19:11-13).

We can use all of the money that we save from travel, books, CDs, DVDs and all those 'love-offerings', 'seed' gifts, 'special donations', to feed the poor, clothe the naked and distribute Gospel material throughout the land. Then Isaiah 58 might just become a reality in our lives.

Oh dear, I think I hear some wailing and gnashing and grinding of teeth from the 'wealth-seeking', 'experience' loving conference-goers!

Let those who are beguiled remain beguiled, but go thou and be all that God calls you to be.

'Let the dead bury their dead: but go thou and preach the kingdom of God.' Luke 9:60

THE RISE
OF
THE GUARDIANS

Chapter Seven

The Rise Of The Guardians

Hidden away, buried under the noise of all the false prophets and wretched misinterpreting teachers of the Bible on a million church and conference platforms, are a unique and special group of men that I shall call 'The Guardians'.

These are 'men that have understanding of the times, to know what Israel [God's people] ought to do.' 1Chronicles 12:32. These are men who know the truth and teach sound doctrine. They have been schooled in the 'old paths' of righteousness. (Jeremiah 6:16; Psalm 23:3)

They might be considered to be 'out of touch' by this compromising and corrupt age, but they are confidently and powerfully in step with God.

They may have been silent for years, unobserved and even disregarded as 'extremists' by some of the church 'hierarchy', but they are God's men for the moment and will come with sword in hand and defy every foe both 'foreign' and 'domestic'.

These men have insight and understand the times that they live in. They know the cause and they know the cure. They see the future and they see the path to deliverance and victory. Good and righteous politicians need these men more than the finest advisors they may have in the Cabinet. (Daniel 5:11-12)

There are indeed many voices who all claim to know what God is saying and what the future holds, but the difference is the 'divine understanding' of the times and the 'real and authentic word' for today. The troupe of false prophets will keep the crowds amused night after night, but they that have godly understanding are like a hammer that will break the rock of heresy in pieces and like a fire that will burn up the false teachers and their admirers.

'Is not my word like as a fire? saith the LORD; and like a hammer that breaketh the rock in pieces?' Jeremiah 23:29

These men know the truth and have held the truth secure in their hearts. They know sound doctrine and have not been moved away by the popularity of the charlatan preachers. They have examined the 'new moves', the 'fresh revelations', the 'third waves' and all the other false claims of various television ministries and have tested, tried and proved them wrong. They refuse to compromise for the 'sake of peace'. They will not abandon the truth just to please the crowd or get themselves onto popular platforms. They are true soldiers of Christ in spite of the fierceness of the battle at times and the weakness of their own flesh. They still remain standing, strong and unflinching in the face of their antagonists and accusers.

Some of these men are 'veterans'; battle-hardened soldiers who have seen the tragic deception of their own people, watched in horror at the vaunted pretence of 'plastic Christianity' on the international stages and seen the slow degradation of their nation before their eyes. They are taken up night and day with the dreadful condition of their society, the ineffectiveness of the church, the sham and disgrace of greed-driven false preachers, the corruption and trickery of their governments and the rise of the beasts of hostile forces seeking to overthrow everything great about their country.

They are not perfect men, but they have perfect hearts that run after God and even though some have fallen in the mud, been crushed by the serpent and mutilated by the accusers, nonetheless, they stand tall and strong in the Lord. It has frustrated them that their voices were never heard and that their so-called 'brothers and sisters' despised them for being 'out of step'. Yet they never gave up, never gave in and never surrendered.

I was given a 'Wobbly Man' when I was very young and this amazing toy was made of plastic with a rounded base filled with sand. This meant that no matter what you did to it, kick it, throw it, roll it, or try to drown it, it would always bounce back to the upright position.

Like that 'Wobbly Man', these Guardians cannot be made to lie down and be silent. They will always come back up and stand on their feet, much to the annoyance of all the loathers of their blood both in the church and outside of it.

Like Nehemiah, their hearts are absorbed continuously with the dreadful state of their country and especially with the deplorable condition of God's 'household'.

'My bowels, my bowels! I am pained at my very heart; my heart maketh a noise in me; I cannot hold my peace, because thou hast heard, O my soul, the sound of the trumpet, the alarm of war.' Jeremiah 4:19

'Oh that my head were waters and mine eyes a fountain of

tears, that I might weep day and night for the slain of the daughter of my people!' Jeremiah 9:1

Their breath is like a sighing in the land (Exodus 2:23); their voice echoes throughout the corridors of time and space; their heartbeat sounds a constant appeal to Heaven for mercy and restoration. Every footstep they take numbers and counts their requests to God and their eyes are constantly looking to the skies for mercy and grace. Herein lies the real evidence, the living proof that such a soul is a true servant of the Lord. Even though they may drift off at times, yet their heart will bring them back to this path of constant prayer, (Ephesians 6:18), to this high calling of God in Christ Jesus, (Philippians 3:14).

When they see the children in the street their hearts rise to God for salvation and protection; when they observe the decadence of the youth and the alcoholic destruction of our young people, their spirit sends out appeals to the Highest; when they read their newspaper, depths of supplication (prayer for favour) and intercession (to plead for someone) comes heavily upon them.

These are called out from the crowd, separated to fulfil a ministry unlike any other and destined to rise at the appropriate moment to complete the task ordained of them by God.

Some of the upcoming Warriors and potential Guardians may be just youngsters who have recently discovered the reality of God and have been baptized with a spirit of prayer and intercession. These are hungering after righteousness and true knowledge. They are not taken in by the 'playschool' mindlessness of contemporary Christianity. They search for the wisdom and depth of understanding that goes beyond the dancing and jiving of the silly crowd around yet another 'Christian' band and its travelling 'miracle-worker'.

They do not feel comfortable in the pretension of a religion that claims to be 'the move of God', but actually has no evidence of the power of God and no sense of the fear of the Lord. They are not fools and will not be tricked into compromising the convictions of their own hearts. They know what is 'real' and they know what is a sham.

These are the 'extra-ordinary' youth who will learn the ways of the King. They find no value or purpose in this passing world, but have harnessed their minds and hearts to those things which are eternal in essence. They are aware of the urgency and desperation of the days we live in and are ready to forsake all and follow Christ.

They are a transformed generation and a transforming generation. Some of the older Guardians must pass the truth on to them and hand the baton into their charge to run the race and raise the royal ensign once more across the nations.

I believe that there is a heavenly 'move' afoot. There is a 'sound of rustling in the leaves of the trees', as though a wind were starting to blow, telling the tale of an approaching storm.

'And let it be, when thou hearest the sound [rumble, distant thunder] of a going [marching] in the tops of the mulberry trees, that then thou shalt bestir thyself: for then shall the LORD go out before thee, to smite the host of the Philistines.' 2Samuel 5:24

There is not just a storm coming, but an army, a powerful

troop of warriors, disciplined, focused, strong and determined. They are the first line of defence, the first battalion of swordsmen and 'the arrow of the LORD's deliverance', (2Kings 13:17). They not only carry the two-edged sword, but they also exercise the high praises of God, the shout of victory and the cry of defiance (Psalm 149).

They are being roused, even now as you read these pages and are preparing the battlefield for the Guardians to rise into their position and destiny. These Guardians are expert in handling the sword, trained and tested in every situation, dignified and confident and contenders for the faith that defines the truth and keeps it pure. There is nothing 'sentimental' or effeminate about them and neither do they use 'emotionalism' to stir up the crowd. They simply deliver the truth fearlessly, yet passionately and live and fight for a cause. They do not know the word 'surrender'.

Throughout the history of the church they have always been there, handing their baton over to the next generation and defending the foundations and 'the pillar and ground of truth', (1Timothy 3:15). They carry the ensign of righteousness amidst the tumult and speak with authority and power. Their words shake the ground, send fire along the floor and drive the clouds of oppression backward. They stand side by side, though sometimes miles apart and strike terror into the enemy's breast. They carry the true Word, deliver the true Word and shake the very gates of hell itself.

There are some who desire this office and play-act the part, spouting and trumpeting themselves in the streets, but pride and arrogance render them ineffective and prove their insignificance. True Guardians are true men, acknowledged by God, known in Heaven, recognised in the counsel meetings of Satan and loathed by the hypocrites.

Who they are and where they all are we do not know, but they will be revealed in their rightful time and will be targeted by every demon in the land.

The first attack will come from the religious and the church leaders, followed quickly by the masses of deceived followers of the platform 'stars' and performers. However, a section of the Warriors will stand in the gap and make up the hedge around the Guardians, but will not necessarily be acknowledged or even be recognised by the marauding hosts. This is the most fearful aspect of what we might call the 'elite' warriors. They are the SAS of the kingdom and work secretly and covertly to destroy the plans of the enemy. These Warriors will learn how to despatch the opposition and thwart their evil words against the servants of God.

Most people want to be recognised for their 'giftings' and spiritual worth, but not so these warriors. Their Commander in Chief is Christ Jesus and their rewards and victory souvenirs are laid up for them in Heaven; and it is their delight to do all his bidding whilst on earth.

These under-cover operatives may never come to light in this world, but be sure of this: they are the ones who are standing between death and life for our children and for our nation. They might be seen on top of the hill in the pouring rain, standing before God on behalf of their country, or perhaps walking in solitude along the beach praying for divine intervention and protection over those on their hearts. They might be seen stood in the centre of their cities defying the works of darkness and standing in the gap for their people. They may be shut up in their own houses with not a friend in the world, but they enjoy direct access to the throne of God.

There is a battle ahead and if God has called you to come to the fight, then you had better ready yourself (Joshua 4:13), get your mind transformed (Romans 12:12) and get your combat gear on, (Ephesians 6:11-13). There is much talk these days about 'spiritual warfare', but in reality, most of it is just another childish 'pseudo-spiritual' game that people play. The true soldiers are praying secretly and they do not need a ministry title to prove their 'spirituality'.

A whole catalogue of 'deliverance ministries' and 'intercession' groups, along with many other amazing titles, fill up the search engines on the internet and social networks, but God's true warriors simply go about their business serving him and not looking for any other reward except the smile on his face. If those so-called 'ministries' were to spend as much time praying as they do filling their computers with 'religious twaddle', perhaps they might actually accomplish something of worth in the earth.

Oops! I hear some more squealing from the 'super-spiritual'; it sounds like hundreds of tom-cats being slowly squeezed through an old hand-mangle!

UNUSUAL AUTHORITY

Chapter Eight

Unusual Authority

The true rulers of a nation are not the 'puppet' figureheads that you see elected into office by vote; neither the dictators who assume that they have a 'divine' right to lead.

A man becomes president or leader of some country somewhere and either does the nation good, or pulls it down and hurts its population. It is the forces of darkness or the forces of light that are behind him that are really in control. Behind the scene there are hidden powers at work, for the real rulers of this world are not made of flesh and blood, but are 'spiritual' beings, either for righteousness or for wickedness. And then there are the Guardians.

The Bible speaks of 'principalities and powers' and the 'rulers of the darkness' of this world. It is referring to demonic entities, even dark princes of violence and evil, of hatred and murder and of corruption and control. They can be perceived only spiritually and must be confronted with the 'spiritual' weapons of battle if indeed things are ever to change.

There are 'powers' out there both good and evil, some of them mighty angels of light and others princes of darkness.

The captains of evil subjugate entire nations and even whole races of people, blinding them to the truth

(2Corinthians 4:4) and making them slaves to rituals and habits, to lusts and perversions and to war and self-destruction.

Jesus came to destroy the works of the devil and to set men free from their captivity. 'For this purpose the Son of God was manifested, that he might destroy the works of the devil.' 1John 3:8

'To proclaim liberty to the captives and the opening of the prison to them that are bound.' Isaiah 61:1

Governments and leaders can be used by the devil to tear down a nation and its Christian faith and heritage, or they can be used by God to establish righteousness and truth throughout the land.

'Righteousness exalteth [lifts up, blesses and prospers] a nation: but sin is a reproach [shame and disfigurement] to any people.' Proverbs 14:34

God always had his Guardians watching over the nation of Israel, ready to speak at the right time and ready to bring a word of rebuke at other moments. Here in England God still has his Guardians hidden away in this beautiful Isle. Throughout our history they have always been there and every now and again they are brought to the forefront to execute His commands and steer the people back to the right way.

They were murdered and burnt alive at the stake by the Roman Catholic Church, yet in the flames they raised their hands and voices in praise to God, because they were still ruling, still reigning over all the evil of that institution. Because of their heroic stand and sacrifice we were freed from the tyranny of Rome at the time of the Reformation. Many in the crowd around those awful sights were struck to the heart, convicted that these men and women were true servants of God and yielded their lives to Christ.

Kings and Queens such as Henry 8th, Edward 6th, Elizabeth 1st and James 1st (in spite perhaps of many failings) came to the defence of the truth and refused to bow to any foreign powers or religions. Men like Wycliffe, William Tyndale, Bunyan, Matthew Henry, Joseph Alleine, Spurgeon and countless others stood in the gap in the midst of heresy and threats. In spite of intimidation from foes within and hostiles outside they preached righteousness and raised the Word of God; over all the screaming adversaries.

Then there was John and Charles Wesley, George Whitfield and William Booth who would not have their voices stifled in the pulpit, but took to the fields and town squares and proclaimed truth to the multitudes. They were besieged and stoned by the mobs, attacked by the 'religious', threatened and accused, but none could stop them or shut them up.

William Booth (founder of the Salvation Army) wrote a book entitled, 'Darkest England and the way out' and through his authority in God tackled the slums of our cities, brought in under-age drinking laws, marched through the towns and cities of this country fearlessly preaching the Gospel and made the government shake in their shoes at the very sound of his name. They actually had him watched day and night for they feared he might wish to take over running the country.

Booth's book was used as the blueprint for the present day welfare state in the United Kingdom when it was

set up by the government in 1948. Many of Booth's ideas were incorporated into our welfare state system.

Countless others went unrecognised, but stood alone on top of mountains, along the streets in our towns and cities, in the corridors of government, in universities and schools and exercised their God-given authority over men and demons.

These Guardians are the real government. They are the government above the government. They are the first and most powerful rulers in the nation. They are the 'chariots and horsemen' that decide whether it will rain or not rain. They are the ones who know the tactics and plans of the enemy even before he has a chance to put them into place. They make the blind see and they cause the 'seeing' to be made blind. Their word destroys the counsel of the wisest of advisers who seek harm to their people, (2Samuel 15:31). They are preserved by God for such a time as this.

Whilst all of Israel was suffering from drought and national disaster, besieged by their hostile neighbours (2Kings 7:24-25), Elisha was sat peacefully in his house with his elders. King Jehoram, despairing of the situation in his country and knowing that this man Elisha was to blame (acknowledging that he was the one who was actually in control), sent messengers to his house to kill him.

'Then he [the king] said, God do so and more also to me, if the head of Elisha the son of Shaphat shall stand on him this day. But Elisha sat in his house and the elders sat with him.' 2 Kings 7:31-32

Here is the place of power. Here is the place of authority. Elisha was not running around the country to every new meeting or every visiting preacher. He was not flustered by the frantic behaviour of his own people or that of the enemy. He knew who he was and knew what he was called to do by God.

The Bible says that Christ is sat down at the right hand of the Majesty on High, from where he reigns and rules.

'Who (Jesus) being the brightness of his glory and the express image of his person and upholding all things by the word of his power, when he had by himself purged our sins, sat down on the right hand of the Majesty on high.' Hebrews 1:3

'But this man, after he had offered one sacrifice for sins for ever, sat down on the right hand of God.' Hebrews 10:12 'Who is gone into heaven and is on the right hand of God; angels and authorities and powers being made subject unto him.' 1Peter 3:22

He upholds and controls all things from where he is seated. The conqueror is seated, for he has won the battle and subdued his enemies. His word now holds everything together and it is sufficient for him to say to his officers and servants, "go here, go there; do this and do that" and they obey him.

Queen Victoria, during the time of the British Empire, did not have to run around the world trying to maintain her extensive realm. She sat on the throne of England and there spoke her commands to all of her officers who carried out her orders explicitly. She was in control, even though her kingdom stretched around the entire planet.

Elisha was sat in the place as one who was in perfect control. Some short time before this event, the king of Syria had decided to attack Israel (see 2Kings 6:8-23). Elisha sent a message to his own king warning him of the precise location of where the attack would begin. This happened on several occasions and in different areas and the king of Syria became very concerned that perhaps he had a spy within his camp. He interrogated his own servants to find out who was the culprit, the traitor, and one of them replied, 'None, my lord, O king: but Elisha, the prophet that is in Israel, telleth the king of Israel the words that thou speakest in thy bedchamber.' 2Kings 6:12

Elisha knew the enemy's plans long before he even discussed them with his generals and was not in the slightest bit concerned when that king sent an entire army to surround the city and seize him. Elisha's servant was more than distressed at the sight of the Syrians that had them pinned in a corner. In fear and dismay he cried, 'Alas, my master! how [what] shall we do?' (2Kings 6:15)

Elisha calmly replied, 'Do not be afraid: for there are far more with us than there are with them'; and the Lord opened the servants eyes to see that the whole of the mountain was filled with angelic warriors, horses and chariots all surrounding God's man.

The prophet understood his call of God and the high calling of his office in the nation of Israel, for he was passed the baton by his predecessor Elijah, (2Kings 2:13).

He had watched in astonishment as Elijah was taken up into Heaven before his very eyes. He beheld the 'chariot of fire and horses of fire' (2Kings 2:11) and the divine whirlwind that lifted his mentor from off the face of the earth. He declared, "My father, my father, the chariot of Israel and the horsemen thereof."

Here indeed was the real army of his country, the father of

his people, the horses and riders of government and true authority! And now he must take up the same 'mantle', pick up the baton and exercise the same awesome office. Here are the true Guardians operating within their righteous spheres. The angels of the Lord stand at their side and encamp round about them. (Psalm 34:7)

Who were these astonishing men? How could it be that the fate of the nation rested in their hands and not that of the ruling power? According to James, Elijah was a man just like you or me, subject to all of the frailty that we know (James 5:17-18), yet walking on a level of understanding and knowledge that few ever discover. They walked with the angels in the supreme corridors of Heaven, brushed against their wings and had them at their disposal whenever they required their help. They heard the discussions and decisions that were made in Heaven's governmental courts day by day and used their seat and veto to plead on behalf of their own wayward country, supplicating for divine grace and favour.

'Thus saith the LORD of hosts; If thou wilt walk in my ways, and if thou wilt keep my charge, then thou shalt also judge [rule, govern] my house and shalt also keep my courts [be seated in my counsel chambers, and I will give thee places to walk among these that stand by [the angels].' Zechariah 3:7

They were not there for any financial gain or getting recognised amongst the famous and influential. They were not 'conference speakers' and in fact would probably have avoided such gatherings and climbed a mountain somewhere to enjoy the company of God. They were the covering for their people, the hedge of protection around them and exercised their priestly office on behalf of the entire nation. They were hidden from view for months, even years and then would somewhat reluctantly immerge into the limelight to deliver a word, or perform a miracle or two. However, just their presence in the nation was the unseen preservation and security of their race, even though judgement and correction were to fall many times upon the people for their sin. They stood before God for the children, for the teenagers, for the young people and future generations, answering the charges, responding to the questions and seeking for God to add grace upon grace to those whom he has set his love upon.

'And I sought for a man among them, that should make up the hedge and stand in the gap before me for the land that I should not destroy it: but I found none.' Ezekiel 22:30

Will God find us willing and faithful in this time of great need and trouble to forsake everything and rise to become those who will build a wall of defence on behalf of our people?

Elijah and Elisha did not live in luxury, have the finest travel arrangements, neither a single bank account to their name, (I just read of yet another self-appointed 'apostle' who has recently gotten himself a private jet so that he can "save the whole world." Ho! Ho! Ho!).

Like John the Baptist out in the wilderness (Mark 1:6) they never had fridges and cupboards filled with nice food but opened their hands to God above and received miraculous supply as and when they needed it. They were not wonderfully clothed in designer suits and crocodile skin shoes and would not be too welcome on our platforms these days, but they were the ambassadors of God, the emissaries of

Christ. They carried the keys of the kingdom and no door could be shut to them which God had opened and no door could be opened which they shut. Their word struck fear into their enemies and spoke life into the dead. They were the gold to the dross, the wheat to the chaff and the genuine to the counterfeit.

Warriors and Guardians are looked upon as rebels, outlaws, too independent and outcasts, but thus it shall always be to those who truly walk with God. They sit reigning in Christ whilst the entire world rocks in distress. They command situations without the need for their voice to be heard but when they do speak, their words bring conviction and disturbance to those that are 'at ease in Zion' (Amos 6:1). They are warriors of the light and stand invincible in the strength of God. Though they fall, yet they do not stay down; they rise again strengthened by the right hand of the Almighty. (Psalm 37:24; Micah 7:8; Luke 22:31-32; Psalm 138:7)

A young Israeli delivered my new passport just a few weeks back. We got to talking about the dire situation here in England and he shared the grave concerns that I did also. I told him however that God has always had 'Guardians' in this land which was entrusted with the Bible and the propagation of the Gospel to the whole world and that they were soon to rise and stand up for the truth. He was amazed and asked whether I was referring to 'spiritual' beings. I told him they were certainly spiritual, but also that they were men who were appointed by God for this time, as in former generations.

I told him about our godly heritage and some of our history that has long been forgotten. He asked me why people did not know the truth anymore and I told him that a devilish plot has been abroad in this land for a long time to destroy both our history and our culture. I also told him that things are going to change. He was excited and wished that he had more time to speak, but was on a tight schedule and had to go.

England still has its secret Guardians and no 'religion' or hostile invasion is going to destroy them or their words, or their extraordinary influence over this land. The 'pretend' church and its heretical preachers cannot destroy them or silence them. To kill them is but to birth a thousand in their place.

If you are such a one and as you read this book you sense that God is speaking to you, then you are now hearing the call to rise, to leave the world and all its toys behind and begin to learn how to co-operate in God's high calling.

Maybe you are not in this country, but hear God speaking clearly to you. America needs the truth, likewise India, Africa, Europe, New Zealand Australia and so on and the Guardians around the world must begin to rise up along with all the sleeping Warriors.

We need to bring back that thing that the glossy televangelists hate so much:

Sound Doctrine

'For the time will come [has come] when they will not endure sound doctrine; but after their own lusts shall they heap to themselves teachers, having itching ears.' 2Timothy 4:3

'But speak thou the things which become sound doctrine.' Titus 2:1

> 'Holding fast the faithful word as he hath been taught, that he may be able by sound doctrine both to exhort and to convince the gainsayers [those who are argumentative].' Titus 1:9
>
> 'Till I come, give attendance to reading, to exhortation, to doctrine.' 1Timothy 4:13

Most Christians do not know what sound doctrine is and their television 'idol' has sneered so much at the phrase that they actually now believe that it is an evil thing. A faith without doctrine is a ship without an anchor. It will be tossed and turned by every whim and imagination.

'My people are destroyed for lack of knowledge.' Hosea 4:6

Switch off the television, even if it is only the 'Christian' programmes that you watch and buy a decent newspaper (not the sordid type with pictures of half-clad girls) and find out what is going on in your country and in the world.

Get your Bible out and look up every verse that I quote or refer to in these three books and become acquainted with God's ways. Ask God to put a passion in your life that flows from His love being shed abroad in your heart, for unless God's love is flowing through you, you will be of no use to him whatsoever.

You might be zealous and eager to do something, but zeal without knowledge and eagerness without compassion is simply a ship without a rudder. It has no way of steering a safe and effective path.

'The love of God is shed abroad in our hearts by the Holy Ghost which is given unto us.' Romans 5:5 'He that loveth not knoweth not God; for God is love.' 1John 4:8

Then learn for yourself sound doctrine, for if you do not know or understand what it is you believe and why it is you believe it, then you are simply a blind soul leading blind souls and all will fall into a ditch. (I have included a very short list of recommended reading at the back of this book).

Dump all the collection of your platform-idol's paperbacks, DVDs, CDs and magazines and open up the Book of Books. Break free from your slavery to the man or woman who has been elevated to some place of 'spirituality' that they never deserved and are not worthy of. You only need Christ.

Pray this prayer (a song I recently wrote):

> Lord, have mercy on this nation,
> Send your Spirit down from Heaven,
> For we need a Reformation,
> A Great Awakening in this land.
>
> Touch our children and our teenagers;
> Save our young people with their families.
> In righteous judgement, remember mercy,
> And save the people of this great land.
>
> Save our young women from the perverts,
> Keep our children from being stolen.
> Confuse the haters who curse our people,
> And bring revival to this land.
>
> Raise an army of fearless soldiers
> Cleansed and washed in Jesus' blood;
> Exalt your Word throughout this nation;
> And send revival like a flood!

Spiritual Contraception

Have you ever noticed how little the 'big name' preachers actually use their Bibles? They talk a lot about themselves and the 'miracles' they have performed and the 'words' that God apparently gives to them and the strange and bizarre experiences they have in their sleep and so on. There are so many 'I am this', 'I did this', 'I said that' and so on in their preaching that it is a wonder God could ever have got near to them.

The noticeable difference between the 'performers' on 'Christian' television and the Guardians and true Warriors is the way the latter point you to Christ and away from themselves. The charlatans are full of themselves and the arena is enthralled with their presence. The only person being sought for a photograph or handshake at the end of the service is the laughing 'entertainer' dancing on the platform, wondering how much he took in tonight's offering.

To meet a Guardian or Warrior is to encounter the presence of Christ, for they only glorify Him and hide behind his majesty. They introduce you to the King of Kings for his handshake and blessing and would sooner leave the building in order that you keep your eyes on Christ rather than run after men.

It is said that John Bunyan (Pilgrim's Progress), having once preached a great message, was greeted by a layman who exclaimed, "That was the most powerful sermon I have ever heard!" Bunyan replied with brute honesty, "Man, you need not tell me that. The devil whispered it to me before I was well out of the pulpit."

It is true that the big names also leave the building as quickly as possible surrounded by their security guards and 'minders'. However, this is only because they do not wish to be 'mithered' by the crowd of their admirers and just need to get to a good restaurant to eat and 'chill-out'.

In the history of real revivals, the preacher would retire to a room to pray for the work that God had just accomplished and to wait on him until He granted leave to go.

You say that I am 'old-fashioned'?

I say that truth never changes.

I mentioned earlier that the reason for the decline of our race here in England is mainly due to abortion and the widespread use of contraceptives. I would enlarge upon this and bring it into the spiritual arena. The great decline in real Christianity, in the true seed of the Gospel is the popular practice of contraception and abortion within the church. Let me explain;

We have shunned the true message of the Bible for something different and offered the people a contraceptive, the condom of 'entertainment' and personal pleasure. We offer bands and travelling 'worship groups', stage-plays and performances, 'conjuring' routines and 'x-factor' stars who get everyone laughing or clapping at their acts.

We offer an alternative 'faith' that costs nothing, demands nothing, (except your hard-earned cash) and carries no responsibility with it either. So long as they are happy and enjoying themselves and of course 'believe' in Jesus, then all is well. We threw away the Holy Bible and got ourselves any old liberal 'translation' that is not 'so scary', leaves us to our own interpretation and gives us licence to live how we like.

We ended up with a whole generation of comfort-zone 'thrill-seekers', but they do not want the responsibility of obeying God, bearing (spiritual) children and living godly lives.

If perchance a child is born who somehow becomes a lover of sound doctrine and righteous living, the church seeks to get rid of them as soon as possible. If they are seen to be militant (wanting to be a soldier of the Cross), or independent thinkers who seek after God for themselves and refuse to be comforted by the laughter of the charismatic hyenas, then they soon dispose of them and seek to abort them as quickly as possible.

Who wants real children these days? That is far too troublesome!

Women were born to have babies and men were designed to increase and populate the earth. The church was born to preach the Gospel and bring a righteous seed from every country on this planet, to fill the whole world with those who know God for themselves.

A recent article in the Daily Telegraph tells us that the question that has 'baffled' the scientists since the time of Charles Darwin – 'What is the point of sex?' – has now been answered. Researchers have now come up with the conclusion that it is to fight off parasites in order that males will exist! So amazing! So incredible! So stupid!

The Bible makes it so simple, so natural and so scientific. God told Adam and Eve to go populate the earth and designed their bodies and impulses in such a way as to do so. Men in their wisdom cannot find God, neither can they find out his knowledge or plans.

'They have not known nor understood: for he hath shut their eyes, that they cannot see; and their hearts, that they cannot understand.' Isaiah 44:18

The church is called to fill the earth with righteous offspring. It is a natural thing to do and a natural 'drive' that is birthed into every true believer.

The majority of Christians these days just run from meeting to meeting to tickle each other, have a good laugh, enjoy the world and pray for increase, blessing and added wealth so that they can feel good about themselves. This is their contraceptive. It produces nothing except arrogance, presumption and deception (three more devils of deceit).

No real babies are born, certainly not the kind that will turn the world upside down or tear down the citadels of darkness, or bring the anointing of Isaiah 61 to a sick and dying age.

'We have been with child [seemingly pregnant], we have been in pain [gone through the physical motions], we have as it were brought forth wind [the body was bloated as one who looked pregnant, but it was just stinking gas]; [the fact is] we have not wrought any deliverance in the earth; neither have the inhabitants of the world fallen.' Isaiah 26:18

The blown-up, exaggerated advertising and promoting of man-made 'revivals' is no more than a build up of carnal 'gas'. It may look like it is 'Christian' and therefore must 'be of God', but a closer inspection will soon burst the balloon and all the squeaky helium-infused voices of the false prophets will fade away in due time.

Carnality seeks only personal pleasure and indulging, but it never comes free. You will always end up paying the Pied-

Piper for his music and dancing; and your entertainment is bought at the door to the conference with your ten percent or however much more the actor can squeeze out of you. But you like being squeezed.

'Let him that hath ears to hear.........'

WHAT ARE WE WAITING FOR?

Chapter Nine

What Are We Waiting For?

It seems like we are all waiting for something to happen. We would like our nation to be restored, for our schools to be better, for righteousness in society, for the immigration situation to change, for economic revival and so on. We wait for a sensible government, for the men at the top to come to their senses and realize that things are out of control. We hope that someone somewhere will take up our cause and fight our corner for us.

We wish that God would raise up a voice in the nation that would speak up on behalf of our Christian heritage and the need to look after our own people. We surrender to the thought that we can do nothing to change our country and we are helpless to influence the outcome of the unjust censorship of free speech.

This is where the enemy has taken full advantage of us, for he comes marching up our streets and roads in the assurance that nobody will do anything to stop him. This is why God is waking up the Warriors and the Guardians.

Will it be the government that ultimately rids our land of the enemies of the Gospel of Jesus Christ? Who is it that will 'put the armies of the aliens to flight'? (Hebrews 11:34)

How will justice, righteousness and equity return to this

land? How will the Word of God be magnified over this entire nation once more?

Who will save our children from the preying 'prostitution-network' foreigners? Who will rescue our young people from alcohol? Who will give us our liberties back again?

It will be the rising of these champions through their resonating voices, their unshakable confidence and above all, their defiant faith.

It is faith that moves the mountains of evil and sin. It is faith that overcomes the screaming of the adversaries.

It is faith that chases out the armies of unbelievers and it is faith that brings deliverance, salvation and hope once again to an ailing people.

In the face of the screaming protestors demanding that our laws get changed, it is faith that will rise up and drown their voices.

In the unashamed determination of those who would see our bloodline annihilated, it is faith that will overcome their plans and ambitions.

It is this outrageous and immovable faith of God inside his people that will change the outcome of a thousand situations, overthrow the unjust determinations of our government, halt the progress of our enemies, change the curriculum in our schools, revive the church from its downward spiral and bring joy and gladness back to our people.

This eternal faith, this amazing and undervalued gift of God has changed the course of history, thrown down unrighteous leaders, removed men and women from office, stopped the enemy's advance, swept thousands into the kingdom of God and raised up generations of godly evangelists, pastors and teachers.

This faith will not yield, submit, or crawl to the insistence of terrorists, tyrants, primitives, or barbarians.

It is the same faith that brought the three young men during Nebuchadnezzar's time into the fiery furnace and delivered them out of it without a hair on their heads being singed. This faith gave Daniel the confidence and assurance to nestle up against the hungry lions and use their fur as his pillow.

In the darkest night, under the most impossible circumstances this faith laughs at the troubles and mocks the enemy's loathing. It counts it a joy to be challenged by trials and difficulties, knowing that God is bigger than all that comes against it and nothing can by any means destroy it.

It rejoices through the stormy night of distress, marches through the blizzard of spite and vindictiveness, lights a flaming beacon along every mile of its journeying and flies a flag of defiance across the battlefield of this world.

It rises to its full strength when faced with insurmountable and overwhelming odds. It discovers its greatest power when seemingly at the point of defeat and failure. It blazes at its brightest when the darkness surrounds and threatens to engulf it completely.

This is the faith that will save our country and our countrymen.

This is the 'force' that will shut up the oppressors; this is the weapon that will subdue all of our enemies under our feet.

'And all this assembly shall know that the LORD saveth not with sword and spear [not with guns and knives, not with violent protests and petrol bombs]: for the battle is the LORD'S and he will give you [our enemies] into our hands.'

1Samuel 17:47

This faith is indefatigable (incapable of being tired out or admitting defeat) and it is this faith that Satan fears most in the people of God. Nothing can stand against it!

This faith of God, this divine gift of the Holy Spirit is living in us, ever-victorious, supremely stronger than any enemy, more influential than the President or Prime Minister and is capable of pulling down the strongest opposition and the most evil of imaginations and conspiracies.

This faith in us is for this world now, not for the world to come, for there we shall need no faith at all. Young people might see this faith like the 'Force' that Star Wars speaks about. This faith is with you and in you and can be used, or can be ignored. It is a shield that surrounds you like a 'force-field'. Nothing can penetrate or destroy it.

'But thou, O LORD, art a shield for me [literally, the 'force-field' of protection all around you]; my glory [my rejoicing and splendour] and the lifter up of mine head.' Psalm 3:3

The Warriors as well as the Guardians will learn how to exercise this faith in a way that they have never done before. They will discover that there are no limits to its power and energy and there is not an army in the world that can resist it when it is operating at God's level. It is supernatural in its essence and is within us, ready and willing to work on our behalf, giving praise to God.

'Have faith in God. For verily I say unto you, That whosoever shall say unto this mountain, Be thou removed and be thou cast into the sea; and shall not doubt in his heart, but shall believe that those things which he saith shall come to pass; he shall have whatsoever he saith. Therefore I say unto you, What things soever ye desire, when ye pray, believe that ye receive them and ye shall have them.' Matthew 11:22-24

You cannot get much clearer than that! Sadly the worldly televangelists have taken these words of Christ and twisted them into a carnal theology that falsely gives you the right to demand money, wealth, houses, cars, planes and a fat belly full of the finest of food. They completely missed the point and turned God into a 'lucky dip' and made faith a superstition for personal greed.

The Warriors and Guardians live for a future inheritance and care not for the dainties of this world. Their task is to fulfil the will of God whilst on earth, engage the enemy in battlefield conditions and propagate the Word of God throughout the land. They are here for a higher purpose and no matter what their earthly employment, their true vocation is to defend the faith, guard the truth and wield the Sword of God's Spirit wherever they go. They are set here on this planet to fulfil their destiny, passing through this time-zone, preparing for a higher service in Heaven.

Faith is not about what they can get, but what they achieve through God and for His glory and for reaching the lost.

The Queen, as the figurehead of our nation is sworn to 'defend the faith' of this country and the Guardians also are sworn to the same objective. Furthermore, they are there for the protection of our people, the future of our line and the blessing and restoration of our land.

When the protestors inform us that we are a 'multicultural society' now, let them also acknowledge that our Queen (or King) stands as the symbol of defence for our historic and ancestral faith. This faith is what we also stand for and defend. It is our faith and if those who wish to come and live here amongst us do not like this fact, then they should go somewhere else where they can feel more comfortable with their surroundings and culture. We are not for changing our history, our faith, or our self-respect. We are coming to take it back.

'Let God arise, let his enemies be scattered: let them also that hate him flee before him. As smoke is driven away, so drive them away: as wax melteth before the fire, so let the wicked perish at the presence of God. But let the righteous be glad; let them rejoice before God: yea, let them exceedingly rejoice.' Psalm 68:1-3

You might speak that out over your nation from time to time.

Back in 2001, Pastor Mark Witherden and I wrote down a Declaration made up of a number of Bible verses. This Declaration was to accompany the flying of a special flag now known as the Crown Flag (www.crownflag.com) and to be spoken over our country every day. Over the last years and especially of late, these words are proving to be right on target to what we believe God is saying and doing in this nation and other nations around the world.

1. 'A sound of battle is in the land!' Jeremiah 50:22
Across this nation and throughout our towns and cities a war is being waged. If you have ears to hear, you can hear

the sound of war, but if your heart is waxed cold and indifferent, then this will just be as the words of an alarmist and an extremist.

'For this people's heart is waxed gross, and their ears are dull of hearing, and their eyes **they have closed**; lest at any time they should see with their eyes, and hear with their ears, and should understand with their heart, and should be converted, and I should heal them.' Mt 13:15

Nonetheless, there is a tumult in this land and there is a fight for the survival and perpetuation of the Gospel as well as for a race of people who have been so blessed of God in all their history. We have engaged the enemy and this word comes to wake up all those who are asleep in Zion and call them to join hand in hand and take back this ground for Christ.

'Blow the trumpet in Zion, sanctify a fast, call a solemn assembly: Gather the people, sanctify the congregation, assemble the elders, gather the children...' Joel 2:15-16

You have been called. The trumpet has been sounded. There are none so deaf as those that do not want to hear.

2. 'The time is fulfilled and the kingdom of God is at hand. Repent and believe the gospel.' Mark 1:15

It is the right time. It is the moment in history when all things are possible, when God is calling us to rise up and obey him.

'When thou saidst, Seek ye my face; my heart said unto thee, Thy face, LORD, will I seek.' Psalm 27:8

There are times and seasons and there are seasons of refreshing.

'To every thing there is a season and a time to every purpose under the heaven.' Ecclesiastes 3:1

There are moments in history when God moves near to do us good, to rescue us from our folly, to save us from our foes. These times are when the kingdom of God comes close and is ready to open the doors of grace to an individual or an entire nation. They are known as times of refreshing and how much we need such a move of God today.

'Repent ye therefore and be converted, that your sins may be blotted out, when the times of refreshing shall come from the presence of the Lord.' Acts 3:19

There are special times when God comes to 'visit' in an unusual way. Let us not miss the opportunity through cynicism, unbelief and pride. Such a triangle of evil can lose us all of the blessings that God so intended for us.

Through sin and backsliding, through casting off our faith and rejecting God's ways, we have found ourselves as a country filled with darkness, oppressed, depressed, lost, lonely, surrounded by hostile enemies of righteousness and without God in our midst.

But this great message comes with a powerful assurance, that if we will listen to the call of God, repent of our waywardness and worldliness, turn back to Him with all of our hearts, then he will save us. His kingdom is at hand. It is ready to open its doors to all the goodness and mercy and supply of Heaven, if we will but hear what the Spirit of God is saying.

'He that hath an ear, let him hear what the Spirit saith unto the churches.' Revelation 3:6

Do you have 'an ear' that can hear the voice of God's Spirit?

You might be able to listen to all the gobbledegook being spouted by your favourite preachers on television, but can you hear the voice that speaks from eternity? (Hebrews 12:25)

The cry of God is that we repent and turn back to him and begin to seek him in full earnest. For those of you who feel you do not have to repent of anything, then go back to sleep. Stay deaf; stay lost; it is your choice.

But for those of you who long for God to move in power in this nation, then turn around and hear the truth, cast off everything that offends your God and prepare the way for him to do something with your life.

'Prepare ye the way of the Lord, make his paths straight.' Mark 1:3

'Go through, go through the gates; prepare ye the way of the people; cast up, cast up the highway [elevate, exalt the way of God]; gather out the stones [the stumbling blocks, sin and rubbish]; lift up a standard [flag, ensign] for the people.' Isaiah 62:10

Repent and believe the good news! From Buckingham Palace down to the cardboard box where a homeless man sleeps, it is time to repent and believe that God has something good in store for us. He can do more than we could ever imagine and there is nothing too hard for him, not even the dreadful condition that we may find ourselves in as individuals or as a people.

There is good news for this land and it is time to take the message to everyone. The Word must be spread once again throughout the entire nation through the printing and distribution of Gospel literature and as many other methods as are possible. You do not need to be famous or well known to do this, but begin your own campaign along with a few others of like mind and make a road of your own to impact the community with truth. God's Word is the truth, (John 17:17).

This is the warrior's sword. We have to take a firm hold of this awesome weapon of righteousness and rediscover its irresistible power as we go out and preach the word.

'It [has] pleased God by the foolishness of preaching to save them that believe.' 1Corinthians 1:21

Notice that it is not through dancing, singing, music or discussion groups that men are saved, but through preaching. 'For the preaching of the cross is to them that perish foolishness; but unto us which are saved it is the power of God.' 1Corinthians 1:18

We need a new generation of preachers who know how to preach the truth with power and irresistible authority. The command is, 'Preach the Word' (2Timothy 4:2), not beg for cash, or 'share some thoughts'.

Maybe you feel like so many others that it is too late for us and we have gone too far down the wrong road. Turn around, look to Jesus Christ the Maker and Master of all things and believe that he is both willing and able to turn the tide, to part the waters, to rescue his people and drown the adversaries just like he did at the Red Sea, (Exodus 15).

'Now unto him that is able to do exceeding abundantly above all that we ask or think [so much better than we could possibly imagine], according to the power that worketh in us.' Ephesians 3:20

3. **'All this assembly shall know that the Lord saveth not with sword and spear: for the battle is the Lord's and He will give you into our hands**.' 1Samuel 17:47

God's own people will see and know for themselves that it is He that fights for us.

'One man of you shall chase a thousand: for the LORD your God, he it is that fighteth for you, as he hath promised you.' Joshua 23:10

All of our adversaries and those who set themselves against us and round about us will be forced to recognise that God fights on our behalf. Those that hate us and despise our blood shall be put to shame at the presence of our God on the battlefield.

'The LORD of hosts is with us; the God of Jacob is our refuge.' Psalm 46:7

'Therefore will not we fear, though the earth be removed and though the mountains be carried into the midst of the sea.' Psalm 46:2

'All nations compassed me about: but in the name of the LORD will I destroy them. They compassed me about; yea, they compassed me about: but in the name of the LORD I will destroy them.' Ps 118:11

'And the LORD opened the eyes of the young man; and he saw: and behold, the mountain was full of horses and chariots of fire round about Elisha.' 2Kings 6:17

This country shall know that God does not save his people through running battles in the streets using physical weapons, but he fights the enemies with the word of his mouth. Just see what is going to happen in the Last Days when all the hostile nations surround Israel for the final conflict. Just when they think that they have the upper hand and are about to triumph over Jerusalem, then Christ will appear adorned in full battle splendour and wipe the smiles from their faces and wipe their memory from off the earth.

'And out of his mouth goeth a sharp sword, that with it he should smite the nations.' Revelation 19:15

'Then shall the LORD go forth and fight against those nations, as when he fought in the day of battle. And his feet shall stand in that day upon the mount of Olives, which is before Jerusalem on the east and the mount of Olives shall cleave in the midst thereof toward the east and toward the west and there shall be a very great valley; and half of the mountain shall remove toward the north and half of it toward the south.' Zechariah 14:3-4

'And this shall be the plague wherewith the LORD will smite all the people that have fought against Jerusalem; Their flesh shall consume away while they stand upon their feet and their eyes shall consume away in their holes and their tongue shall consume away in their mouth.' Zechariah 14:12

And if God is going to do that for Jerusalem, then be sure that he is going to fight for us when we cry unto him for our nation.

All those who live among us seeking our hurt and destruction shall know that God is risen up on our behalf and now the battle belongs to the Lord and he will give them into our hands!

'Call unto me and I will answer thee and shew thee great

and mighty things, which thou knowest not [could not even imagine].' Jeremiah 33:3

'Call upon me in the day of trouble: I will deliver thee and thou shalt glorify me.' Psalm 50:15

God is bigger than our adversaries. His voice is louder than their whining, their chanting and their mocking.

'The LORD thundered from heaven and the most High uttered his voice. And he sent out arrows and scattered them; lightning and discomfited [confused and troubled] them.' 2Samuel 22:14-15

Let us pray these words:

> *'Keep not thou silence, O God: hold not thy peace and be not still, O God. For, lo, thine enemies make a tumult: and they that hate thee have lifted up the head. They have taken crafty counsel against thy people [even us] and consulted against thy hidden ones [even the Warriors and Guardians of truth]. They have said, Come and let us cut them off from being a nation; that the name of Israel [even England also] may be no more in remembrance.' Psalm 83:1-4*

> *'As the fire burneth a wood and as the flame setteth the mountains on fire; so persecute them with thy tempest and make them afraid with thy storm. Fill their faces with shame; that they may seek thy name, O LORD. Let them be confounded and troubled for ever; yea, let them be put to shame and perish: That men may know that thou, whose name alone is JEHOVAH, art the most high over all the earth.' Psalm 83:14-18*

4. **'Lift up your heads, O ye gates; and be ye lifted up, ye everlasting doors; and the King of Glory shall come in. Who is this king of glory? The Lord strong and mighty, the Lord mighty in battle.**' Psalm 24:7-8

You, who long for God to do something, whose hearts are burdened with the awful state of the church and the misery of your own people, lift up your heads.

To every Warrior and every Guardian who may wonder whether there is any hope left for us, whether these things can be true, lift up your faith and expectations!

You are the gates of this nation, the doorways of righteousness and deliverance. The future of your people is in your hands. Satan has slammed the doors shut for too many years now and it is time to make a change and bring in the kingdom of God in all of its power.

The devil has laughed in our faces, belittled us, shut out our voices from being heard and has vaunted himself telling us that he is now in charge. He claims that this country is now his and all of those pledged to him will soon wipe out our memory from these shores. He boasts that he has established citadels of religious defiance throughout the land, changed our laws and regulations, deceived the government and leaders and nobody can now turn the tide back.

But he has not accounted for the Sleepers, even the Guardians! The tide will turn, because it is the law of the tide. Even the tsunami must return to its place.

I watched with so many others as the dreadful tsunami hit Sri Lanka and the South India coast some years back. I had in my mind the picture of one man stood in front of that overwhelming flood holding firmly the royal standard of the Crown Flag and the waters passing each side of him, but not able to overcome him. Imagine this picture, if you will, but with thousands upon thousands of faithful warriors all standing against the daunting waves of evil that now seek to engulf our great country.

As an irresistible wall of defiance and authority, glorious flags flying in the wind, the entire ocean of hatred and rebellion could be sent backward, even as the waters of the Red Sea were held back to allow the Israelites to cross safely. After all, we do not stand alone, but the hosts of the Lord's angels are with us, surrounding us and fighting next to us.

Let the Warriors and Guardians lift up their heads and lift up the everlasting doors of their destiny. They are the hope of this country, known of God and called by him before the world was ever created. 'According as he hath chosen us in him before the foundation of the world.' Ephesians 1:4

'Thou whom I have taken from the ends of the earth and called thee from the chief men thereof and said unto thee, Thou art my servant; I have chosen thee and not cast thee away. Fear thou not; for I am with thee: be not dismayed; for I am thy God: I will strengthen thee; yea, I will help thee; yea, I will uphold thee with the right hand of my righteousness. Behold, all they that were incensed against thee shall be ashamed and confounded: they shall be as nothing; and they that strive with thee shall perish.' Isaiah 41:9-11

'Elect according to the foreknowledge of God the Father, through sanctification of the Spirit, unto obedience and sprinkling of the blood of Jesus Christ: Grace unto you and peace, be multiplied.' 1Peter 1:2 ,

'But ye are a chosen generation, a royal priesthood, an holy nation, a peculiar people; that ye should shew forth the praises of him who hath called you out of darkness into his marvellous light.; 1Peter 2:9

When you lift up your heads and lift up the eternal doors of your heritage, your authority and your right, then the King of Glory shall come in. He shall come into your life, into your house and into your country. He shall come as a man of war, as a victorious conqueror, as the fearful and overcoming Deliverer of his people.

For this you were called and for this time in the history of the world are you here. He will come when you prepare the way for him.

Stand up for your hope and faith, your dream and vision. Rise up and lift up the eternal plan that God has for you in Christ Jesus. Claim back this wonderful country for the glory of God and declare this day that you have engaged the enemy and you will not be stepping down nor running away. The King is coming to this place and you are his emissary and the voice of one in the wilderness declaring, 'Prepare ye the way of the Lord'.

5. **'Lift up your heads, O ye gates; even lift them up, ye everlasting doors; and the king of Glory shall come in. Who is this King of Glory? The Lord of hosts, He is the King of Glory**.' Psalm 24:9-10

And if it was not enough to state it once, the Holy Scriptures reinforce the command to you. 'Lift up your heads, O ye gates; even lift them up, ye everlasting doors.'

Who is it that will come through these gates to the city and march in power and majesty through these everlasting doors? It is the LORD of hosts. His armies of angels, of horsemen and swordsmen are too numerous to count, too majestic to ignore and too fearsome to defy. These are the hosts of God who obey his every command who run through the towns and cities, climb over the walls and barricades and enter the houses and homes of all those who loathe his glorious name. They ride and fly before the glory of his presence, breaking the opposition in pieces, binding the strong man and his companions and making a highway for our God.

It is for the Warriors and Guardians to wake up, lift up their heads, lift up their voices, stand in their high and noble calling over the nation and lift up the eternal gates of deliverance for their people. They are the highway into the nation. The kingdom of God is ready to come here if we will do what God calls us to do.

6. **'This is the generation of them that seek Him, that seek thy face, O Jacob.'** Psalm 24:6

Do not wait for another time or another person to stand in the gap. We are the generation; we are the people that must seek the face of God. No matter what we may have been, no matter where we might have been going, we are now the generation that seek the face of God, who look back to the unique and eternal call of Jacob as he lay his head upon the stone out on the hillside. He saw the angels ascending and descending from Heaven (Genesis 28:12), wrestled with the greatest of all Warriors on top of the mountain (Genesis 32:24), had his name changed to Israel and was blessed of God beyond all measure, (Genesis 32:28).

7. '**Open ye the gates that the righteous nation, which keepeth the truth, may enter in**.' Isaiah 26:2

Here is a command from God's servants. "Open the gates to this nation and to this people!"

"We are coming in and we are taking back what is ours."

It is the command and demand of the Guardians who keep and guard the truth, who are the defenders of the faith, who are the custodians of the unadulterated Word (the Holy Bible) and of sound doctrine.

'The righteous nation [people, watchmen], which keepeth [guards, preserves, protects], the truth.'

These ensure that the truth is delivered to their people and handed on to the next generation.

Open the gates to the Guardians!

'I will open my mouth in a parable: I will utter dark sayings [difficult questions] of old: which we have heard and known and our fathers have told us. **We will not hide them from their** [our] **children, shewing to the generation to come the praises of the LORD and his strength and his wonderful works that he hath done**.

For he established [raised up] a testimony [witness] in Jacob and appointed a law [instruction] in Israel, which he commanded our fathers, that they should make them known to their children: [so] **that the generation to come might know them, even the children which should be**

born; who should arise and declare them to their children: That they might set their hope in God and not forget the works of God, but keep his commandments: and might not be as their fathers, [who were] a stubborn and rebellious generation; a generation that set not their heart aright and whose spirit was not steadfast [faithful] with God.' Psalm 78:2-8

'And there arose another generation after them, which knew not the LORD, nor yet the works which he had done for Israel.' Judges 2:10

'O God, forsake me not; until I have shewed thy strength unto this generation and thy power to every one that is to come.' Psalm 71:18

'This shall be written for the generation to come: and the people which shall be created shall praise the LORD. For he hath looked down from the height of his sanctuary; from heaven did the LORD behold the earth; to hear the groaning of the prisoner; to loose those that are appointed to death.' Psalm 102:18-20

When the Warriors and Guardians begin to speak with one accord and raise their voices into the cloud of darkness that covers our nation and declare, 'Open the gates, so that the righteous people, who guard the truth, may enter in', then we shall see a dynamic change begin, a shaking and trembling in the ground and the light of God piercing the gloom and darkness that Satan has cast over us.

"Open those gates that have been shut in our faces for too long. Open the gates that say we cannot preach the Gospel. Open the gates to our schools and colleges, to our towns and cities, to our government and official offices, to our police force and our judicial system. Open the gates of our history and our culture; open the gates to our destiny and calling. Open the gates of liberty and freedom; open the gates that our enemies have built to defy us and keep us out. Open the gates of righteousness that will expose the corruption at every level and the secret plans for hurting us as a people. Open the gates that will bring a godliness that will exalt this nation once again. Open the gates of influence, of government, of communication, of authority, of the military and of finance and enablement."

Shout it out Warriors: "OPEN YE THE GATES!"

And cry this cry of triumph I shall,
And scatter light as shining seeds
Across the blackened furrows
That gouge this planet's face.
For this the Gospel is,
And this the work the kingdom does,
Advancing on the enemy's camp,
Releasing souls from Satan's grip,
Delivering the captives,
And healing wounded hearts;
Declaring TIME UP!
Declaring grace;
Declaring this the day of conquering!

8. 'THY KINGDOM COME; THY WILL BE DONE,' IN MY LIFE, IN MY FAMILY, IN THIS TOWN, IN THIS NATION, in all the earth, as it is done in Heaven. Matthew 6:10

This is the essence and sum of the whole matter. It is that God's will is done in our nation, in the Royal household, in

Parliament, in our families, in our communities and in our lives.

'I exhort therefore, that, first of all, supplications, prayers, intercessions and giving of thanks, be made for all men; For kings and for all that are in authority; that we may lead a quiet and peaceable life in all godliness and honesty. For this is good and acceptable in the sight of God our Saviour; who will have all men to be saved and to come unto the knowledge of the truth.' 1Timothy 2:1

For, '**When the righteous are in authority, the people rejoice: but when the wicked beareth rule, the people mourn**.' Proverbs 29:2

Speaking of the kingdom of God, Daniel speaks of it as a rock that destroys all that gets in its way:

'And the stone that smote the image became a great mountain and filled the whole earth. And in the days of these kings shall the God of heaven set up a kingdom, which shall never be destroyed: and the kingdom shall not be left to other people, but it shall break in pieces and consume all these kingdoms and it shall stand for ever.' Daniel 2:35+44

Jesus told his disciples, 'Upon this rock [Christ the Rock, His Godhead an unchangeable fact] I will build my church; and the gates of hell [death] shall not prevail against it. And I will give unto thee the keys of the kingdom of heaven: and whatsoever thou shalt bind on earth shall be bound in heaven: and whatsoever thou shalt loose on earth shall be loosed in heaven.' Matthew 16:18-19

'And he sent them to preach the kingdom of God and to heal the sick.' Luke 9:2

RISING INTO THE PLACE OF POWER

Chapter Ten

Rising Into The Place Of Power

For some, this may mean literally moving from where they are and relocating somewhere so they can do what they have to do. This may mean leaving the town or city that you are in and finding a place where you can wait on God and get into the fight. Maybe it means that you just rent a bed-sit or a shed out in the countryside so that you can get away at weekends for a protracted time to do what God has called you to do.

In this mind-boggling age of rush and tear it is hard to find a place where we can be alone.

'Woe unto them that join house to house, that lay field to field, till there be no place, that they may be placed alone in the midst of the earth!' Isaiah 5:8

Coming away from the crowd, walking into the wilderness, the field, or the deserted coastline allows us to 'find' God again. It also enables us to cut out all the distractions and voices that demand our constant attention and keep us away from our most high and holy calling.

Yes, you may have to leave home. Yes, you may have to go somewhere strange and out of 'phase' with what you normally do. The soldiers who went to fight for King and country left their comfort zones, their nice happy and sweet environments and took off to ready themselves for blood and war. They did not look back, but engaged their full senses into what was to be a fight for their children and future. Nothing else mattered except to do their Commander in Chief's bidding and come back a living hero, or a legend of the kingdom having given their life for such a glorious and noble cause.

'And Jesus answered and said, Verily I say unto you, There is no man that hath left house, or brethren, or sisters, or father, or mother, or wife, or children, or lands, for my sake and the gospel's, but he shall receive an hundredfold now in this time, houses and brethren and sisters and mothers and children and lands, with persecutions; and in the world to come eternal life.' Mark 10:29-30

If God calls you to stay in the city, then you need to locate a place to seek him where you can switch off all other communication devices and know that you will not be disturbed. This is a most holy place and a most holy time between you and God. Let nothing interrupt it or challenge it for first place. Here you will learn to hear the voice of God like never before. There is no rush in this place. When in Bombay I get myself up to the rooftop 'far from the madding crowd'.

Warriors and Guardians need to prepare their hearts and minds for what is going to happen. They need to know what the Bible says, not what the preacher on television says. They need to get acquainted with the needs and find the directions to deal with them. They need to learn how to fight and how to attack the citadels of evil and wickedness. They need to know who they are in Christ and what power and authority is at their fingertips. They need to start practising with and learn how to handle the Sword of the Spirit in battlefield conditions.

It is time to change your clothes. What you have been wearing is not suitable or worthy of the work ahead of you. 'Put on thy beautiful garments.' Isaiah 52:1. It is time to ditch the pyjamas and night clothes, time to put off the dirty and torn garments of half-hearted Christianity and habitual backsliding and get bathed, get cleaned and put on the robes and tunic that befit a soldier of Christ, an ambassador of Heaven.

'And that, knowing [realizing] the time, that now it is high time to awake out of sleep: for now is our salvation nearer than when we believed. The night is far spent [long gone], the day is at hand: let us therefore cast off the works of darkness [the sloth and carelessness of sin, the night garments which are only suited to the darkness] and let us put on the armour of light.' Romans 13:11-12

It is time to adorn our royal robes of righteousness and princely authority. It is time to put on the armour of light which is clean from contamination and worldliness. It is time to put on the full armour of God, ready to engage the enemy and tear him apart. It is time to quit our sleep. We have had far too much of it and our spiritual muscles have gone all sloppy and are become useless through lack of use.

'Therefore let us not sleep, as do others; but let us watch and be sober.' 1Thessalonians5:6

'For they that sleep sleep in the night; and they that be drunken are drunken in the night.' 1Tessaloniansh 5:7

It is time for us to arise and shine!

'Arise, shine; for thy light is come and the glory of the LORD is risen upon thee.' Isaiah 60:1

Warriors, Guardians, hear the word of the Lord! You do not need to look for the light when the word of God comes to you. You just need to arise and shine with the glory that God has put upon you.

The rising of the Warriors and the Guardians will be the key to the light and glory of God coming into this nation. We have to get up, or nothing will happen. The Guardians must arise from their slumber, from their doubts and fears, from their unbelief and dress themselves with the light of God's glory. They must go out from where they have been living, open the doors of their constrictions and run to the centre of the battlefield. This is their destiny and God's purpose for them in this world.

If your right hand is withered and ineffective like the poor man in Luke 6:6, then all you need do is stretch it out and it will be made wonderfully whole. The right hand symbolizes the hand of strength and authority and maybe for years you have been unable to exercise your calling of God because nothing seems to happen when you try.

Faith overcomes your disability and restores health and vitality to your soul. This is the time for you to stretch forth your hand and see the accompanying power of God at work in your life.

Stretch forth your hand!

You may have been lying on the ground like the disappointed man by the well of Bethesda. He had been there for more years than he could remember, hoping that someone would lift him up and put him into the rippling water after it was miraculously stirred up by an unseen force. He had been unable to do anything for thirty eight years, was crippled and could only dream of a better future. Then Jesus the Son of the living God appeared on the scene! He need wait no longer. The miracle was in his hand!

Jesus said, 'Rise [get up], take up thy bed and walk. And immediately the man was made whole and took up his bed and walked.' John 5:8-9

You may feel called of God to do something, been wondering for countless years how or when it might happen, but TODAY this word comes to you through these very pages you are reading. You do not need the strange 'water' offered by the big preachers, or the strange phenomena that occurs in the weird meetings on 'Christian' television.

Right now, God is calling the Warriors and Guardians to stand up upon their own two feet, refuse the lies that they have been told about themselves and cast off the images of their failures and inconsistencies.

The word comes to you: "In the name of Jesus Christ of Nazareth, RISE UP and WALK! NO LONGER BE CRIPPLED BY UNBELIEF AND DOUBT. THIS IS YOUR DESTINY; THIS IS YOUR TIME."

'For, behold, the darkness shall cover the earth, and gross darkness the people: but the LORD shall arise upon thee, and his glory shall be seen upon thee.' Isaiah 60:2

Look at this! When darkness and wickedness engulf the population and when black darkness seems to obliterate the light of the Gospel and plunges us all into fear and anxiety, then God shall arise upon his servants brighter than the morning sun in all of its wonderful radiance. When we arise from our complacency and our fumbling at everyday survival, God's own glory will become visible upon our lives and it will be noticed and observed by those around us. As the light draws the moths to its shining, so God's glory upon us will draw those lost in the night to his presence. All we need do is obey the command to arise.

'**And the Gentiles shall come to thy light and kings to the brightness of thy rising**.' Isaiah 60:3

The unsaved and heathen will come to you when the light of God is upon you. They may not seek you for your good looks, but when the brilliance of Christ is beaming upon your face, it is as a heavenly magnet, an irresistible force that demands their attention.

Kings, leaders, businessmen and women, the high and mighty, the influential and noble will be drawn to you because God is all over you.

'Kings will come to thy rising'. Notice that the light and glory comes only when we obey the call of God to get up from the dust (our history of going nowhere), shake off the cobwebs of monotony, the bad influences that kept us back and stand firmly on the ground as those that are both ready and prepared to serve the Lord.

'Shake thyself from the dust; arise and sit down, O Jerusalem: loose thyself from the bands of thy neck, O captive daughter of Zion.' Isaiah 52:2

It is now time to move from where you have been for so

long. 'Ye have compassed this mountain long enough: turn you northward.' Deuteronomy 2:3

We cannot go anywhere unless we leave somewhere.

That is a fact. If we stay where we are, then we shall die where we are. We cannot get to fulfil our destiny unless we cut the ties and leave the rubbish behind. We cannot have Christ unless we forsake the world; We cannot engage our vision unless we get up from our sleep. If we choose to carry on in our slumber, then one day they will find us dead in bed. What a useless end to such a great potential.

'How long wilt thou sleep, O sluggard? when wilt thou arise out of thy sleep?' Proverbs 6:9

You have to get up, get changed, pack a simple case and shut the door behind you if you are going to go somewhere for God.

CUSTODIANS
OF
THE TRUTH

Chapter Eleven

Custodians Of The Truth

England, this little country whose language is spoken throughout the world, which once ruled over a quarter of the world's population and dominated the seas with her shipping vessels, was surely given the outstanding privilege of being the guardians of the Word of God, the divine Oracle, in particular the New Testament.

It is a part of our history but more importantly our identity and destiny that has long been ignored or forgotten.

God entrusted us with the Bible, with its translation into English and with its perpetual propagation throughout the earth. This is a sacred trust, not in any way different to that which was given to Israel with the Old Testament.

In Romans Paul poses the question, 'What advantage then hath the Jew? or what profit is there of circumcision?' Romans 3:1

He was speaking in the light of the Gospel and the place of the Jew in this respect. He answered himself thus: 'Much every way: chiefly, because that unto them were committed the oracles [law, testimony, words] of God.' Romans 3:2

Why is England so unique and so blessed in many ways? Why is it such an important nation? We might well answer, "Because unto us was committed the sacred trust of the Oracle, the Gospel – the Bible." It is a God-given responsibility and we still hold the office. So what if this nation is 'unbelieving' and far away from God at present? God always has his remnant in waiting.

'For what if some did not believe? shall their unbelief make the faith of God without effect? God forbid: yea, let God be true, but every man a liar; as it is written, That thou mightest be justified in thy sayings and mightest overcome when thou art judged.' Romans 3:3-4

God still entrusts us with its safe-keeping in purity and reverence, in spite of all the nonsense that is being taught today throughout man-made churches and so-called 'revivals' and in spite of all of the new translations that seek to undermine the authority and trustworthiness of the written Word.

It seems that everyone wants to write their own version of the Bible these days, but none of them, not one, has the grandeur, the hallmark, the bloody and violent pedigree and the proof of divine providence and divine intervention that the King James Version has.

Don't like that? Too bad. It is true.

The New International Version is owned by the now infamous Rupert Murdoch's unholy corporation and each purchase just makes him a little bit richer.

Wonderful men, women and children died and made the ultimate sacrifice to ensure that the Bible was free and freely available to everybody. The Roman Catholic Church murdered multitudes in their determination to stop ordinary folk discovering the truth that would set them free from the clutches of the priests and pontiffs.

England fought with her blood to rid this land from the control of the pope and his murdering Inquisitors. We have the Bible in our hands today only because of such heroism and faith. Political correctness and satanic manipulation has buried our real history and painted a different picture of who we are and of our true heritage. There is far more to us than meets the eye!

What other religion in the whole world despises their sacred and historic foundations?

Only silly 'Christians' and pseudo-intellectuals cast away and dismiss the corner-stones of their own history. The blood of every martyr screams in your face when you spit upon the memory and acts of their valour for future generations such as ours.

They died that we might live. They sacrificed their blood so that the Word of God would be unfettered and delivered in purity to a hungry world. What have you done with the shallow existence of your church-going habits in comparison to their heroism and Heaven-honoured acts of faith?

The Muslim may not understand a word of Arabic; nevertheless he honours and reveres the Koran and will fight for its respect with his life.

Ignoble and carnal 'Christians' hardly ever touch their Bibles, refuse to address it with the capital letter it deserves (Bible, not bible), place their television magazines on top of it, or chuck it down on the floor somewhere in all of their mess. They are not worthy to even hold the Book in their hands, let alone make some comment that they think the King James Version is rubbish. Have they read the King James Version cover to cover, or do they just think themselves too simple or insufficiently educated to understand it? When it was first printed, the majority of folk in this land were illiterate, yet they learned to read and discovered the truth from the pages of that Sacred text.

You may indeed use no end of other versions if you please, but to disparage or mock the King James Version just shows ignorance and contempt for God and his glorious and greatly beloved heroes. Dare you spit upon their memory and gallant obedience just because you cannot understand 'thee' and 'thou'? I heard a well-known speaker at a conference mocking the King James from the platform and suggesting that the only place to put it was the dustbin. He then went on to extol the 'merits' of some vague contemporary mis-interpretation of the Bible called 'the message'. Maybe he will get saved one day and repent of his pride. Maybe he won't.

When people ask "why should this country be called 'Great' Britain?", we may well answer them "That unto us was given the solemn charge of being the custodians of the Word of God".

That is truly what makes us 'Great'. Greatly blessed and highly favoured. Who can comprehend why God should choose us?

God still has some men in this country who are the Guardians of the Word in this age of the Gospel and it will soon be their time to herald a new movement to raise the standard high once again and earnestly contend for the faith which was once (and once was sufficient) delivered to the saints.

'Beloved, when I gave all diligence to write unto you of the common salvation, it was needful for me to write unto you and exhort you that ye should earnestly contend for the faith which was once [Greek: once for all] delivered unto the saints.' Jude 1:3

It is not America that is going to save the world, no matter how many films Hollywood produces to make themselves out to be the heroes in every situation. It is the Word of God that alone has the power to deliver, restore and save a single soul or an entire nation. And anyway, where did the Pilgrim Fathers come from when they sailed to the Americas in 1620 to build a new country and future? Was it not originally from this little island of Great Britain?

Have you ever wondered why there is so much hatred towards the Anglo-Saxons, or why there is so much contempt expressed toward us and this nation?

It is in great part because we took the Word of God to the world and spread the mighty Gospel of Jesus throughout the nations.

There are also other awesome reasons that I shall not go into at this time. Have you ever wondered why some rather aggressive religions seek to abolish our faith and try to make our nation submissive to their claims and practises?

They hate the truth and would burn every single copy of the Bible if they possibly could.

There is a spiritual battle constantly being waged against this country to thwart, hinder and ultimately wipe the Word of God out of existence.

It was the living Word (Jesus) who was attacked during his years on earth and it is the written Word which has been under attack ever since.

It is always the religious type of people who lead the assault and then persuade the mob to run with them. As it was with Christ during his pilgrimage on earth, so it is with us. But nothing can destroy the Word.

What they do not understand is this: that 'the Word of the Lord endureth forever.' 1Peter 1:25

'If the foundations be destroyed, what can the righteous do?' Psalm 11:3

But the foundations can never be destroyed, for God 'has magnified [his] word above all his name' (Psalm 138:2) and let the Word of God be once more magnified over all this nation!

God still watches over this country.

IT'S ALL ABOUT FOCUS

Chapter Twelve

It's All About Focus

Time is too short and the future too grim for wasting our lives on the inferior materialistic dreams of a bored and indifferent generation.

Whilst you and I are sat at home wondering what we can do to entertain ourselves, the enemies of all goodness and grace are eagerly plotting how they might destroy our democratic freedom and Christian heritage.

And before you think that this is just another alarmist trying to express his personal convictions, do yourself a favour and get educated about what is really happening in your country and across the world right now under your nose.

The enemy of truth is within. He is not a thousand miles away, but living in the same street, working in the same office or factory, claiming the same benefits from our all too generous government and possibly plotting your destruction and the murder of your children's futures. Even worse, he uses our freedoms, our ridiculous toleration and our taxes to finance his advance and spits in our faces without fear of recrimination because we are too kind and nice to stand up and deal with him properly.

Over the last thirty years we opened our doors to numerous Trojan horses that brought hidden agendas and secret plans to ultimately destroy us as a people. They have already done terrible damage socially, economically and culturally; and our sin and backsliding has escalated their ability to do us much more harm. Our worldliness and our indifference towards God's holy laws have left the hedge of protection around this nation broken down and in severe disrepair. If we are to prevent any further goodness pouring out and stop the floodtide of evil pouring in upon us, we must return to our God in humility and repentance. We must begin to repair the walls that are being destroyed every day by our adversaries, (Nehemiah 4:6)

'If my people, which are called by my name, shall humble themselves, and pray and seek my face, and turn from their wicked ways; then [**and then only**] will I hear from heaven, and will forgive their sin, and will heal their land.' 2 Chronicles 7:14

This is a verse that gets quoted time and time again, but THAT IS ALL THAT HAPPENS.

We have experienced the harshness of war in Europe on more than one occasion, but the subtlety and diversity of the campaign to subjugate and crush Great Britain's sovereignty today is far more serious than all of them put together. At least we could see and smell the enemy before, but now they come disguised in cloaks of 'European directives', 'Human rights' and 'Religious victimization'.

Maybe you expect to be dead long before such calamities come, but that is the very attitude that the enemy depends on to accomplish his goal.

Procrastination and ignorance are two vices that offer our enemies the right to do as they please. Complaining to each other about their vile behaviour accomplishes nothing and we can only blame ourselves for failing to act when we should have.

You are needed right now to get up and fight for your country, your family, your friends and every good citizen of this great nation.

Play the silly religious church games if you like, but they mean absolutely nothing and will leave a damning judgement against you for cowardice, selfishness and arrogance (three more wretched devils of destruction).

'**Awake thou that sleepest, and arise from the dead, and Christ shall give thee light**.' Ephesians 5:14

I speak to every one who is called of God to stand in these days and fight. You may be a sleeping Guardian, a sin-enslaved Warrior, or a lowly pilgrim cleaning offices who stopped praying because you saw no results. If we will humble ourselves before God, if we will begin again to pray and if we put our lives right by clearing out each and every thing that offends our Lord, then we shall see the 'walls of Jerusalem' being rebuilt and restored and God's gracious healing beginning to flow in our land once again. (Psalm 51:18)

Some say that it is too late to do anything and there are not enough of us anymore. What nonsense. It is never too late. Read some of our wonderful history and see what amazing victories and accomplishments have been delivered even in the most unlikely circumstances. Read the story (or see the film, 'Into the Storm') of Winston Churchill. Read the book of Nehemiah.

Numbers are not the key. One shall chase a thousand and

two shall drive out ten thousand. In the darkest night, all it takes is one hero to break through the overwhelming forces of evil and deliver a mighty destructive blow to their diabolical plans and proposals.

Read the Bible and see what God can do with just a few dedicated and true men who are ready to forsake everything for His cause.

Ah, but here is the challenge! Who is there who would leave everything, give up their sinful habits, sell all that he has, put on the uniform of the soldier of Jesus Christ the Glorious Son of God, the Sovereign of Heaven, the conquering Saviour, the Prince of Peace, the Lion of Judah and follow Him into the valley of death and do or die?

Such a one is dead to this world and all its toys. Such a soldier has distanced himself from the vanity and frivolity of ordinary life and set his focus on pleasing his Captain and fulfilling his destiny. He is not ready to 'settle down' and live like every one else. His commitment and future is nailed firmly to the path that God chooses for him and he can never find rest or satisfaction in this world or its expectations. He knows more of his future home than he does of any resting place here and the road he travels is the path of pilgrims, but not just some religious duty or 'spiritual' pilgrimage, for he is a warrior, seeking only the kingdom of God and its expansion throughout the entire earth. He may be mocked and ridiculed for his 'strange' behaviour and 'bizarre' beliefs, but he laughs at troubles and shakes the disdain from off him as water off a duck's back.

Nothing in this world compares to the love he has to his King and his duty as an officer in the King's army.

'No man that warreth [enlists and goes to war] entangleth [gets involved, indulged, focuses] himself with the affairs of this life; [so] that he may please him who hath chosen him to be a soldier.' 2Timothy 2:4

Even though he fail and fall a thousand times (Psalm 37:4), yet he will rise again and face the storm and bitter wind of adversity, grit his teeth and harness himself to march on forward towards the only beacon of hope in the dark and cold night.

Loneliness and isolation are common to him and every encounter with a like-hearted soldier on his journey is as the sweet nectar of Heaven spurring him onward. He is not for giving up, though at times he may feel like shutting his eyes never to wake again in this world of trouble. He may not be famous upon earth, but in the kingdom of heaven his name is heralded amongst the angels of God.

He is a stranger in the earth (Psalm 119:19) and often misunderstood and misinterpreted by those presumed his allies. He is seen as a threat by the self-appointed church 'commanders' and they feel uncomfortable when he enters their congregations, especially when he receives more response from the people than they do as the ministers and leaders. In his heart he has the unwavering certainty that he is more than a conqueror through Christ who loves him and if he just stays firm to God's plan, then nothing is too big or impossible to him.

'But cleave unto the LORD your God, as ye have done unto this day. For the LORD hath driven out from before you great nations and strong: but as for you, no man hath been able to stand before you unto this day.

One man of you shall chase a thousand: for the LORD your God, he it is that fighteth for you, as he hath promised you.' Joshua 23:8-10

So what happens when these warriors start to get together?

> *'And five of you shall chase an hundred and an hundred of you shall put ten thousand to flight: and your enemies shall fall before you by the sword.'*
>
> *Leviticus 26:8*

It is a simple matter of mathematics. Their unity creates an impenetrable and unmovable force in the land. Every warrior that joins forces adds a dimension of authority, resistance and justice that sends a trembling through the divisions of the enemy. Just add some noughts to the figure every time you add a true warrior. You see, with God it is nothing (0), just another nothing he adds on the end.

The difference between £100 and £10,000 is simply two 'nothings' added to the end. Two are better than one and when three come together, it is next to impossible to break their resolve or plans. (Ecclesiastes 4:12)

'LORD, **it is nothing with thee to help**, whether with many, or with them that have no power: help us, O LORD our God; for we rest on thee and in thy name we go against this multitude. O LORD, thou art our God; let not man prevail against thee.' 2Chronicles 14:11

King David's 'valiant men' were trained in battlefield conditions and were not taken from the high and mighty, or rich and influential. They were those who were in debt, distressed, depressed and disillusioned with the current state of their nation. They hid in caves, slept in the open, scurried round the countryside looking for something to eat and were as outcasts or outlaws within their own community.

And another thing, they worked together in unity, not squabbling for position and recognition and demanding to be the leader. Too many 'potentials' out there will never actually fulfil their potential because they are too proud, too arrogant and too full of themselves.

It is always sad to see those who have great promise never fulfilling their destiny simply because they will not work with somebody else. Unbroken horses are a danger to everyone and are quite unusable on the battlefield. Eventually they break free from all restraint and go haring off across the countryside with their heads up in the air, thinking themselves as something amazing.

One 'potential' whom I knew and worked with told me that unless he was the leader, he could not minister with me. He told me categorically that he and his wife just had to be in control. Well, that sort of finished that then. It is still my hope and prayer that he might see fit one day to work together for the glory of God, for he also showed me much kindness from time to time.

There is power in unity. When a government speaks with one voice and stops the bickering and infighting, then nothing can stand against it.

David's men did not have nice houses, wide-screen televisions, comfortable armchairs and sleep-easy mattresses. Yet they were the chosen of God and righteous men.

'And every one that was in distress and every one that was in debt and every one that was discontented, gathered themselves unto him; and he became a captain over them: and there were with him about four hundred men.' 1Samuel 22:2

It sort of exposes all the nonsense these days of the 'prosperity' teaching that has mesmerized the masses.

These men ate with their king, slept in the same field, fought the same battles, conversed and discussed the details with him face to face. They were acquainted with his ways and knew exactly where his fortresses and secret places were. They were trustworthy and loyal.

His command and expectations came first, even before their own families and loved ones. (That just has to upset all the modern Christian counsellors and pastors who tell you that wife and family are first, then God's call somewhere down the list and after that your own self).

They were together in all that they did, often despised and unwanted by those who should have admired them, looked upon as vagabonds and rebels, but God was with them and His purposes **and the future of the nation was in their hands**.

They were not afraid of hardship, hard work, battle and fatigue. They were ready to die for their king and would risk their lives to please him.

These men were not perfect, but they had perfect hearts and like Peter, even when he was rebuked by Jesus (Matthew 16:22-23) ran hard after their leader and never gave up.

They did not have to run home to go do the shopping with their wives every week, nor have to beg them to be allowed to join their team to have a prayer meeting. These were men. These were soldiers. None had a softer heart than David himself, yet none was a greater warrior and soldier than David. (2Samuel 18:33).

Gentleness is not weakness. It is greatness. Gentleness does not turn the mighty and strong into sentimental effeminacy. Strength and power go hand in hand with gentleness and gentlemanliness. Mercy and grace find no contradiction with warfare and heroism.

God is a God of judgment and retribution, yet He is also a God of mercy and forgiveness, full of grace and truth.

At her Coronation, our Queen held two swords in her hands. One is the sword of justice, the other (with its tip symbolically 'blunted') is the sword of mercy.

Judgment is surely coming, yet mercy is still free to each and every soul who will believe.

This message may fall upon a million deafened ears and foolish hearts, but somewhere in this world it might just capture one soul who is ready to follow Christ into battle. **And be sure of this, that we are in the midst of the greatest and gravest battle this nation has ever fought and the only way to win and conquer is through the supernatural arsenal that God has provided us with through the power of the Holy Spirit and His word**.

We are not fighting against men and women, but against demonic principalities and satanic powers which carry out their rule and plans through the bodies of those we live amongst. Such devilish entities require human 'hosts' to carry out their threats against God's people.

We have to learn how to put on the full armour of God and train and practise in the use of the flaming, double-edged

Sword of the Spirit. To wield this Sword we must have clean hands and a pure heart and our souls freed and cleansed from pride and presumption. For who shall ascend into the hill of the Lord the King? Who shall dwell with Him and feast at his table and listen to His directives? Only those who are bid welcome and only those whose souls are distressed with sin and evil and focused upon the kingdom of God and His righteousness.

Let us turn again unto the Lord, seek his face with true desperation, put away everything that is wrong, cleanse our hands and our hearts, confess and forsake our sins and submit ourselves to God; then indeed He will hear from Heaven, forgive our sin and heal our land. It is His promise and He never breaks His promises.

It is not a five second prayer, nor a five minute emotional response, but a thorough repentance and putting things right and in order in our lives. It is a true forsaking of the world and all of its rebellious ways from our homes and our hearts.

'Then all the congregation answered and said with a loud voice, As thou hast said, so must we do. But the people are many and it is a time of much rain and we are not able to stand without, neither is this a work of one day or two: for we are many that have transgressed in this thing.' Ezra 10:12-13

God help us at this time.

THERE IS STILL HOPE FOR US

Chapter Thirteen

There Is Still Hope For Us

A word came on the wind just yesterday in the middle of my labour. It has been a long time (very many years) since I have heard anything good spoken over or to my life and I certainly was not expecting any positive encouragement under the uncertain clouds that press me in. I might also add that this word came from a most unlikely source and I had no idea that they ever thought about me or had any consideration as to any value in my life.

I was told that there are a few men in this country whom God has called, who have been targets of Satan since the day of their birth. Before they were ever born or ever formed, they were called of God to fulfil a certain commission and ministry. Like Jeremiah, they were set apart to become prophets (preachers) to the nation and the indestructible passion that drives them ever onward is an evident proof of this destiny.

I was told that I must come back to full-time in the work of God and that I have never experienced or seen even ten percent of the potential that God has waiting for me in ministry.

A few days back they had watched a short video that I was preaching on ('The Winning Combination') and felt constrained to tell me what they sensed God say to them.

They also asked me a couple of direct questions which I was happy to consider and rather than seek to defend my borders, I actually was relieved that someone had for the first time ever the right motives to approach me and be honest with me.

I have always loved this country that I was privileged to be born in and since the day of my conversion I have longed for God to send revival and mercy to its shores. I care especially for my own people and I see them overcome with evil and sin, yet often despised and sneered at by the multitudes of foreigners flooding our land. Sadly, also, I see many foreign churches in this country with their ministers standing aloof in their fat buildings pretending that they care about us, but actually looking down their noses as though we were nothing in the sight of God.

One night, as I walked through London, two Arab youths walked by and deliberately spat at my feet in quite obvious contempt and I asked God how long we have to put up with such hatred here on our own native soil.

I was told yesterday by this same Nigerian minister (which also confirmed my strong conviction), that it will take a few indigenous Anglo-Saxon men, born of this Island to turn this nation back to God. Whilst a multitude of shouting and screeching preachers from parts of the world which my forefathers took the Gospel message tell us that they are the only hope for this country, I know in my heart that the seed of life and reviving hope will ultimately spring forth from the roots of this ground.

If they indeed have any real care for us then let them join hand in hand with those who would weep for the plight of this nation. Only those who truly love this country and truly love its historic people and are willing to lay down their lives for them will ever discover a way to reach them and bring them back. Such souls are unique and extremely rare these days, but I believe there may be some.

'Hearken to me, ye that follow after righteousness, ye that seek the LORD: look unto the rock whence ye are hewn and to the hole of the pit whence ye are digged. Look unto Abraham your father and unto Sarah that bare you: for I called him alone and blessed him and increased him.' Isaiah 51:1-2

Look to the history and the deep roots of this nation and recognise the good hand of God upon us throughout our long and extraordinary existence. What other nation apart from Israel has seen such outstanding goodness and grace bestowed upon it?

I am not writing here to show off or pretend to be somebody and I am very reluctant to include this episode in this volume. I am just recording the things that happen to me and the things that God shows me along my journeying. Who knows, but it might just be the word that you need to hear from God as well? God always has some men scattered around the nation waiting for his time and it may just be possible that this is the time for them to arise and heed the call of God in this desperate hour. David had his 'valiant men' and God has his men hidden away, being prepared for the day of his power. They are probably unknown, maybe not even on the platforms, but they are being trained in his Life-Academy for their finest hour. They may have been failures, backsliders, rejected or ignored, seen as 'extremists' or 'narrow-minded' by other believers, but the Spirit of the LORD God rests upon them and it is He who shall be exalted through them.

'For ye see your calling, brethren, how that not many wise men after the flesh, not many mighty, not many noble, are called: But God hath chosen the foolish things of the world to confound the wise; And God hath chosen the weak things of the world to confound the things which are mighty; And base things of the world and things which are despised, hath God chosen, yea and things which are not, to bring to nought things that are: That no flesh should glory in his presence.' 1Corinthians 1:26-28

'One man of you shall chase a thousand: for the LORD your God, he it is that fighteth for you, as he hath promised you.' Joshua 23:10 (but look at the previous verses to see the conditions).

The call of God and the continued preservation of his people is far greater than any demonic threat or vile plan of Satan for their destruction. Let those sneer, accuse and curse who so choose, but the blessing of the LORD is still upon his people. (Psalm 3:8)

'Then the word of the LORD came unto me, saying, Before I formed thee in the belly I knew thee; and before thou camest forth out of the womb I sanctified thee [set you apart] and I ordained thee a prophet unto the nations. Then said I, Ah, Lord GOD! behold, I cannot speak: for I am a child.

But the LORD said unto me, Say not, I am a child: for thou shalt go to all that I shall send thee and whatsoever I command thee thou shalt speak. Be not afraid of their faces: for I am with thee to deliver thee, saith the LORD. Then the

LORD put forth his hand and touched my mouth.
And the LORD said unto me, Behold, I have put my words in thy mouth. See, I have this day set thee over the nations and over the kingdoms, to root out and to pull down and to destroy and to throw down, to build and to plant.

Moreover the word of the LORD came unto me, saying, Jeremiah, what seest thou? And I said, I see a rod of an almond tree. Then said the LORD unto me, Thou hast well seen: for I will hasten [watch over] my word to perform it [accomplish it].' Jeremiah 1:1-12

'And they shall fight against thee; but they shall not [ultimately] prevail against thee; for I am with thee, saith the LORD, to deliver thee.' Jeremiah 1:19

They shall fight and war against anyone who is called by God to exercise such a ministry, especially if that ministry flies in the face of heresy and the false prophets; but they will not ultimately overcome or destroy the servants of God.

It may not be appreciated, but Jeremiah's seven-faceted ministry was more about judgement and destruction than it was about Sunday morning love-songs and momentary happiness. Firstly, he was given authority over the nations and the kingdoms, then the rooting out of wickedness, pulling down the citadels of defiance, destroying the myths and nonsense of false teaching and throwing down the pride and presumption of rebellion against God.

Only the last two facets of his ministry were 'building and planting'. This does not fit in too well with today's 'prophesying of good things', of smooth things and things that do not disturb the conscience.

'This is a rebellious people, lying children, children that will not hear the law of the LORD: which say to the seers, See not; and to the prophets, Prophesy not unto us right things, speak unto us smooth things, prophesy deceits.' Isaiah 30:9-10

This really does sum up the nature and character of the Western church. To speak out against the modern trait of 'cheap' Christianity' and false preachers will without doubt stir up a storm of hatred and opposition. To dare to take on the false teachers and prophets of wealth and success will ignite the true nature of the deceivers. Hatred, anger and foot-stomping retaliation will fly from the mouths of the dressed-up televangelists and they shall fight against the word of God, but they shall not overcome or prevail against God's servants.

'And they shall fight against thee; but they shall not prevail against thee; for I am with thee, saith the LORD, to deliver thee.' Jeremiah 1:19

'And I will make thee unto this people a fenced brasen wall: and they shall fight against thee, but they shall not prevail against thee: for I am with thee to save thee and to deliver thee, saith the LORD.' Jeremiah 15:20

Truth is never comfortable to those who are caught up in lies and falsehood. The true word of God will always come as light into the hiding places of darkness; and men prefer to stay in the darkness because their deeds are evil (John 3:19). It comes as exposure to the cloak of deception, as clarity into the depravity of ignorance and as confusion to the pride of the lying prophets.

What will they and their followers do when their world begins to collapse all around them and all their comforts and securities vanish in front of their faces?

'The prophet that hath a dream, let him tell a dream; and he that hath my word, let him speak my word faithfully. What is the chaff to the wheat? saith the LORD. Is not my word like as a fire? saith the LORD; and like a hammer that breaketh the rock in pieces?' Jeremiah 23:28-29

The true word of God does not require a television show neither a pretty 'cheer leader' (worship leader), neither slick advertising, personal bodyguards, henchmen, hit-men, or whatever else you might like to call them. It is a hammer that bricks the hardest and most proud and stubborn antagonist into shards. It is a fire that consumes the screaming, ranting paddy of the raving, conceited evangelist and it runs like molten lava along the ground against all the 'cluck-clucking' followers of the cheating prophets.

It is the wheat and wholesome kernel of God's own grain and remains pertinent and powerful long after the irritating and useless chaff of plasticized religion is blown away.

It is the threshing teeth of God's harvester that tears down the mountains of presumption and arrogance, that beats down the hills of haughtiness and defiance and that levels the valleys of carnality and double standards.

It is the wind of the Spirit; the haunting and unnerving whisper of God's disdain at hypocrisy and it is the whirlwind of his righteousness against all unrighteousness, especially that which is done in the abuse of his holy name.

'Behold, I will make thee [into] a new sharp threshing instrument having teeth: thou shalt thresh the mountains and beat them small and shalt make the hills as chaff. Thou shalt fan them and the wind shall carry them away and the whirlwind shall scatter them.' Isaiah 41:15-16

'The voice of him that crieth in the wilderness, Prepare ye the way of the LORD, make straight in the desert a highway for our God. Every valley shall be exalted [raised] and every mountain and hill shall be made low [levelled]: and the crooked shall be made straight and the rough places plain [smooth].' Isaiah 40:3-4

If ever there is to be a highway for our God, if ever a place where he will come with his reviving power and not the supercilious pretensions of man-made revivals, then there will first of all come a clearing of the ground, a tearing down, a breaking down, a pulling down and a destroying of all that is man-elevating and not God-exalting. The crooked, twisting deceit of man's false interpretations shall be corrected and put right and the cunning deception of the money-grubbing charlatans shall be exposed and slapped to the floor once and for all.

'Prepare ye the way of the LORD.' Matthew 3:3

It is us that have to prepare the way, that have to remove the stones and boulders of stumbling, the filth and dirt of contaminating sin.

'Go through, go through the gates; prepare ye the way of the people; cast up, cast up the highway; gather out the stones; lift up a standard [a flag] for the people.' Isaiah 62:10

It is time to raise a standard, an ensign over this nation of ours and make a way for the people to come to the truth.

However, fire must come before the latter rain will ever fall upon the barren and dry wilderness of our professed Christianity. Fire must first purge the silver and gold before the King will ever grace our homes. Fire must rage through the plague of worldly and carnal indifference and cleanse the holy city of the leprosy of greed, self-ambition and fame-seeking. Fire must burn up all our time and life-wasting habits.

I have witnessed the first raindrops falling from heaven in a late-night meeting in Ireland and seen, not the laughter of people gone mad, but the weeping of hearts broken by the presence of holiness. I have felt the ground shake under my feet and seen the trembling of conviction in the lives of both young and old alike. I have felt the immeasurable 'weight' as the presence of God draws near and seen grown men and women crumble to their knees and onto their faces before the majesty of God's purity.

I have seen tears flowing like rivers when the whisper of God comes into the house, bringing exposure of sin and unrighteousness; and I have watched as a congregation repented of its rebellion and refusal to hear God. There were no weird 'manifestations', no wild and insane shaking of the heads, no stewards waiting to catch people falling over, but deliberate, conscious acts of obedience and putting things right one with another and with God.

None of today's 'strange' commotions where men and women prance around the stage blithering about what God is supposedly 'telling them', can compare in the slightest with the real and genuine work of the Holy Spirit. The conference 'mystics' may put on a good show, but the world does it better.

You won't be laughing when the real fire falls. You won't be lying on your back giggling or cackling like an imbecile when the Almighty presence enters the room. You will be running for somewhere to hide.

'And the kings of the earth and the great men and the rich men and the chief captains and the mighty men and every bondman and every free man, hid themselves in the dens and in the rocks of the mountains; And said to the mountains and rocks, Fall on us and hide us from the face of him that sitteth on the throne and from the wrath of the Lamb.' Revelation 6:15-16

Do you find this type of language 'scary', or 'not in touch with what God is doing'? Then your heart is far from God and you need to get right with him, (and me just saying that will make you very angry indeed!)

However, if you find that it witnesses with your spirit and excites and stirs you up inside, then God is calling you to come out from the crowd and seek his face until he be found of you and the rain of grace comes down from Heaven.

A sound of battle is in the land; the time is fulfilled and the kingdom of God is at hand. Repent and believe the Gospel.

God protect and preserve the throne of England.

God save Prince William, Prince Harry and Her Royal Highness The Duchess of Cambridge (Kate).

God save Great Britain.

THE MISSING MULTITUDES

Chapter Fourteen

The Missing Multitudes

The Church of England recently said that unless something radical happens and urgently, it would be 'wiped out as a significant national force'. Having lost over fifty percent of its members over the last 40 years and having witnessed a loss of over 80% of children regularly attending services, its future hangs precariously in the balances.

Most of the Christian denominations in Great Britain have seen significant decline at the same time and in spite of varied efforts and the introduction of dozens of 'Christian' television channels during the same period, things continue to look grim.

Many African churches boast that they are now the only viable representation of Christianity in England but such pumped up arrogance is just the rattle of a broken cymbal and their influence in the population is restricted mostly to their own race. I have written more extensively on this in '21st Century Pilgrim's Progress'.

The great majority of the indigenous population have no interest in the church and even less interest in the screaming preachers telling them how bad and wicked they are.

The truth of the matter is that there are tens of thousands of people both young and old who once upon a time attended a local church, but who have now abandoned it and go nowhere at all for their spiritual nourishment. They did not necessarily abandon their personal faith, but neither did they pursue the practice of reading their Bibles and seeking after God's will for their life as they might have.

There are actually millions of folk in this country who truly believe in God, who have some witness in their hearts that Jesus Christ is God's only Son, but they do not want to be associated with all that calls itself 'Christianity' and they wish to avoid any identification with those who prance around calling themselves 'Christians'.

Of course, a war would change much of this and rally the spirit of this nation once again to look to God for their help and deliverance. The trouble is, there is a war already raging in this country, but nobody is willing to openly identify it and worse, they do not know how to begin to put a stop to it. They feel lost, hopeless and abandoned both by their government and by God.

There are a number of reasons that we have been brought to the state that we now find ourselves languishing in and many more reasons why so many have turned away from our national faith.

Firstly, we are in this dreadful condition because of our sin and our deliberate walking away from God. When we turn our back on God, then we had better consider that God may indeed turn his back on us.

'The LORD is with you, while ye be with him; and if ye seek him, he will be found of you; but if ye forsake him, he will forsake you.' 2Chronicles 15:2

Through our abandonment of God we brought upon ourselves a multitude of evils and opened the floodgates of wickedness and oppression such as we have never known before as a people. We look out of our windows at the results of our national denial of God's ways and God's Word. Our cities and towns have been turned into cesspools of violence, perversion, bigotry and hatred, with masses of humanity and a mixed multitude all churning in their own vomit and rebellion toward the one true God and his righteousness.

We look and our hearts sink in despair and dejection, not seeing any possibility of restoration or a return to the right paths for a people to walk in. We are a nation besieged from within and it seems that we have lost our ability or determination to turn things around and make this a country worthy of its good name.

Hundreds of thousands have fled these shores looking for a better life somewhere else in the world. The vacuum left behind is soon filled with everything alien to our wonderful culture and history. Many of us wish we could either start this land of ours all over again, or go and discover another island where we could all take ourselves. That way we could rid ourselves of all the anguish of having to live under the heavy burden that presses down upon us daily and the continual scorning and despising of our people and our heritage.

'Multiculturalism' is just a political word trying to explain the confusion of our integrated (but not so integrated) society. Remember the Tower of Babel (Babel means 'confusion), where everyone lived together all seeking a common 'god' and goal? God stepped in and turned their plans into nonsense and bewilderment. (Genesis 11)

This is what sin has done to us and this is what happens when we turn away from what is good for us and ignore the pleadings of God to repent of our wicked ways and simply trust his Word.

But let us look at the reasons behind the general demise of the Christian faith in this country and see what lies at the root. We all know that 'materialism' and self-worship stole away our minds and hearts from things that were more noble and 'vocational'. Money became everything and the billion or more 'gadgets' and 'gimmicks' flooding out of Japan, China and America stole our creative energy and replaced the 'pioneering' spirit of our forefathers with 'living for the now' and pleasing only ourselves.

Our children were brought up on designer-wear and computer games and missed out on a childhood of innocence and fun. They were fed a diet of filth, violence and perversion by the television 'soaps' and given access to such things on the internet as the mind could only boggle at.

Nowadays a child of seven knows more about sex and perversion than I had ever heard of at the age of eighteen. Sin has stolen the beauty of their early years and deranged government officials demand that they are taught at school the gross immorality of an age gone bankrupt of all moral restraints. I am sure we all know exactly to what I am referring. What is not right even to commonsense and so obviously against the 'natural' design of the human composition, is and always shall be wrong. See Romans 1:24-28 and observe God's judgment on the whole of this 'controversial' matter; and remember, it is only 'controversial' to those who refuse to hear or accept the truth.

Now, the priests and the politicians can argue over these matters until they are blue in the face and steaming at the ears, but what the Bible expressly teaches cannot be changed and that is why ordinary self-respecting people still squint or laugh embarrassingly at such disgusting folly. It is not the majority of people who think it is 'normal', but as always, just a very 'loud' and aggressive minority trying to convince us all that we have got it all wrong and they are the only 'right' ones.

Thank goodness we are all so 'wrong' on this matter. The vast majority of us (not just Bible-believers) are actually disgusted at the grossness of such a dereliction of normal and 'right' human behaviour. The trouble is that this little crowd of antagonists all demanding their 'rights' to livc how they please get the headlines and front pages of our newspapers ahead of everything else. This is because the 'spirit' of this age is bent on defying God and his laws and seeks to contaminate every mind on the planet with his dirt. It is a spirit of lawlessness that refuses God's way and rebels against His word.

'Know ye not [do you not realize] that the unrighteous shall not inherit the kingdom of God? Be not deceived [don't be fooled]: neither fornicators [sexually immoral], nor idolaters [worshipers of idols], nor adulterers, nor effeminate [soft, 'gay', a homosexual prostitute], nor abusers of themselves with mankind [a sodomite, homosexual]... shall inherit the kingdom of God.' 1Corinthians 6:9-10

Hmm... so why are the bishops having such trouble trying to work out whether it is acceptable to receive such people into the 'ministry'? Maybe they should just take the Bible, believe it is God's authoritative word as did their distinguished and godly predecessors, and do what it says.

The Bible says it and that is the end of the matter to faith. That is what our faith is all about after all. We believe the Scriptures to be the infallible word of God to us.

As that great Jewish Bible scholar Adolph Saphir wrote: '*We believe that Scripture is given by inspiration of God. We do not believe that it is possible that this book, worldwide and eternal in character, could have been written by "holy men", unless they were moved by the Spirit, who searched the deep things of God and guided by Him who was and is and is to come.*

We believe the Scriptures to be inspired and our faith in the inspiration of Scripture has its basis and root in our faith in God Himself. It is because we have experienced the divine power of the truth Scripture contains and because in the reading of Scripture we have heard the voice of God. It is because God speaks to us in this written word, that we believe it is God's.

This faith is a conviction, an inward beholding and seeing, a knowledge that far transcends in height and strength, in certainty and firmness, all human evidence and argument.

We can not pass on this faith to our neighbours; for faith is the gift of God and "they shall be all (and each) taught of God". We can only testify of it and give reason for the knowledge that is in us.

On no lower ground can we build our assertion that Scripture is God-inspired.

The inspiration of the Scriptures is an object of faith; and faith can only rest in the Word of God, the testimony of the Holy Spirit to the soul. It is impossible for us to form a the-

ory of inspiration. Even of that gracious influence of the Spirit of which we possess personal experience in our own conversation and daily renewal, it would be impossible for us to frame a theory; for the work of the Spirit is mysterious. We cannot trace the beginning nor the end of His path.'

And then we got rid of the Bible from our school curriculum and introduced a whole slather of strange religions and myths just to confuse and confound their little minds. We taught them self-assertion and independence and now wonder why we have a generation of teenagers who demand everything, but do not wish to work for it and earn it. All of our evangelistic efforts and projects over the last thirty years (not that there have been that many of any substance or merit), have utterly failed to touch or impress our young people and rather than attract them to the truth of God, the strange and sometimes quite revolting attitudes of 'believers' have driven them further away.

Whilst on the subject of 'attitudes', I might well say that it is those same attitudes that have been the main reason that so many have fled from church meetings and settled down to watch television instead. They now want absolutely nothing to do with church or its strange attempts at wooing people into its boring or stereotyped and predictable programmes.

Many a soul has run from the church after meeting the 'real' character of the leaders and elders who make themselves out to be something they certainly are not. There are tens of thousands of wounded, torn and abused lives around this country, still reeling from the 'treatment' they received in the place they should have found comfort and encouragement.

They just got fed up with the lies, the deceit, the trickery, the thieving and the self-righteous hypocrisy of people who pretended to be more 'spiritual' than anybody else.

They met the stinking 'we are holier than thou' attitudes and saw that these people were no better than anyone else out there and in fact on the whole, were a great deal more 'nasty' and vindictive.

They trusted some of their secrets and personal problems to pastors who went round breaking confidences and gossiping about them to other church members. They saw the sneers and despising looks, they heard the hurtful things being said about them in the 'fellowship'. (By the way, a pastor or elder who breaks a confidence should not remain in office for one more single day).

In some churches, they always hoped that they might one day be allowed to do something for God, but watched silently as the platform, the band the choir and the office filled all of its positions with newcomers, whilst they were passed by.

Many of the white people left their churches as the congregations become predominately 'black' and rather than feel that they were being judgemental or prejudiced in their minds, they would sooner leave and stay quietly at home. They began to feel out of place and strangers in their own assembly.

It is not, as some might presume that they have backslidden or were never true believers, but simply because they did not wish to be stressed-out every Sunday and then spend the rest of the week worrying about their having to go again the following weekend.

You may not like what I am saying, but amongst the missing multitudes there will be a great many who agree with me.

Integration is one thing, dismissing our culture is another. At the launch of a certain 'British' Christian television station some while back, I realised that there were was just one English person there apart from myself and I asked him why everyone and everything was 'black'-oriented. He told me that the whites were not interested in God and so they had geared everything to the black community.

Then, because I refused to jump and dance and wail during the 'worship time' at the celebration the same evening, the African leader suggested to his audience that I was obviously not 'in the Spirit'. I like being who I am. I love the fact that God loves me for who I am. If I do not wish to raise my hands with everyone else, then that is up to me. If I do not want to shout 'Alleluia', or 'Amen' every time the preacher says something, then that is my choice. It makes me no less 'spiritual' than anybody else there. All the dancing, jiving and screaming in the world can never compare to the awe of standing in the presence of the King and listening to His voice.

I visited one church in London where there was a really good and healthy balance of nationalities and cultures. The church was thriving and a good and vibrant spirit was in the place. Some few years later I returned to find that I was one of only a very small handful of white folk left in the congregation. The band the choir, the ushers, deacons and elders were all black, and the music, the style of worship, the atmosphere and culture of the church were now totally different and typically 'African' in practise. Where had all the white people gone? Perhaps to some other church, but more likely they would be at home reminiscing of better days when things were not so 'complicated'. It was not a matter of being prejudiced, but simply feeling pushed out of the doors of their 'home' all in the name of 'God'. Of course, the current congregation just assumed that those who left could not have been of God, quoting (misquoting) the verse from 1John 2:19 and suggesting that they were 'not in the Spirit'.

'They went out from us, but they were not of us; for if they had been of us, they would no doubt have continued with us.'

Such arrogant misinterpretation always uses this typical excuse for an unwillingness to love one another in the same way that Christ loves us (Romans 12:10; Romans 15:7; Ephesians 4:2; Ephesians 4:32; Colossians 3:13).

The congregation and its leaders have forgotten all those who are now missing, too engrossed with their own sense of self-importance and consigning all those who left to the 'spiritual' trash heap.

I am simply telling it like it is. Many African pastors have asked me how they can encourage the white folk to come to their churches. I always reply that they cannot, but perhaps if they have an Englishman, a Chinese man and an Indian on the leadership team all as equals with the same salary as the resident pastor, then indeed these other nationalities might be happy to attend. Sadly, this was never something that any of these ministers were willing to facilitate. As in most churches, whatever their cultural identity, the pastor guards his position with great care and only feels secure if his team remains subservient to him. The lust for 'control' and being 'in charge' will always outweigh the desperate need of working together in unity.

'Feed the flock of God which is among you, taking the oversight [care] thereof, not by constraint, but willingly; not for filthy lucre [self interests, personal gain or money], but of a ready mind; Neither as being lords [masters, controllers, bosses] over God's heritage [inheritance, possession], but being ensamples [role models] to the flock.' 1Peter 5:3

Christ washed the feet of His disciples and raised them up to sit in heavenly places with Him, showering them with His glory and turning them into the heroes of faith that we still read of today, some thousands of years later. Christ knew who He was and did not need to defend His position. He came to raise fallen man to the throne of God, to clothe him with righteousness and honour and make him a priest and king even whilst here on earth.

So, 'Let this mind be in you, which was also in Christ Jesus: Who, being in the form of God [being God Himself], thought it not robbery [did not need to claim or defend his right, or consider it necessary to prove Himself] to be equal with God: But made himself of no reputation [did not boast about who He was, but disguised His glory and majesty] and took upon him the form of a servant and was made in the likeness of men: And being found in fashion [nature] as a man, he humbled himself [even further] and became obedient unto death, even the death of the cross.' Philippians 2:5-8

For, 'except [unless] a corn [grain] of wheat fall into the ground and die, it abideth alone: but if it die, it bringeth forth much fruit.' John 12:24

So Christ came not to be ministered unto, not to be waited on and served and bowed to, but to give His life away, to be nothing and less than a worm, so that he might raise up the poor from the dunghill, the prostitute from the whore-house, the drunkard from the ditch and to save them and lift them up to be among princes, (Matthew 20:28; Psalm 22:6; 1Samuel 2:8).

Now there is a lesson for the minister. Unless we die (die to self-love, die to pride, die to vanity and the need of adulation), we remain alone and once we have gone from this world, we shall leave nothing behind except the fading praises of men-worshippers and a few soon-forgotten tears at our graveside, (John 13:14-17; Isaiah 53:9-12).

A word for the pastors, ministers and elders: the so-called 'shepherds' throughout this country.

'Thus saith the Lord GOD unto the shepherds [pastors, leaders]; Woe be to the shepherds of Israel that do feed [look after, nourish and think only of] themselves! should not the shepherds feed the flocks? Ye eat the fat [take everything you can] and ye clothe you with the wool [strip them of everything that you can get out of them], ye kill them that are fed [use and abuse those that have something to offer, then dump them]: but ye feed not the flock. The diseased [the weak, the wounded] have ye not strengthened, neither have ye healed that which was sick, neither have ye bound up [restored, mended] that which was broken [hurt and damaged], **neither have ye brought again that which was driven away, neither have ye sought that which was lost; but with force and with cruelty have ye ruled them**. And they were scattered [just as the missing multitudes are today], because there is no shepherd [not one that actually cares]: and they became meat [prey, victims, targets] to all the beasts of the field [the devil and all of his wretched agents], when they were scattered. My sheep wandered through all the mountains and upon every high hill [looking for some solace, help or comfort in anything they could]: yea, my flock was scattered upon all the face of the earth and none did search or seek after them.' Ezekiel 34:2-6

And there are so many lost sheep out there looking for an answer, wondering if there is anyone in the whole world of seven billion other people who really cares.

'Because ye have thrust with side and with shoulder [asserting yourselves and indifferent to the pains of the people] and pushed all the diseased with your horns [pomposity], till ye have scattered them abroad; Therefore will I save my flock and they shall no more be a prey [either to you or the enemy out there].' Ezekiel 34:21-22

God himself is going to get back all the casualties of the local churches and their leaders. He is going to dismiss those who should have been out there bringing healing and hope to the poor in spirit, but who instead are just feasting with the wealthy, looking out for the 'middle-class' and gathering their ten percents every week to better themselves.

God is going to bring back those however who you dismissed, who you thought were outcasts and rejects and elevate them to a place of honour right in front of your nose.God is going to mend and heal those who you damaged through your pompous attitude and nasty snide talk. He will turn them into the diamonds in his crown and lift them higher than you ever went. He will bring again those who you mocked and belittled in your fear and inferiority complex.

God himself will elevate to leadership, to teaching and to preaching those who you thought were beyond His redemption and who were far too lowly in your estimation to be ministers or servants of Christ. God is going to go for the missing multitudes around this nation as surely as the Good Shepherd went out from the safety of the fold to find the one lost sheep that went astray.

God will bring back the backsliders and those who are sunk in sin and cover them with his glory and power and show you that these are his gems and precious treasures.

He is going to separate the fat cattle from the thin cattle and cast out the impostors and charlatans.

'I will seek that which was lost and bring again that which was driven away and will bind up that which was broken and will strengthen that which was sick: but I will destroy the fat and the strong; I will feed them with judgment.' Ezekiel 34:16

'Therefore thus saith the Lord GOD unto them; Behold, I, even I, will judge between the fat cattle and between the lean cattle.' Ezekiel 34:20

God himself will deal with all the false prophets, the greedy 'ministers', the unholy platform crooks and the religious slave masters who have brought shame and contempt upon the real Gospel of Christ. One by one they will meet with His judgments and all those who follow their pernicious [destructive, money oriented] ways (2Peter 2:2) shall also come to nothing.

Every church building in the country could be filled to overflowing with these missing multitudes if there was just a little of God's love in those who profess His name. God's love is not the sentimental slushy stuff that wants to go round giving everyone a 'spiritual' hug and welcoming them at the door. That means as little as the brief second that it took to perform and was as empty as the supercilious pretence that it was given in.

The love of God is rugged, strong as a mountain, long as the universe is wide, always consistent and without hypocrisy. It is a high tower, a fortress and a safe-hold for every poor soul to run into and hide. It does not show favour to those who are better dressed or have bigger purses and wallets, but receives each child as they come, with all their faults and blemishes.

It is, above all, the love of God and not some emotional expression shown just because we think our church is great, or because we are happy that a new person has come into our assembly. Such love that flows from Heaven is superior to anything this world can ever offer. It is what mankind is missing and it is of such a nature that there will never be a satisfactory substitute for it. No 'professional' worship bands or soloists can come anywhere near to it and no clever preaching or articulate rhetoric can in any way counterfeit it.

The true proof of the baptism of the Holy Spirit is not whether one 'speaks in tongues' or performs miracles. I have seen false cults, spiritualists and crazy people do these things, but it does not make them right. Just because someone can throw you on your back when they pray for you does not mean that they are either righteous or filled with God's love, In fact, it proves absolutely nothing at all except that the gullible congregation would sooner seek for a 'sign' or some phenomena than seek the face of God for a holy life.

The real evidence is surely that 'the love of God is shed abroad in our hearts by the Holy Ghost which [who] is given to us', (Romans 5:5).

Now, a man or woman may make a lot of noise about how righteous they are. They may sing in the worship group, give 'prophetic' words, preach, dance, pray, be known for some special 'ministry', but if the real love of God is not wall to wall and floor to ceiling in their lives, they are absolutely nothing more than a crashing or tinkling cymbal.

The preacher who is more interested in how they look on the platform than seeking to know how to bring light to those in darkness, or how to lift the poor old beggar from the dunghill of his dreadful experience and give him some money, is just a 'performer'. He may weep tears, make a great commotion, raise his voice to the rafters, twist his body and act out his part to the very highest level of his skill, but he is just an actor at the end of the day. He does his 'show', gets applauded, gets bowed to and goes home patting himself on the back thinking himself very 'anointed'.

There are plenty of 'professional' pastors and preachers these days and you have to be able to do something a little out of the ordinary to be elevated to their dinner tables. If you aspire to reach their group, then you will have to do a lot of dancing and 'acting' yourself.

It is only those who are sucked into their little game, who follow them and sing their praises that are fooled. Those who cry for reality and long for the true evidence of God's presence see through the disguises and walk away.

The missing multitudes are those who so longed for an encounter with the God of glory, but met with the cold sham of religion and ritual. They met with disgusting and judgemental attitudes and found nothing better than the world offers. In fact they found that there was more concern, friendship and love in the people outside of church than within the Christian community. The poor around them were far more generous than the middleclass and rich that parked all of their fancy vehicles outside their glamorous church buildings.

I had an old van which a lovely Colombian lady bought for me when I was in dire need and completely homeless, but when I went to preach at the well-dressed churches, I had to hide it out of the way in case the rich-suited congregation saw what I was driving and where I was living. They would have sneered at me and rejected anything I had to say. When I eventually got a decent jeep, an African elder said, "Oh, this is great! Now the churches will know you are somebody." What a lot of nonsense. I felt like getting my old van back. At this moment in time I do not have any form of transport, but it makes me no less the child of God I truly am.

Even in the Pentecostal and charismatic movements, meetings have become just another form of 'ritual' and entertainment to try and hold onto the uncertain and not always so loyal congregation. When did God really last show up? When did his glory and presence reduce the congregation to humility and tears, to repentance and confession and to holiness and righteous living? Yes, I know you sing for hours, roll on the floor and have a good laugh, feel warm and 'fuzzy', but that has nothing to do with the love that drove God's only Son to the cross to carry away our sins in his own body. Such love breaks a man's heart and brings him to his knees. It revolutionises the soul and disposition of the most hardened and unkind person. It renders the aggressive and hostile fighter a gentleman, full of grace and truth.

Love only can the conquest win,
The strength of sin subdue
(Mine own unconquerable sin),
And form my soul anew.
Love can bow down the stubborn neck,
The stone to flesh convert;
Soften and melt and pierce and break
An adamantine heart. *(Charles Wesley)*

This love disregards and disdains personal goals for wealth and prosperity and accepts the contentment that says, 'If I have Christ, then I have everything'.

It searches and hunts out the needy, not waiting for the poor to come to them for help. It calls and goes the extra mile to discover how that missing life is doing, whether they have enough food, whether their children are suffering. It sees and feels the pain of the lost and foundering soul long before they ever think about coming to church. It does not demand that they join their fellowship, but simply longs for them to find the same amazing love that God has filled their own lives with.

It is an unconditional love that is selfless and fearless. It is not passive, 'squishy', changeable or impure. It is active, kind, strong, unlimited, unbiased, always available and always consistent. It does not get jealous, never laughs at tragedy or violence, is not proud or big-headed, does not rejoice and revel in sin, but is patient and puts up with the many troubles that it sometimes has to bear, (1Corinthians 13:1-7 'charity'=love). It goes the extra mile, weeps with those who weep (Romans 12:15), rejoices with those who rejoice and carries the burden and sorrow of those who are bowed down (Galatians 6:2). According to 1Corinthians 13:8, such love never fails.

Now, if the church were to truly experience a baptism of this love, then the whole of our country would be won over to the claims of Christ. 'Revival' is the coming again of such love to the church through repentance and returning to God and his Word. Everything else is just a noise that many of us wish would just go away. At least with the television you can simply turn off all the rowdy and often 'mental-looking' 'Christian' nonsense that is aired every day to a completely disinterested and unimpressed world.

The life-transforming 'power' of the church is the demonstration of the self-sacrificing love of God in its midst, and the simple preaching of the Gospel. The baptism of the Spirit is a baptism of love. If you don't have that, then you have nothing whatsoever.

'By this shall all men know that ye are my disciples, if ye have love one to another.' John 13:35

'And the multitude of them that believed were of one heart and of one soul: neither said any of them that ought of the things which he possessed was his own; but they had all things common.' Acts 4:32

'Neither was there any among them that lacked: for as many as were possessors of lands or houses sold them and brought the prices of the things that were sold and laid them down at the apostles' feet: and distribution was made unto every man according as he had need.' Acts 4:34-35

'And believers were the more added to the Lord, multitudes both of men and women.' Acts 5:14

Here was a brand of Christianity that was real. It is the original product and the only valid Biblical hallmark of true faith. It draws a dismissive line across all of the pretensions of today's religious merry-go-round. They looked for a world to come and were not living their lives for what this world had to offer them.

Should a soul go home from church to a hungry house, wondering how he must feed his little ones? Should my brother have to walk everywhere in his worn-out shoes because he has no transport, whilst I have at least two beautiful vehicles to show off in? Should that one on the end of my row of seats, who loves God, have to put up with raging toothache night after night just because he cannot afford a dentist?

My father-in-law knew that my dad was driving around in a car which had no road tax on it (this was very many years ago before my father, who was very poorly went to be with the Lord). Now, instead of doing what most church-goers would do, which would be to frown and show their 'righteous' indignation, he went out and bought my dad some road tax, but not only that, he also bought him a newer car to go with, it as he saw that the vehicle was getting old and unreliable.

True faith finds its expression and progression in extravagant and sometimes flamboyant acts of love and grace. It matters not whether anyone else sees or knows about the things it does. It is an outpouring of love toward God in touching his children for good. It is never done to show off its own vaunted 'spirituality'.

Selfishness, on the other hand hangs on to everything it now possesses and fears for the future. It is too scared to give, just in case there is not enough cake left to take care of its own needs and demands, (1Kings 17:10-14). God's love gives without thought for its own welfare, and fears not the future because it is made perfect in that same love.

'There is no fear in love; but perfect love casteth out fear: because fear hath torment. He that feareth is not made perfect in love.' 1John 4:18

'He that hath pity upon the poor lendeth unto the LORD; and that which he hath given will he [God] pay him again.' Proverbs 19:17

'For whosoever will save his life shall lose it: and whosoever will lose his life for my sake shall find it.' Matthew 16:25

It is so easy and usual to invite all our 'buddies' or 'middleclass' Christian friends out for a 'Chinese', but when did we invite that poor soul who we do not know or particularly care for, out for a meal? He has been in our church before, but who is he to us?

I remember meeting up with the Principal of a Bible college at some gathering a few years back. He said: "Where have you been John? I have not seen you for ages; you have been lost."

I replied: "Well, John (his name was the same as mine), sometimes you just need somebody to care enough to come out and find you." He lowered his head and said, "True."

'Thus saith the Lord GOD; Behold, I am against the shepherds; and I will require my flock at their hand and cause them to cease from feeding the flock; neither shall the shepherds feed themselves any more; for I will deliver my flock from their mouth, that they may not be meat for them. For thus saith the Lord GOD; Behold, I, even I, will both search my sheep and seek them out.

As a shepherd seeketh out his flock in the day that he is among his sheep that are scattered; so will I seek out my sheep and will deliver them out of all places where they have been scattered in the cloudy and dark day.' Ezekiel 34:10-12

In every street in our nation there is somebody sat there waiting for someone to care enough, to love enough, and to be kind enough to come and 'find' them. Many of these are those who once went to church, perhaps as a child, or young adult, but nobody came to look for them when they never returned.

Some of them are now old and lonely, locked in their own little worlds of remembering how things were when they were happier. Nobody cares about them anymore and the modern church of dancers, foot-tappers, hoppers and screaming 'prophets' are more interested in the music and getting 'blessed', than they are in those poor lost souls.

Deceiving cults like the Jehovah's Witnesses and the Latter Day Saints (Mormons) knock on their doors trying to attract them into their 'families', but the local church locks itself behind the safety of its four walls, pretending that things are not really as bad as they seem.

As I have said before, the real church is probably sat at home on Sundays wondering where the real church is.

THE REAL FATHERS OF THE NATION

Chapter Fifteen

The Real Fathers Of The Nation

One of the most moving stories in the life of David was when Absalom his son was killed in battle.

The love of a mother is maternal, sensitive, fussy to an extreme at times, protective and sheltering. It is a beautiful thing to behold when a mother watches over her young ones, seeking to protect them from all the harms that life can offer and carrying on this duty until the day she dies.

But the love of a father is something quite different.

The love of a father toward his offspring is strength itself. This is no simple emotional-based maternal 'feeling'. It is not a soppy sentimental expression of weakness which some may suppose it is.

Just look at King David. His son Absalom had rebelled against him and sought only to disgrace his father and have him removed from the throne of Israel. His anger and hatred grew so bad that he planned and plotted his own father's death. His father loved him in spite of this and would have done anything for him if he could (2 Samuel 17+18). A battle ensued between Absalom's men and the king's soldiers and the young man was killed in the heat of the conflict.

Were the valiant men of David's army jubilant? Yes, for their enemy was dead and the usurper was dismissed. Did they return to Jerusalem triumphant and ready to proclaim a great victory? Yes indeed. Did they not rush to the king and tell him the news, anticipating the relief that the beleaguered sovereign would feel?

Did the king rejoice? Was David at last relieved that the troubles were over and now he could ascend once more to his throne and position?

No, for here was a father who had lost his son, a life which was so much part of his own, so much of his essence, so much of his own blood. This was a beloved and beautiful son who was the apple of his father's eye, now gone forever and for what reason?

Did David have a party? Did he call a council meeting?

No.

Instead, we find him climbing the steps to the wall of the city pouring his heart out with the bitterest of tears for his son. 'O my son Absalom, my son, my son Absalom! would God I had died for thee, O Absalom, my son, my son!' 2Samuel 18:33

Oh the depth of a father's love! Though despised, rejected, hated, conspired against and chased out of his own house by his own boy, yet this father still loves, still cherishes, still adores his rebellious offspring. Who can fathom such love or comprehend the pain of such a loss?

He wished he had died in his son's place. He would even now swap his life for this his son if only he could. Others saw this young man as contemptible, selfish and fit to die, but not so his father. He yearned for him and longed for him to somehow come through the doors and defy the stories of his death.

Is this weakness? Is this effeminacy? Is this David 'getting in touch with his feminine side' (as some silly people might suggest)?

Never! This is the power of love, the extremity of a father's heart. Who can understand such a thing? Who can dare interfere with it? Who would be stupid enough to belittle it? It is higher than the heavens, deeper than the sea, stronger than iron and more furious than a furnace. It is a man of war avenging his beloved, a raging storm defying the darkness, an ocean flooding over the nations and a cry of anguish piercing through the silence of the universe. 'For love is strong as death.' Song of Solomon 7:6

Spiritually ignorant people try to make God into a woman, or seek to impress the gullible that the love of 'Mother Mary' is what they need in their lives.

But the Bible says that 'God [Himself] so loved the world, that he gave his only Begotten Son', (John 3:16).

What the world needs now, what our young people need now and what the church needs to know now is not 'mother church' (which is just another form of slavery), but the fatherhood, the father-heart of God!

The love of our Father in Heaven is not some wishy-washy cuddle from a kindly gentleman with a white beard, but is eternal in its essence, boundless in its measure, faultless in its compassion, more extensive than the cosmos, more amazing than the sunset in all its glory, more powerful than the grave and utterly inexhaustible.

Floods of misery cannot drown it, the raging waves of hatred cannot diminish it, death cannot defeat it and a billion words can never express it.

It is stronger than titanium, more powerful than every neutron bomb put together, is reliable, trustworthy, never failing, never faltering, never changing, forever the same; holy, pure, outstanding and beyond anything this world can imagine. It is manly, noble, magnificent and extends to me and to you at every moment of every day of every year of our lives. It embraces us in our weakness, lifts us up when we have fallen, raises us up to the highest places of Heaven and rejoices all over us in front of millions of angels.

This love is deep, you cannot find the bottom. No matter how far down the valley of despair you sink, it will reach you even there. You cannot outrun it, nor flee from its touch. It is a tsunami of goodness and grace, of mercy and kindness. It will find you in the lowest pit, the darkest night, the loneliest desert and in the saddest moments of your life.

Well did the hymn-writer sing:

Oh, the love that drew salvation's plan;
Oh, the grace that brought it down to man;
Oh, the mighty gulf that God did span
At Calvary.

Such love of a Father that drew up a plan to rescue the sons of God, lost and dead in sin!

Such grace from a Father that made a way for it to be brought to earth in His own hands in the person of his Son Jesus Christ!

Such a mighty bridge that a Father built himself across such a dreadful chasm to rescue these wretched sinful creatures, so unworthy of his love!

And at Calvary, at the cross where Jesus yielded up his life:

Mercy there was great and grace was free;
Pardon there was multiplied to me.
There my burdened soul found liberty!
At Calvary.

The Father devised a supreme plan to make a way for us to be restored to Himself. It was elaborate, profound, majestic, dignified, overwhelming, beyond comprehension and brimming over with divine compassion and mercy. Yet it was simple enough for you and I to apprehend (lay hold and take) for ourselves.

Out of His fathomless love He sought for and found a way to bridge the mighty gap that sin had made in separating us from Himself.

Bigger than the Grand Canyon, deeper than a black hole in space, yet the Cross of Jesus spanned the mighty abyss and placed the hand of the Father into the hand of the sinner. The Father's great love snatched this lost wretch from Hell's mouth itself and brought him into the everlasting arms through Christ the Creator of all things, forever.

'Like as a father pitieth his children, so the LORD pitieth them that fear him. For he knoweth our frame [he knows what we are made of]; he remembereth that we are dust.' Psalm 103:13-14

'A father of the fatherless and a judge [protector] of the widows, is God in his holy habitation.' Psalm 68:5

It is no wonder then that God, through the prophet Malachi uttered this cry: 'Behold, I will send you Elijah the prophet before the coming of the great and dreadful day of the LORD: And he shall turn the heart of the fathers to the children and the heart of the children to their fathers, lest

I come and smite the earth with a curse.' Malachi 4:5-6

'Our Father, who art in heaven', is how the Lord Jesus taught his disciples to begin their prayer. Children need a dad and we are at the best but helpless children, lost droplets in a fathomless ocean, grains of sand upon the vast seashore of life and only a heavenly Father can search us out, lift us up, make us right and carry us home to where we belong.

Our government needs a father. Our children need a father; our nation needs fathers, our young men and lads need a father. The church needs fathers, not the ones titled 'Father', but the real spiritual fathers who know how to be true fathers. With a father comes care, wisdom, years of experience, understanding, patience, love, gracious correction and the power to save us when we have messed everything up.

The Guardians are the true 'fathers' of this nation who watch over it day and night. Their preoccupation is the welfare and protection of their people. Elisha acknowledged his natural father Shaphat, but recognised his 'spiritual' father in Elijah the prophet of the Most High. (1Kings 19:20; 2Kings 2:12) 'And Elijah went up by a whirlwind into heaven. And Elisha saw it and he cried, My father, my father, the chariot of Israel and the horsemen thereof.'

Turn the heart of the fathers to the children and the heart of the children to their fathers. Turn all of our hearts to our amazing and wonderful Father in heaven.

WAR OF THE WORLDS

Chapter Sixteen

War Of The Worlds

Two worlds are at war. The world of righteousness and light and the world of evil and darkness are set one against the other and the battleground is Earth and the human race. One is a world of angelic warriors and universal supremacy with an Almighty Champion who is King of Kings and Lord of Lords, the other a kingdom of outcasts and renegades who were thrown out of Heaven with their rebellious leader Beelzebub, Lucifer, Satan (to name but a few names he goes by).

Under him there are countless dark fallen angels who do his bidding and wander throughout the earth looking for a place to rest, a human home, a body from where they can have some sport and recreation (Luke 11:24).

'And there was war in heaven [right at the beginning of time]: Michael [Kingdom of Light] and his angels fought against the dragon [the devil, Kingdom of Darkness]; and the dragon fought and his angels [against God's armies] and prevailed not [lost the fight]; neither was their place [presence, residence] found any more in heaven .

And the great dragon was cast out, that old serpent, called the Devil and Satan, which deceiveth the whole world: he was cast out into the earth and his angels were cast out with him.' Revelation 12:7-9

Arriving on earth they discovered the most beautiful of all God's creations – Adam and Eve, the first of a new type of 'being', made in God's own image (Genesis 1:27).

With raging animosity and vindictiveness in his mind, he sets about seeking to destroy the thing that God loved the most. If he can turn this wonderful design for God's own enjoyment into something that is as rebellious as he is, then he will bring grief and sadness to the heart of the King and destroy this object which He so highly treasures (Genesis chapter 3).

As we know, Adam and Eve fell from their position of innocence and communion with God by siding with the devil. They chose to rebel against the truth and listened to the liar rather than obeying their Creator. Consequentially, every one of Adam's offspring have been born as rebels and sinners in the sight of God. They are lost, blinded to the truth, dead towards God and under the dominion of sin and Satan.

And ever since that day it has been the devil's hatred that has driven him to wreak havoc and destruction on earth through those who possess the same rebellious spirit that he himself is. That is why Jesus said to his opponents, 'Ye are of your father the devil and the lusts of your father ye will do. He was a murderer from the beginning and abode not in the truth, because there is no truth in him. When he speaketh a lie, he speaketh of his own: for he is a liar and the father of it.' John 8:44

Only the truth can set us free.

Man was designed for the enjoyment of his Creator and his future was planned for everlasting blessing and happiness.

Hell was not made for man, but was to be the final destiny of the devil and all his angels and followers.

'Then shall he say also unto them on the left hand Depart from me, ye cursed, into everlasting fire, prepared for the devil and his angels.' Matthew 25:41

But since the moment man listened to Satan instead of God, he fell from his place of friendship and companionship with God and became a slave of the devil.

The Gospel of Jesus Christ (the good news, that is), tells us that if we believe on Jesus Christ as the Son of God, receive Him as our Saviour and Lord, we shall be freed from the grip of Satan and transferred from the slavery of the kingdom of darkness into the kingdom of Light.

'Who hath delivered us from the power of darkness and hath translated us into the kingdom of his dear Son.' Colossians 1:13

This is what the Gospel is all about.

'To open their eyes and to turn them from darkness to light and from the power of Satan unto God, that they may receive forgiveness of sins and inheritance among them which are sanctified [made holy, made righteous] by faith...' Acts 26:18

'And ye shall know the truth and the truth shall make you free.' John 8:32

'Jesus saith unto him, I am the way, the truth and the life: no man cometh unto the Father, but [except] by me.' John 14:6

No religion in the world can save us; denominations cannot save us; superstition and charms cannot save us.

'Believe on the Lord Jesus Christ and thou shalt be saved and thy house [household].' Acts 16:31

Saved *from* what?

Saved from the captivity of Satan and his kingdom of evil; saved from sin and its dominating power over our lives; saved from the coming judgement of this world; saved from the wrath of God against a sinful and rebellious race; saved from the Final Destination – the Lake of Fire (Hell).

Saved *for* what?

Saved to become the children of the Living God (John 1:12); Saved, to become light in the Lord (Matthew 5:14); saved to know God personally (John 17:3); saved to be raised up with Christ Jesus into heavenly places (Ephesians 2:6); saved to live for ever in Heaven where there will be no more death, no more pain, no more crying and no more tears.

'And God shall wipe away all tears from their eyes; and there shall be no more death, neither sorrow, nor crying, neither shall there be any more pain: for the former things are passed away.' Revelation 21:4

'For God so loved the world, that he gave his only begotten Son [to this world, for this world of lost sinners], [so] that **whosoever believeth** in him should not perish, but have everlasting life.' John 3:16

Around the earth this very day there is a gigantic battle raging over the nations and throughout entire continents. It is engineered by top level demonic principalities and unseen rulers of the darkness of this world. The riots and violence, the looting and thieving, the criminal damage and arson even in this country from time to time are all part of their campaign of terror to bring about their wishes and plans for how this world should be run.

Part of their objective is to demoralise the populations, grow fear amongst their inhabitants and spread a plague of violence and murder throughout the towns and cities. Man is already desperately wicked in his heart and the devil simply handcuffs his evil desires to the 'anti-God' rebellious nature within each person and persuades him to carry out acts of depravity and unrighteousness.

This in no way ever excuses man from his own responsibility. He always has a choice, but he chooses evil over good, preferring darkness to light, because his heart is utterly wicked. He would sooner give his allegiance to a false god than to the One true God who expressed Himself perfectly in the Person of His Son Jesus Christ.

'And this is the condemnation [judgement], that light is come into the world and men loved darkness rather than light, because their deeds were evil. For every one that doeth evil hateth the light, neither cometh to the light, lest his deeds should be reproved [exposed, corrected].' John 3:19-20

'The heart is deceitful above all things and desperately wicked: who can know [understand or comprehend] it?' Jeremiah 17:9

What you see at street level, what you read in the newspapers, what you observe on the television news channels is all part of a much more sinister plan than what you may at first observe. From the highest offices in government to the lowest criminal in the street, the powers of darkness manipulate and encourage evil through willing individuals wherever they can. You have to look beyond the destructive and controlling politicians and money lenders who seek to enslave the populations of the world. You have to look beyond the violent thugs and bloodthirsty dictators who love to murder, maim, or abuse other fellow humans.

There are greater shadows in the background. That is where the real fight is.

'Woe to the inhabiters of the earth and of the sea! for the devil is come down unto you, having great wrath, because he knoweth that he hath but a short time.' Revelation 12:12

The devil is known as 'the prince of the power of the air' (Ephesians 2:2). This is a very interesting title for the arch-enemy of God, but fully expresses certain aspects of his territory, movements and strategies for wreaking havoc and anguish upon the human race. The single greatest means for inciting a riot or gathering the slaves of earth together to battle these days is the air.

I refer of course to our incredible ability through modern technology to communicate with each other in milliseconds. There are social networks, texting, mobile phones and all sorts of instant-contact methods that use the airways to harness a crowd for evil. Satanic powers (hidden from physical sight, but as real as you and me) incite, influence and encourage their minions to do all their bidding and entice these unsaved and degenerate hordes to carry out their commands. What would have taken weeks, months or even years to bring about just thirty years ago can be organized in minutes or even seconds these days.

Now, if the world can use such sophistications, why do the Christians still wait to go to church on Sunday to have a little meeting to complain about the troubles in their village? During the disgusting riots here in the UK not so long ago, the Sikhs in one town decided that they would make a stand against any mindless thugs who might dare come into their area to cause a disturbance and threaten their welfare. They marshalled themselves outside their temple and homes with swords and hockey sticks and they stood through the night to defend the peace. I am not advocating violence here, but what did or does the church do in such dire circumstances? Nothing. Where is its voice? Silent.

What lies beneath?

Democracy, along with law and order is a very fragile membrane that is stretched extremely thinly over the fury of anarchy and the unruliness of man's naturally sinful nature.

Our governments and politicians seek to maintain its integrity, but of late we have seen awful rips in its fabric revealing the extent of evil that lies just beneath its protection offered to a civilized society.

The whole of the world lies in sin and darkness and thankfully here in England it is very much down to our Christian heritage which established our laws and government, that we still manage to keep order and uphold safety and peace for all of our inhabitants. It is this faith (our historic Christian faith) which is in fact the best 'defender' of all the other faiths or those with no faith whatsoever who choose to come and abide under its umbrella.

However, this is now become a very volatile situation and the so-called 'multiculturalism' that was created by previous governments is now threatening to utterly tear apart the security and safeguards afforded by this same protective skin.

The whole of humanity is a restless, surging sea of rebellion against God and His ways and these fearful glimpses into what the world would be like without any moral constraints and national laws highlight the reality of what lies just beneath.

Imagine for a moment what would happen if our banking systems went to meltdown and all of the ATMs were shut down. This nearly happened here in 2008 and it was only just avoided by the government during a weekend emergency session when banks, apparently were just hours away from a complete collapse. The country would have become a war-zone within minutes as uncontrolled desperation, greed and violence swept through entire areas.

Powerful princes of darkness are manipulating complete sections of the community, instilling hatred and rage, or just sheer mindlessness and primitive tribal madness into the hearts and minds of those they take captive. Suddenly they will rise up and form a mob and rally themselves as a drunken troop, attacking anything they see fit, even destroying the very place they have to live in.

It is like a form of insanity, but in fact is the work of dark and vile unseen forces. If your children or family are part of the crowd then you can be sure that they have fallen under the spell of such demon princes and you need to get in the gap and pray them out of there.

The only answer to our country is a return to the ways of God, to humble ourselves, and to pray and seek him with all of our hearts.

Then we need a restoration of the Bible (God's Word) in the church and in government, and the propagation of the same word of the Gospel throughout the nation.

If we will return to God, then He will return to us.

'Return unto me and I will return unto you, saith the LORD of hosts.' Malachi 3:7. There is no other answer that will restore the 'Great' back into Great Britain again.

This I know however, that if true revival comes to this country, then the whole world will see, feel and know its impact and its fire will sweep the globe. The devil also knows this and that is why we are under such constant oppression here and why he does all he can to keep us from hearing the true word of the Lord.

Right now, as you read this book, the devil is raising distractions to pull you away from doing something about your own life and your future. No matter how convicted you may feel, or how concerned you are to do something to change both yourself and the world around you, there will come something else to divert you from the path to godly success. You can count on it.

It may be a phone call, something online, some relationship or family matter, or a multitude of other things. Your enemy is scared of you, especially when your heart and mind get re-tuned to serving God with all of your strength

He knows that if you actually dare rise up at this time, you will pose a mighty threat to him and his plans for this nation.

He will use the greatest ploys ever to make sure you do not get to do or be what God has planned and ordained for you. Something will catch your eye and draw you away from pursuing the call upon your life. Your attention will get diverted by one of a million possibilities and quickly the hopes and aspirations that are being developed in your heart will fade and lose their image and focus.

Your time will get stolen.(John 10:10), your mind will get tired (Matthew 26:40-41), your life will become filled with anxieties and worries about other things (Mark 4:19) and the devil will sit back satisfied that he has quashed and dampened any flames of zeal that might have been kindled by the promptings of the Holy Spirit (Mark 4:15).

Do not let this happen; and if you have already been drawn away, then stop what you are doing and come back to what God is saying.

The devil will only attack those who he fears; and he fears us greatly and fears us as a nation which has such a wonderful heritage. So take it as an encouragement that he thinks you worthy enough a contender to bother with. If he has found ways to distract you and divert you from this message, then he certainly knows that you are one of the rare and true Believers that pose a great threat to his diabolical plans. He will try to stop any of the Warriors and Guardians from waking up and stirring themselves to get hold of God's power.

You can be quite sure that he will muster a storm and a war against you if you dare to pursue God's call to you at this time.

So, if you are about to give up because it seems impossible to keep moving forward, take this as a proof that the enemy thinks of you as dangerous, even a dreadful threat to his dark empire. Perhaps you have already been knocked down after believing that this is the time of your rising. Well, just get right back up again, look the adversary in the face, recognise that God has not made any mistake in calling you to the front line. Press forward into victory!

THE PRINCE OF PERSIA

Chapter Seventeen

The Prince Of Persia

Whilst Daniel prayed and sought God for wisdom and understanding (Daniel 9:3) a huge battle was being waged some many miles away; but this was no earthly war. It was a supernatural contest for dominion and control over lands and peoples.

It was a conflict that was headed up by demonical principalities and the rulers of the wickedness of this world (Ephesians 6:12). Two princes were embroiled in some contention for the control of entire regions and populations and down on the ground, not a soul was aware of what was actually going on.

The angels of God had engaged in battle with these wretched beasts and it seemed that light and darkness were pitted against each other in an extraordinary altercation.

Daniel needed answers and could not understand why his prayers were not being heard or why God was not responding to his cries. It would be three weeks before he would find out the reason for the delay. Surely Daniel himself was a Guardian of his time and stood in the gap for his nation.

The angel that appeared to Daniel whilst he was praying said that whilst he was heading to him with the answers a great ruler of the darkness encountered him and withstood him for twenty one days, preventing him from getting there. The engagement was so severe that it took another mighty angel called Michael to come and assist him in the fight (Daniel 10:12-14).

The angel also spoke of the 'kings of Persia', showing that there was a strong spiritual kingdom throughout that region with a diversity of rulers and power-hungry generals. Indeed, it would seem that there were principalities and rulers of darkness very active within that area, because the angel went on to say that after speaking with Daniel, he must return once again to the conflict to fight with the Prince of Persia. He spoke of another prince also who he would then encounter called the Prince of Grecia (Daniel 10:20).

It throws so much light on Ephesians 6:10-18 and opens the door to see what is really going on behind the politics and battles of this world. If you look at the newspapers over the last few years and indeed months, you will observe the great demonic conflict that is brewing up a dark and ferocious storm throughout that same region today.

Who, or what is really behind all of this unrest and uprisings? What is it that mustered these screaming and hyperventilating crowds in city after city?

The atrocities committed in Norway in 2011 which saw the murder of so many precious lives, was not about one man's personal vendetta. There was without doubt a very subtle and clever plan behind his actions, but masterminded and inspired by the devil himself. The one who carried out the act was simply a puppet in the hands of a greater evil. Blame was apportioned as usual to Christians, right-wing

Fundamentalists and even Israel. However, it was actually nothing to do with any of these, but simply another deliberate and strategic move to stop the Christian community from speaking out against things that are afoot within Europe and to give one particular prince of darkness an upper hand in his over-riding programme to dominate the region.

It is a spiritual war that we are engaged in and it can only be dealt with by a spiritual offensive. How quickly the press took up against Christians and how unbelievable was the sympathy-card played by those of the other religion living amongst us who abuse our hard-won liberties and freedom of speech, claiming once again 'victimization' (over what exactly I am not sure). Unless we see what is really going on behind the scenes we will never be able to understand why certain things are happening in our world. You can watch the news and become dismayed and confounded at all that you see, or you can study the Bible, get alone with God and learn what is really going on behind the curtains of the physical and material world. Only then does the news make any sense.

I state again, our warfare is not one of guns, bombs or any other form of physical weapon, for the weapons that we have are far superior to anything the world can offer and they are exercised through faith and obedience.

Many years ago I took a job in a sawmill to earn some money during my studies with the Colonel. On one particular morning I was minding my own business and getting on with my job, when for no apparent reason one of the new guys working there came over and punched me in the mouth, breaking one of my teeth. I was shocked and stunned and all of the other men were as well. I did not know what to do really and everyone expected a confrontation at that point. I committed myself to the Lord, asking Him why this had just happened. I was very happy when many hours later I was able to go home. I lived with my parents at that time and on arriving at the house I avoided dinner and instead went off over the fields.

I needed to get an answer from God and as I was walking I asked him about it. I was both annoyed and embarrassed by the incident and distressed by the whole situation and what I was meant to do, especially as I had to go back the next day and work alongside the same fellow.

I sensed God ask me a question. “Am I not your Father?” Speaking out, I said: “Yes”. Then came the next question: “Are you not my son?”

I got my answer and that was all I needed to know about the whole situation. I went home and had my dinner. Why should I worry of these things? Why should I be stressed out by such an incident? God was my Father and I was His son, so I could give it all to Him and trust Him with the outcome.

The Bible says, ‘Commit thy way unto [roll yourself upon] the LORD; trust also in him; and he shall bring it to pass [He shall deal with the situation].’ Psalm 37:5

I went back to work the next day and was happily surprised to see that someone had scrawled ‘John is a Christian’ above my work area. I also noticed that the chap who hit me was very quiet and hung his head low that morning and so I asked one of the young men if he knew what was troubling the aggressive one.

He said: "Oh, haven't you heard? His car went underneath an articulated lorry last night and quite miraculously he escaped death and is lucky to be alive today!"

I do not need to retaliate, do not need to punch or stab anybody, but simply have to stand in the place of authority and faith and let God deal with my enemies. I had no further trouble from him and it was not long before he went from the place.

If we get where God is and stand in the gap for our people and this nation, then we shall watch as the Lord fights our battles for us.

'And all this assembly shall know that the LORD saveth not with sword and spear [not with violence and murder, not with guns and bullets]: for the battle is the LORD'S and he will give you into our hands.' 1Samuel 17:47

We know that in the end days there will arise certain evil spirits that will deceive the nations and draw them into the great and final conflict.

'And the great dragon was cast out, that old serpent, called the Devil and Satan, which deceiveth the whole world: he was cast out into the earth and his angels were cast out with him.' Revelation 12:9

'And I saw three unclean spirits [a trilogy of evil] like frogs come out of the mouth of the dragon and out of the mouth of the beast and out of the mouth of the false prophet. For they are the spirits of devils, working miracles, which go forth unto the kings [rulers] of the earth and of the whole world, to gather them to the battle of that great day of God Almighty.' Revelation 16:13-14

Behind the scenes, hidden from sight, whilst you and I play

silly games with our lives, a deadly and vicious war is being fought for this our country and for the destruction of Christianity from off the face of the earth.

You may smirk at such a statement, but if you do, then it just goes to prove that you are already taken captive and have had your eyes blinded by three tricky spirits: 'Deception', 'False teaching' and 'Carnal comforts'.

'In whom the god of this world hath blinded the minds of them which believe not.' 2 Corinthians 4:4

Do you really think that the devil and his legions care two hoots about you going to 'conference' or how many worship CDs you own? He is more than happy for you to spend your time and leisure on such things, but he is very scared of the young man who might throw everything away, put on his uniform and come into the spiritual arena where true faith fights the historic battles of the future.

Our young people will understand something of what I am saying, for they are already wise to the dark side of things and actually comprehend the reality of another dimension and not just what we can see with our physical eyes.

Church was never about sitting down in a building on Sunday singing hymns. Church was about a unique and radical family, but also about the army of the Lord; an army that would become the most feared power on earth by the 'dark side'.

The church should be everywhere, in every town and street, every nation and continent, a defiant opposition to all evil and wickedness. The church is given the keys to God's kingdom and arsenal and possesses authority over every evil power that exists. It is the light in the darkness. Just look at this:

'And I will give unto thee the keys of the kingdom of heaven: and whatsoever thou shalt bind on earth shall be bound in heaven: and whatsoever thou shalt loose on earth shall be loosed in heaven.' Matthew 16:19

'Verily [truly] I say unto you, Whatsoever ye shall bind on earth shall be bound in heaven: and whatsoever ye shall loose on earth shall be loosed in heaven.' Matthew 18:18

'Behold, I give unto you power [authority] to tread on serpents and scorpions and over all the power of the enemy: and nothing shall by any means hurt you.' Luke 10:19

In other words, what we do and say here in this world shall be effective in the spiritual realm though God's signature and seal upon our lives. What we say and do within the faculties of our bodies and spirits whilst on this earth, God will already have executed in the heavenly realms on our behalf. Our voice should be heard above all the din and commotion of the millions of godless voices that fill the air.

We are not talking about getting a new car or a better job here. All those things are so subjective. Seek ye first the kingdom of God and His righteousness and all these things [what you need, not what you crave] shall be added unto you. (Matthew 6:31-33)

The prince of Persia has not disappeared, nor did he die. He is a spirit after all, an evil entity whose eventual destiny is the Lake of Fire. He has in these last three decades sought to extend his kingdom from the east (along with all the other dark rulers) and invade the Western world. He is building his forces and strengthening his position right here, right now, right under our noses. He is a most dark and sinister ruler who holds multitudes of human captives in spiritual darkness and blindness. His ways and methods of domination are the cruellest and most inhumane imaginable. You can mark his murderous history down through the ages of this world and read of the violence and rage of his human armies.

These are they who are 'taken captive by him at his will [whenever and wherever he chooses].' 2Timothy 2:26. They have little mind of their own except to submit to everything that he says.

What men like Stalin and Hitler sought to do in their brief time in this life, he has accomplished in millions of lives worldwide.

The prince of Persia is in this nation seeking dominance and subjugation of the people here.

He hates what this country represents and despises our history, for everywhere he has gone around this planet he has encountered the results of the Gospel that left these shores in the suitcases and in the lives of thousands of missionaries and Bible teachers.

Those who are here following his commands and instruction are his slaves. They would not accept this, for delusion corrupts sensibility and common-sense. They are victims themselves and will happily throw away their lives to please him, even though they do not see his true colours, for he comes as an angel of light.

'And no marvel; for Satan himself is transformed into an angel of light. Therefore it is no great thing if his ministers [prophets, preachers, teachers] also be transformed [appear and masquerade] as the ministers of righteousness; whose end shall be according to their works.' 2Corinthians11:14-15

Only the Word of God, the Gospel of light can free them from such a slavery and control and sometimes this can only be accomplished through prayer and fasting. (Matthew 9:17-29)

If you are going to fight, then you need a uniform and weapons. Both have been given to you by the Holy Spirit, but they are still most likely packed in your spiritual suitcase and have yet to see the light of day.

With the Sword of the Spirit in our hands we can learn to speak truth in unity into the midst of the deceit of deception. We can rise up in the light and glory of God and become a lighthouse over the roaring seas of destruction. We can be a flaming beacon on the hills overlooking the putrid and writhing confusion of humanity in our cities. We can speak life into our 'matrix' societies of death, hope into the forgotten communities of misery and faith into all those who have given up already. We can become the wall of defence and the towers of defiance against all of our hostile foes that lift their heads cockily as though they would march right over us.

God can save to the uttermost and can transform both the individual and society.

'In meekness [not 'weakness', but gentleness] instructing those that oppose themselves; if God peradventure [haply, indeed] will give them repentance to the acknowledging [recognition and understanding] of the truth; and that they may recover themselves out of the snare [trap] of the devil, who are taken captive by him at his will.' 2imothy 2:25-26

Let us, however, understand that the troubles and violent warfare that is being waged over and in this nation is because we have left God and turned our attention and desires upon the things of the world. We have not just forgotten who we are supposed to be, but have rebelled against the Word of God and sought us out an alternative lifestyle that suits our carnal and selfish nature. We want the world and the kingdom of God, but we can actually only have one of those. The lying prophets have taught everyone that to follow Christ means you can claim anything and everything you desire and the proof that you are righteous is the money in your bank and the job that you now have.

We have opened the front door to sin and left the back door open for evil and judgment.

We should take good notice of what Matthew Henry (the great Bible Commentator) had to say: 'Sin makes a gap in the hedge of protection that is round about a people through which good things run out from them, and evil things pour in upon them, a gap by which God enters to destroy them.

There is a way of standing in the gap and making up the breach against the judgments of God, by repentance, prayer and reformation. Moses stood in the gap when he made intercession for Israel to turn away the wrath of God (Psalm 106:23).

When God is coming forth against a sinful people to destroy them he expects somebody to intercede for them and enquires if there is but one person that does; so much is it his desire and delight to show mercy. If there is but a man that stands in the gap, as Abraham did for Sodom, God will see him and be well pleased with him.'

'Run ye to and fro through the streets of Jerusalem and see now and know and seek in the broad places thereof, if ye can find a man, if there be any that executeth judgment, that seeketh the truth; and I will pardon it.' Jeremiah 5:1

Now, I know there will be the supercilious, super-duper pseudo 'spiritual' folk who say, "Oh, I only read the Bible; I do not need any of man's comments." They of course do not read the newspaper, watch the television, read the ingredients on their food packets, blow their noses, watch god-tv, or go shopping to the carnal supermarkets for their food. They walk down the highways with their eyes covered, never drive a car, never use the bank and have no electricity in their homes. Likely story!

But for the rest of us who just long for a God-given revival where no man gets any glory and no screaming preacher fleeces the congregation of their cash, we lift up our hands in honesty and say, "Lord, have mercy upon us and our nation. Forgive our iniquities and sin and restore us once again to Divine favour; and please teach me how to stand in the gap for my people." And we do not mind searching out the 'old paths' that the saints trod, to discover the way back to truth and righteousness.

'It is time to seek the LORD, till he come and rain righteousness upon you.' Hosea 10:12

Let every Guardian and every Warrior within this land begin a prayer meeting in their own town or street for revival to come to this beautiful Isle now ravaged by wickedness at every level. You do not need permission from anyone (not even the pastor) to do this. Any true minister of God would be absolutely delighted to find that someone in his congregation is obeying God and doing something so vital and needful. Sadly, you will be opposed, but only by those who think that they know better than God and are scared of losing the control they believe they have over your life. We do not need man's permission to come together to pray or preach or praise.

Just hire a local church, or a hall, or use your home, or meet in a cow shed, out in the field or down on the beach and invite all those whose hearts are broken and concerned with the destruction and dreadful condition of our country.

CONFLICT

Chapter Eighteen

Conflict

If you have stirred yourself up to take hold of God (Isaiah 64:7; Ezekiel 22:30) and find his purpose for your life; if you have gotten yourself out of your slumber of death (Proverbs 24:33-34; Isaiah 56:10) and roused your heart and mind to the eternal purposes of Christ in you (1Corinthians 15:34), then be very certain of this: you have entered the battleground.

You will be tried and tested in every area and find yourself in conflict and close combat. Things will face you that before did not come near you.

The mountains may seem higher than they were and the valleys may appear even deeper, but all this is because you have moved from your bed of laziness and carnal comfort and engaged yourself in the plan and purpose of God for your life. You are now nearer the challenges and are beginning to experience what it means to be a soldier of Jesus Christ.

I will not pretend that it is going to be a pleasant stroll down country lanes and a gentle walk through the meadows and pastures. The battle is in the wilderness at times, even in the parched and dry land where no water is. This is where the demons and princes of darkness all hang out and this is where Christ came on his earthly ministry to destroy the works of the devil. (1John 3:8) Did you really think that the devil was just going to let you march on in and take back everything that he has stolen over the last fifty years? Did you imagine that you would be able to just storm in here and in a few moments or a few days accomplish a victory that would turn the world upside down and allow you to go back home a victor?

This is an engagement, a long-term, life-long strategic war that will only be won through perseverance, dedication and diligent, persistent, obstinate progress. Many of the dark shadows of the past will seem to resurrect and try to frighten you away and you will hear whispers and talk of slander and threatening opposition.

'For I have heard the slander of many: fear was on every side: while they took counsel together against me, they devised to take away my life.' Psalm 31:13

Your enemy will seek to get at every area of your life, distract you by whatever means he can in the hope that you will run back home to your safe little existence and give him no more trouble. He will stir up strife and contention, money troubles and bills, family problems and distresses, tiredness and fatigue, diversions and deceptions and doubt and fear. He is a master of such strategies and knows how to discourage the fighter from his duty and take his focus off the call of God.

But you are called to be the servant of Christ (Romans 1:1) and looking unto Jesus the beginner and completer of our faith (Hebrews 12:2-5), the Captain of our salvation (Joshua 5:14), the Angel of the Lord who goes before us (Exodus 23:23), we are certain of success and triumph against the most foul, despicable and overwhelming enemy who seeks to destroy us (John 10:10).

No weapon formed against you shall succeed. All the accusers and slanderers who come to point the finger, you yourself shall condemn. This is the heritage of God's servants and your righteousness is from the LORD, His gift and covering upon your life. (Isaiah 54:17)

There will be sin and temptation and the lure of the flesh all seeking to draw you away from what you should be keeping your mind on, in an effort to win over your affections and bodily lusts. You might think that you have conquered all of those and are shocked at their appearance and strength yet again in your thinking and life.

The answer to all these is the same: turn away your eyes and mind from dwelling upon sin and ask God for grace and the ability to get back up and put such things behind you. Dust yourself off, wash your hands and heart (James 4:8) and get right back into the thick of the fight. They say that the best thing for you if you fall off a horse, is to clean your wounds, rub your bruises and get right back in the saddle before fear and unbelief keep you from ever riding again.

Set up a place (a room, garden shed, study etc.) where you can write out everything that God speaks to you about and pin it up boldly on the walls. Print out Scripture verses that remind you of your call and vocation and compass yourself with encouragements and instructions. Take cuttings from the newspapers and stick pictures on your notice-board that will help to reinforce your prayer-life with passion and concern.

Abraham was told to look at the stars in the heavens; Nehemiah went and looked at the desolation of Jerusalem; the disciples were told to look at the fields ripe unto harvest.

Set your face, as Jesus did, like a flint (Isaiah 50:7), determined, unshakable, unmovable and unstoppable. Like the 'Terminator', you may be shot, beaten, knocked back time and time again, but they will soon discover that you are indestructible in your faith and perseverance. If they kill you, then you just become greater and more blessed and more powerful than ever, for death will never touch you again.

As Billy Graham once said, "*Someday you will read or hear that Billy Graham is dead. Don't you dare believe a word of it! I shall be more alive than I am now. I will just have changed my address. I will have gone into the presence of God.*"

No Weapon sent to destroy you shall succeed

Here is the assurance, the daily maintenance of 'I am with thee', (Isaiah 41:10).

We do not go to fight alone; we do not run to the battlefield unless our Commander fights for us. In Isaiah 54:15, we are told that, 'they shall surely gather together [come to fight against you], but not by me [not at the request of God, neither with his blessing]: whosoever shall gather against thee shall fall for thy sake.'

It is the nature of warfare that our enemy seeks to destroy us, but we may stand in confidence and certainty that though they gather in their thousands to bring us to the ground, nevertheless it is they who shall fall and we that shall remain steadfast and standing.

And it is 'for our sakes' that they shall utterly fail in their hatred toward us, for we are the sons and daughters of the Almighty. 'Since thou wast precious in my sight, thou hast been honourable and I have loved thee: therefore will I give men for thee and people for thy life.' Isaiah 43:4

'For he that toucheth you toucheth the apple of his eye.' Zechariah 2:8

Perhaps you can look back over your life and see the many times where your enemies sought to dismiss you, to suggest that you were a failure and unworthy to be called by the name of God. Maybe their animosities toward you made you give up on your dreams and hopes and made you forget trying to serve God or do something in the kingdom. Your own inconsistencies seemed to disqualify you forever.

A few words from unkind lips can do severe damage to a tender soul and backstabbing from the people you trust is desperately injurious.

Those who hold office and preach on the platforms are the most dangerous of all because they use their 'suit' to ruin your name and make it nigh-on impossible to fulfil the vision that God gave to you. These are proud and nasty people who make much ado about their own 'ministry', but are dreadfully jealous at what you have. Shame and disgrace be upon them.

The anointing and grace that rests on you convicts them of their own absence of the presence of God and so they set themselves to become your opposition. They talk badly of you when you are out of sight, but pretend to like you when they meet you face to face.

Anyone know what I'm talking about?

The opposition is not always the man in the street or the criminal going about his naughtiness. More often than not it is the one who makes himself or herself out to be 'religious' and good and gathers around them those whom he can hoodwink into his deception. It happens at platform level from pastors through to the choir leader. It happens with those we sometimes put too much trust in.

'Trust ye not in a friend, put ye not confidence in a guide [teacher]: keep the doors of thy mouth from her that lieth in thy bosom [the one you should be able to trust]. Micah 7:5 'A man's foes shall be they of his own household.' Matthew 10:36

Well, here's another consideration for you: forget the things that are past and reach out to all that God has in store for you in the future and stand on your feet and get ready to march on this land that God has already given to you.

'Behold, the LORD thy God hath set the land before thee: go up and possess it, as the LORD God of thy fathers hath said unto thee; fear not, neither be discouraged.' Deuteronomy 1:21

'All the commandments which I command thee this day shall ye observe to do, that ye may live and multiply and go in and possess the land which the LORD sware unto your fathers.' Deuteronomy 8:1

Paint a new picture of yourself

I was watching an artist painting a caricature of a young man seated in front of him in Leicester Square, London, one evening. His client had no clue as to how he was portraying him on the paper, but to all of the onlookers, the distortions and twisted outlines of what was supposed to be his better features brought only amusement and laughter. I certainly would not wish to sit for this scribbler, for his work was only derogatory and a deliberate misinterpretation of the truth.

The fact is, we are all being painted and presented in so many different ways by so many different people in life. Some of those images have influenced our thinking and left lasting impressions upon us, not necessarily for good or constructive use.

We may actually be living our lives by the pictures which we have been told represent us, but in truth, have nothing whatsoever to do with the reality of who we are in God. The devil loves to get us to believe the negative and hopeless image that he paints of us and having convinced us he is right, he then sells it to us so that we can hang it in front of our faces day by day.

I had been looking at all those portraits that others painted of me and having looked at them so often before, I came to believe that the artist's impressions must have been right. Their images became my mirror, so I stopped looking some time ago because I did not like what I saw.

But they are a lie. That which they painted is but an imagination of their own hearts and worse still, perhaps a reflection of their own lives. They use their brushes to mock and despise, to ridicule and belittle that which they are afraid of.

It is time to cast down their imaginations and their high thoughts of presumption against this child of God (2Corinthians 10:5). It is time to tear down the accuser's depictions from where they have been hung for so long, douse them with petrol and burn them with fire. Somewhere today amidst the grime of this world, walking the streets through the contamination of this evil age, a prince of Heaven presses resolutely forward (Genesis 32:28) and a messenger of the Highest is just a set of clothes away from being seen to be the heavenly ambassador he actually is (1John 3:1-2; Romans 8:19).

I shall therefore fill my room instead with all the paintings that God Himself has done of me and hang them on gilded frames for all the world to see. In fact, I might even open a gallery and charge admission to any who wish to behold the beauty of His handiwork. After-all, the brutish depicters hang their wretched drawings for free wherever and whenever they wish and I am quite sure they would not care to pay anything to see the gloriously outrageous visions that the hand of the Master has portrayed over my life.

I shall not cast my pearls before swine though, for pigs would only tear up the canvass and make a foul, stinking mess everywhere. Let them hang their ugly pictures in the darkened alleys and backstreets, but I shall live in the brightly lit gallery up on the hill of God's blessing and righteousness. All those who are dignified will pass by their second-rate efforts and head for the lights of my new home.

I shall welcome freely those who admire the works of my great Artist and friend and who are loving students of all His masterpieces; for they alone shall be my companions and acquaintances. For surely 'the ungodly shall not stand in the judgment [deciding of a case], nor sinners in the congregation [company] of the righteous. For the LORD knoweth the way of the righteous: but the way of the ungodly shall perish.' Psalm 1:5-6. For, 'I am a companion of all them that fear thee and of them that keep thy precepts.' Psalm 119:63

'He that walketh with wise men shall be wise: but a companion of fools shall be destroyed.' Proverbs 13:20

Somebody painted me as a failure.
God paints me as a hero!
Somebody painted me as sinful
God paints me as righteous!
Somebody painted me as a loser
God paints me as an over-comer!
Somebody painted me as a tramp
God paints me as a prince!
Somebody painted me as a backslider
God paints me as a man of God!
Somebody painted me as unwanted
God paints me as loved and welcomed in Heaven!
Somebody painted me as outside the 'church'
God paints me as chosen and called amongst His beloved!
Somebody painted me as poor
God paints me as an heir to all that Christ owns!
Somebody painted me as a cripple and broken
God paints me as whole and healed!
Somebody painted me as insignificant
God paints me as indispensable!
Somebody painted me without a future
God paints me with the world at my fingertips!

Somebody painted me as one without a ministry

God paints me as an oracle and a symphony of truth!

Somebody painted me as one who has no influence

God paints me as a ruler over the nations!

Somebody painted me as lost and lonely

God paints me as seated next to Him in heavenly places!

You do not need the cheap and distorted prints of the back-street market stalls when you already have original and priceless works of art, hand-painted by the Master Himself. Take the rubbish out of your life, cast it into the deepest sea of forgetfulness and gaze upon the beauty and nobility that God portrays over your future. 'Lift up your heads, O ye gates; and be ye lift up, ye everlasting doors; and the King of glory shall come in.' Psalm 24:7

Don't just sit there waiting for a miracle

'And there was a great famine in Samaria.' 2Kings 6:25

Let us just look at this passage again, for here is a part of the Bible that I have read numerous times and spoken about at meetings and conferences everywhere.

It shows both the power and ability of God to intervene in our circumstances, even when things seem absolutely impossible and beyond our control. It also shows that God is waiting for one person to get up, dare to be different and step out into the unknown, so that He can show His power and glory in breath-taking ways!

Because of Israeli's sin and rebellion against God, they were brought into a state of desperation, poverty and discomfort. There is always a remedy for sin, but we do not like to take God's prescription because it goes against our pride, our lust and our stubborn wills. Thank God for righteous men like Elisha, who 'stand in the gap' and intercede (earnestly pray on behalf) for a nation or individual. Thank God for Jesus, who intercedes on behalf of His people even now, who intercedes for me!

'And he bare the sin of many and made intercession for the transgressors.' Isaiah 53:12

'Who is he that condemneth? It is Christ that died, yea rather, that is risen again, who is even at the right hand of God, who also maketh intercession for us.' Romans 8:34

'Wherefore he is able also to save them to the uttermost that come unto God by him, seeing he ever liveth to make intercession for them.' Hebrews 7:25

When there is no one who cares about your soul; when there is nobody who wants to know you, Christ Jesus Himself intercedes for you in Heaven!

'And he saw that there was no man and wondered that there was no intercessor: therefore his arm brought salvation unto him; and his righteousness, it sustained him.' Isaiah 59:16

During this crisis in Israel, when the whole nation was in distress and the king was out of his mind with worry, the prophet Elisha sat in his house, quite unruffled by the situation.

'But Elisha sat in his house and the elders sat with him.' 2Kings 6:32

He was unperturbed by the commotion because he was in

the right place, at the right time, doing the right thing. He was waiting on God and interceding for his nation to repent and turn back to the Lord.

But let us look specifically at the way God chose to answer prayer and change the circumstances because of one faithful intercessor. 'The effectual fervent prayer of a righteous man availeth much.' James 5:16

'And there were four leprous men at the entering in of the gate: and they said one to another, **Why sit we here until we die**? If we say, We will enter into the city, then the famine is in the city and we shall die there: and if we sit still here, we die also. Now therefore come and let us fall unto the host of the Syrians: if they save us alive, we shall live; and if they kill us we shall but die. And they rose up in the twilight, to go unto the camp of the Syrians.' 2 Kings 3-5

See here four lepers. What was their condition? What was their mindset? They had all but given up. They were 'outcasts' in any case and basically lived with a 'survival' mentality. They were more than aware of their own personal crisis and were dependant upon other people's goodwill and charity to survive each passing day. But that benevolence and generosity was now dried up! They were depressed, resigned, and unmotivated and were left in a lethargic and incapacitated state.

They had given up on any good coming their way and had accepted that nobody cared for them at all. Their situation was hopeless. But one of them could not sleep that night and began to use his brain a bit more than usual. There is no doubt whatsoever that it was the prompting of the Holy Spirit, but that same prompting requires our response.

He asked himself: "Why are we just sitting here waiting to die?" He shook his companions awake and said: "What are we doing here? Why do we just wait for the worst? Why are we doing nothing except expecting the inevitable?"

He questioned his own common-sense and began to reason with his own heart. He challenged his fellows and addressed his own thought process. "If we just sit here doing nothing, waiting for the end, for strength and breath to run out, then we will die! That is a fact."

"I do not want to die", he declared. Good start to the road of recovery.

"If we go back to the city, to what we have always done to survive, there is no one to help us even if they wanted to. Everyone else is in trouble too! We will die there just as well as if we sit here."

They must do something.

What should they do?

Who has the food? Who has the resources?

The enemy!

But they will kill lepers, especially Israeli lepers!

"So what? What have we got to lose by trying? We are going to die anyway. Better to get stabbed quickly than to suffer a long agonising death lying out in the sun with no food or water."

Nobody was coming to help these poor wretches. There were no friends in the city who even gave them a thought. No one knew them, wanted them, or cared for them. It is just the same today for many who look to the church for answers, or who hope that some great deliverance will come when the preacher gets jumping and squeaking 'words from God'. However, there is nothing in the city, nothing coming from the camp and the worthless 'prophecies' from the conferences and 'worship' fantasias produce nothing to change the national dilemma.

They could just sit there languishing in self-pity, dreaming some imaginary dream that they might win the lottery or come into an inheritance suddenly, - or they could get up and do something themselves.

'Cannot be bothered', is the surest way to poverty and death.

Procrastination is the quickest way to others stealing your dreams, ideas and inventions.

Be bothered! Be very bothered and get up off your backside quickly and make decisions to do something about your life and circumstances, lest there be no remedy to your lethargy and no future to your hopes and plans.

Use what you have in front of you. Look around your house and your life and make an inventory.

Do not wait for what you do not have.

'And the LORD said unto him [Moses], What is that in thine hand? And he said, A rod [a stick].' Exodus 4:2-4

The poor widow woman said, 'I have not [even] a cake, but [just] an handful of meal in a barrel and a little oil in a cruse.' 1Kings 17:12-14

Another was asked, 'Tell me, what hast thou in the house? And she said, Thine handmaid hath not any thing in the house, save [except] a pot of oil.' 2Kings 4:2

Jesus asked the disciples what they had. They replied, 'There is a lad here, which hath five barley loaves and two **small** fishes: but what are they among so many?' John 6:9

What you already have is where your miracle is buried!

The seeds of success are in your hand in the little pot of oil, the small jar of meal, the 5 loaves and two little fishes, or the brilliant 'idea' you once had that you did nothing about!

Do not let anyone steal what is yours, or dampen your determination to activate the seeds of harvest! Pick up what you have, bring it to God, do what he says and watch the miracle happen.

Throw the stick on the floor! (Exodus 4:1-4)

Pour out the little oil! (1Kings 17)

Distribute the five loaves and two small fish! (John 6)

Use what you have to ignite the promise of God. Get up and do something if you want things to change.

Waiting for them to change into a miracle will see no results.

Take what you have in all of its imperfection, its weakness, its smallness, its insignificance, because the miracle will not happen until you release it, pour it out, pass it on, give it away and let it loose! God takes the next to nothing that we despise or consider inadequate and he performs the miraculous, so that we give all the glory to him. Make a phone call; get on the train; write the letter; visit the forgotten; get up and fight for your future!

The disciples could not minister to the vast crowd of thousands until they took the crumbs of those five loaves in their hands and began to distribute their unbelievable insignificance.

Do not wait for someone in the church to let you in, give you a chance to speak, or invite you to the platform, but go to the enemy camp, for that is where the miracle is.

The moment that the lepers decided to get up was the moment that the miracle began to take place, even before they got within sight of the enemy! God begins His extraordinary work the moment we trust and step out in obedience.

Now, I must point out that it was 'twilight' when they arose from their place. Nothing is ever clear in such half-light and everything seems to melt into a grey blur. It is the same in the spiritual sense. We wait for the bright light of day to give us some clarity of what to do in our circumstances, but God calls us forward when things are not clear and when there appears no definition or humanly possible guarantee of success.

Faith steps out into the darkness and climbs down onto the troubled waters, not waiting for a better day to come, but trusting that God will make a way through the raging seas, the barren desert and the lonely wilderness.

So, why do we sit here all day just waiting to die? Let us arise, turn the impossible into possible, turn defeat into victory and turn the darkness of fear and doubt into the light of faith and daring.

Let us '*storm the forts of darkness and bring them down*'.

AGAINST ALL ODDS

Chapter Nineteen

Against All Odds

Is it really possible to turn the tide in this nation and see righteousness and commonsense restored to this nightmarish society we find ourselves in? Is there any dim chance that we might avoid the coming turbulence and violence that is gathering momentum every day due to reckless immigration, injustice, violent and hostile extremism and man's plain greed and selfishness? Can we withstand the onslaught of the enemies of the Gospel both from outside our little Island and from the devil's wretched armies already spreading themselves throughout our towns and cities? Is it possible to turn this land back to the Lord and see the Word of God exalted and proclaimed throughout every community and age-group?

The true answer to all of these is 'no', unless something of a miraculous nature happens.

Let us not doubt for a moment that a mighty army, indeed rampant armies have spread themselves in the valleys and hillsides around and in this wonderful country and whether they be false religions, anarchists, atheists, devilish 'church' organizations, perverts and despots, or political and financial war machines, they are all set as antagonists and loathers of the truth, that is, of 'the faith that was once delivered to the saints'; the faith of this country. Jude 1:3

They have set themselves in array to destroy the royal seed of the family of God (1Peter 2:9), to extinguish the light of the true Gospel and to enforce their stinking corruption and violent demands throughout our shores. Some of them may claim to be on our side and even say they believe in Jesus, but as Christ Himself said, 'He that is not with me is against me'. Luke 11:20

Many centuries ago, a huge Ethiopian army surrounded the much smaller army of Israel, taunting them to come and fight, knowing full well that they completely outnumbered King Asa and his troops.

'Then Asa went out against him and they set the battle in array in the valley of Zephathah at Mareshah. And Asa cried unto the LORD his God and said, LORD, **it is nothing with thee to help, whether with many, or with them that have no power: help us, O LORD our God; for we rest on thee and in thy name we go against this multitude**. O LORD, thou art our God; let not man prevail against thee. So the LORD smote the Ethiopians before Asa and before Judah; and the Ethiopians fled. And Asa and the people that were with him pursued them unto Gerar: and the Ethiopians were overthrown, that they could not recover themselves; for they were destroyed before the LORD and before his host.'

Notice, King Asa's confidence was not in his own abilities neither that of the experience of his army. He knew full well that numbers are not of importance to God, for whether it be many or few, the battle belongs to the Lord. (1Samuel 17:47)

Secondly, see how he prayed and rested in the assurance

that God was with him and then got up and charged toward the enemy, taking the battle to their camp instead of waiting for the inevitable to come to him.

See also how the enemy was completely destroyed before the Lord and His hosts. It was not just the somewhat insignificant band of warriors from Israel that sent the Ethiopians to their graves, but the hosts of the Lord which were encamped around about God's people and who invaded the enemy's regiments even before King Asa's men got there.

God's hosts of angels get up and fight on behalf of His servants the moment they rally themselves and run to the enemy camp.

Sitting, waiting for God's deliverance is never going to achieve anything. We have to get up and do something before the miracle of victory will ever come.

Moses told the people to 'stand still and see the salvation of the Lord', when they were trapped at the Red Sea by the Egyptian soldiers. God told Moses to get up off his knees and march the people forward into the impossible (Exodus 14:13-15). The miracle begins when we dare to believe and when we get off our lazy hides and obey the command to get up and fight.

The walls of Jericho came down, not by the shout of the Israelites (Joshua 6), but by the power of God through the obedience of His people to go and march around that great city. The walls would not have come down if they had just sat there having a prayer meeting about the situation. Faith necessitates obedience. Obedience necessitates action. Action is the catalyst that sees the miracle take place before our eyes.

'Rise up and walk', is the only way to receive the miracle (Acts 3:6). Even Lazarus, dead and bound up in his grave-clothes had to arise and walk out of the tomb if he wanted to see the land of the living once again. Jesus did not pick him up and carry him out of the cave. If you want your nation saved, then you need to do something about it.

Gideon's 300 men knew that they were absolutely nothing compared with the multitudes of Midianites that mocked them, (Judges 7). However, in spite of their weakness and against insurmountable odds, they dared to believe that their God was greater than any situation, no matter how impossible and illogical it might seem.

Was it the candles in their clay jars, the shout of victory, or their simple obedience that wrought such a mighty victory for them that day? It was of course their faith and obedience and the moment they broke the clay jars on that hillside and shouted a cry of triumph, the angels of the Lord stormed into the enemy camp and drove them all to confusion, so much so that the Midiantites went round stabbing each other with their own swords! (Judges 7:20)

There is another fantastic example of this in 1Samuel 14. Jonathan and his armour-bearer dared to take on an entire garrison of the enemy. They had to climb a very steep hill on their hands and knees before getting within fighting distance of the soldiers, but through their faith, courage and daring to take the battle to the enemy, they slew twenty fully armed swordsmen and then began to chase the thousands of soldiers that were garrisoned behind them. Once more we see the angels of the Lord mysteriously bringing confusion and madness into the enemy's heads that they began to hack each other to death with their own weapons! (1Samuel 14:16)

God can do what we cannot, but he requires our obedience and faith to do what we should in order for his miracle of intervention to take place.

The odds stacked against us in this country are indeed great and daunting, but they are nothing once the Lord of Hosts marches in with His people to do battle. But who will rise to be a soldier of Jesus Christ? Who will set himself apart from the cares and attractions of this world to save our country and our people?

I was speaking with a young unconverted man about this nation and our need to win it back and see it restored and he said, "When you raise your army, count me in! I love this nation." The same evening I spoke with another young fellow who was also unsaved, about beginning a new type of church and he said to let him know when to be ready to come.

A sound of battle is in the land – for those of us who can hear and for those who cannot.

God can bring judgement on a city, a town, a people and a race. He can cause plague upon the Egyptians and yet keep the Israelites in perfect health within the same city and country.

In the Book of Exodus we read how God sent a plague of locusts throughout the Egyptian coasts that devoured and destroyed every living plant. He then sent swarms of flies that would completely overtake the entire Egyptian population, yet miraculously not one fly would enter the area where God's people lived! He put a strange and uncanny darkness upon all of the Egyptians for three days and so dark was it that they could not even go out to visit each other. However, at the same time, the Israelites had light in all of their dwellings, even though they lived in the same region at that time.

Then He sent a ferocious lightning storm and giant hail that killed thousands of cattle and livestock as well as people and destroyed their crops, yet in the Israelite's housing area there was not one single hailstone, nor one casualty.

The Lord knows how to segregate and deliver righteous judgement to communities as well as nations.

See what the Lord says to his people:

'If thou wilt diligently hearken to the voice of the LORD thy God and wilt do that which is right in his sight and wilt give ear to his commandments and keep all his statutes, I will put none of these diseases upon thee, which I have brought upon the Egyptians: for I am the LORD that healeth thee.' Exodus 15:26

'And the LORD will take away from thee all sickness and will put none of the evil diseases of Egypt, which thou knowest, upon thee; but will lay them upon all them that hate thee.' Deuteronomy 7:15

The Lord separated Lot and his family from Sodom and Gomorrah before sending destruction upon it. He brought his people out of the Red Sea before the waters returned to drown the Egyptians. He knows how to deal with the enemies of the light and even segregate house from house as He did when the firstborn were killed throughout the land of Egypt. Those without the blood of the lamb upon their doorposts and lintel were visited by death. He sent 'emerods' (some form of genital disease or plague) into the men who dared to challenge His glory in 1Samuel 5. Maybe God will send some of that to the vile perverts who are 'grooming' and stealing our children for the sex trade.

In the end times God will separate the sheep from the goats, the wheat from the chaff, the corn from the weeds and the righteous from the unrighteous.

Even now, God has the power to intervene in our most troubled situations and disturbing environments and make changes and consequences which we might think inconceivable. He can revive Great Britain, break the power of evil, destroy the haters of righteousness, restore our heritage and beautify the future for our children. All things are possible to him who can believe and in that believing rise up to do whatever He tells us to do.

TIME

IS PRECIOUS

Chapter Twenty

Time Is Precious

Sitting there gawping at Facebook or some other time wasting, friendship-breaking, sin-encouraging social network is like selling your soul to the devil.

God has placed in you the amazing ability to be creative and do something amazing and outstanding in this world. Time is all that you really have and as you spend it, so it gets less and less and soon you will find yourself 'bankrupt', with eternity beckoning you to leave this world and come away. Then you will look back in astonishment at all the rubbish that you 'spent' your time on. As I have said before, time is the finest and most expensive of all commodities and yet we are happy to squander it as though it meant nothing and had no value.

I walked into a house the other day and saw three young men sat on the settees in the room. Two of them were holding control-sticks in their hands for a game they were playing on the television screen. The third was deeply engaged with something on his latest mobile phone.

I had hoped that I might get a cup of tea there, but they were all far too busy and employed with what they were doing to ever consider stopping for one moment to do anything useful and 'normal'.

The game they were playing had taken them over and the

way they were getting stressed and even distressed when things were not going in their favour led you to believe that they actually thought that these insane moving images on the television screen were actually 'real'.

This is all they could find to do with their lives and rather than explore their God-given talents and unique abilities, they had succumbed to the 'spirit of this age'.

This 'spirit', without any doubt, is of a demonic nature, for it is destructive, wasteful, selfish and utterly empty of any value either in this world or for the world to come. It steals the souls of our young people and absorbs them into its mass of pointless and purposeless living, where everything real and potentially good is replaced with mindless and profitless occupations.

When the television got boring, it seems the enemy of mankind inspired his minions to invent a multitude of devises that would capture the thoughts and creativity of a whole generation of potential world-changers and turn them into 'zombified' halfwits, who sit fiddling with bits of plastic, screaming and shouting at something that does not even exist.

Of course, the quickest cure to all of this enforced dementia is to turn the power supply off, i.e. press the 'off' switch, or smash the stupid gadget and get a life.

Billions of pounds are spent every year on worthless and senseless games, from a pretend car that stays in the middle of the screen whilst unreal images made up of millions of little light-cells make you think that you are really driving it, to pretend soldiers who shoot pretend guns, making pretend victories from bits of silicon and plastic on a printed circuit board.

What would happen if the electricity were to fail in this country for say six months? There would be millions of 'zombies' wandering the streets and fields wondering what to do or where to go. They would not know how to do anything constructive like planting vegetables or crops, because they thought that it all came from their freezer and never knew that it had to be grown.

Giving all those hours and days to a computer or television screen is the same as selling your soul to the devil. If you do not have the capacity, energy, determination or power to break free from such controlling devices and mind-numbing occupations, then you are already Satan's slave.

Some computer games give you the chance to 'pretend' that you are a musician and can play an instrument by manically pressing plastic buttons on another piece of Chinese-made cheap nonsense. Why not spend the same time actually learning to play the guitar or piano using a real instrument? You might just astonish yourself at what you are able to accomplish.

If you are sitting up half the night, glued to the screen throughout the day, lost in the artificial 'matrix'-type world of a false reality, then you are under the power of demonic control and you need Christ to set you free. I dare not mince my words on this matter. God gave you life and his desire is that you have life 'more abundantly'.

Your life is only as long as the time allotted to you and in the course of that time period you are permitted to spend the hours and minutes as you seem fit. It is up to you to decide what the most profitable thing to invest your time in is and what value that investment might add to you and to others. The Bible tells us to value our time and redeem it. To redeem our time means that we should not just throw it away, but highly prize it and recognise its worth.

Listen to what that wise old King Solomon had to say:

'Whatsoever thy hand findeth to do, do it with thy might; for there is no work, nor device, nor knowledge, nor wisdom, in the grave, whither thou goest.' Ecclesiastes 9:10

And here's another thing: all of these electronic gizmos are dependent on the silicon chips that make them function, but silicon comes from sand and you know what happened to the man who built his house upon the sand? Yes! It fell down (Luke 6:47-49). We have built our lives upon sand and soon the rains will come.

You are worth more than the stupid computer game. You do not actually own the farm that you are spending so many waking hours 'attending' on the computer! You do not really have an army under your command that is really fighting any battles for you on the war games you play. If you spent the same amount of time actually growing real fruit and vegetables and renting a bit of land somewhere to do it, then you might indeed accomplish something of true value and be proud of your success. If you were really engaged in the spiritual war that ravishes our nation right now, then you might indeed have something to boast about, but the digital connections on your screen are nothing, mean nothing and accomplish nothing. They simply steal away bucket-loads of your amazing potential.

The terrorists who are plotting the next outrage of defiance in our country are delighted that you are engaged in such pointless pastimes. Whilst you are playing, they are building bombs and planning the destruction of your countrymen. Whilst you are sitting there, quite unconcerned about your future, the extremists are busy discussing and secretly inventing plans to destroy Christianity and our great Christian heritage, right under our noses. Whilst you squander your days and weeks and months, they are spreading their influence and demands throughout our society and growing an 'army' of babies to one day change the government and obliterate the culture of this country. You, your children and future offspring are a problem for them and what you do now with your life will decide whether they succeed in their purposes or not. There is a cloud of darkness and evil expanding across our cities and towns and no one seems concerned enough to do anything about it. Who will rise up in faith and put the armies of these aliens to flight? Hebrews 11:34

Your life is of so much greater value than you can imagine. Why allow Satan to laugh at you whilst he mesmerizes you with nonsense and steals yet another day of your life?

You are made in the image of God and that means that you have both creative energy and untapped capabilities which you have yet to discover.

Over the last centuries here in Great Britain, thousands of world-changing discoveries, inventions, ideas, cures and strategies have transformed lives and nations around the globe. This was because people, ordinary people like you and me spent our time doing something constructive and creative instead of sitting in the sun (not that we have very much of that) or drifting the days away in pointless pursuits. As a child I was taught how to use everyday tools like screwdrivers, saws and hammers. I was taught at school how to plant vegetables and use a garden fork. I learned from my father which plants out in the wild were good for food and which were poisonous. I became creative and invented things and I had a 'Plan' book which I always kept with me.

We did not sit indoors watching television every day and losing our precious childhood. In fact, we did not have a television until I was fifteen years old. Watching the screen does not take much brain power, but reading a sensible and informative book turns all the lights on inside the outstanding 'sealed-unit' on top of our shoulders. Writing down our thoughts and inspirations sets those lights flashing and twinkling and begins the creative processes.

Right now in this nation there are literally millions of potential miracles waiting to happen, multitudes of life-saving ideas, brilliant minds and inventive thinkers all sat down doing nothing about the gifts and abilities just waiting to be released inside them.

Turn off the rubbish. Throw it away if you have to and get up from where you are; stretch those legs and arms and go for a long walk and allow your mind to begin to exercise in the way it was designed to. Ask God to forgive you for the wasted hours, days and months and for ignoring his claim to your time and life. Ask him to fill you with inspiration and clarity and give you wisdom and understanding.

'If any of you lack wisdom, let him ask of God, that giveth to all men liberally and upbraideth not [does not refuse]; and it shall be given him. But let him ask in faith, nothing wavering [doubting]. For he that wavereth [doubts or double-minded] is like a wave of the sea driven with the wind and tossed.' James 1:6

Make a resolution that you will not return to be a slave of Lucifer ever again.

'If the Son therefore shall make you free, ye shall be free indeed.' John 8:36

Maybe you are an inventor, a writer, a painter, a musician, an engineer, a chemist, a discoverer, a preacher, a pioneer, or one of a million things not listed here. Maybe it is you who will change this nation or some other place in the world, but you are just sat there not even knowing your own true value, throwing away the years of your strength.

Who will save our young people? Who will reach our children for Christ? Who will help the homeless, the desperate, the needy and the lonely? Who will make jobs for those in dire distress? Who will think up a plan to create new businesses and opportunities for our youngsters to do something with their lives?

Who is on the Lord's side and who will come and fight against the powers of darkness that seek to extinguish the lamp of the Gospel in this great country?

Who will take up the cause of bringing the good news to millions of kids who have been brainwashed at school and by the media to believe there is no God? Who will deal with the despots who are stealing our children into the sex-trade after 'street-grooming' them?

Who will get to where our young teenagers are and bring them some real respect and love and win them to Christ?

Who will reach our older folk, bring them a 'quality' of life and give them something to do of real value in their twilight years?

Who will begin a national prayer campaign for this nation? (Forget the 'big names' and the platform 'stars'. God does not need any of them at all and most of their prayers never get answered anyway.)

Who will start a Temperance movement that will rescue our youngsters from alcohol? Who will write the next Gospel Tracts and newspapers that really will impact the lives of those who read them?

Who will get into Parliament to exercise a godly and righteous ministry there?

Who will do something about the growing numbers of homeless people around our nation? Who will build the barns to store food and clothing for distribution to the poor when things begin to get too hard?

Who will find cures to the diseases which are baffling our scientists?

Who will invent ways of tackling the global issues that governments use to tax and control the populations?

Who will save the young women of this country from the vice of alcohol and foreign abuse? Who will rescue our children from being dragged away into the 'flesh-trade'?

Who will make sure that the Bible, God's Word is once more magnified throughout this land? Who will become a missionary to some of the parts of the world that still have not heard the Gospel, like India's 1.2 billion people?

Who will join the new Reformation, to see righteousness and truth and sound doctrine back in the church?

Who will dare to sell their lives for the cause of truth?

Everyone wants to start a 'worship group', but the world does not need a band it needs the truth. Simple Gospel songs and anointed (not professional) singers is all that is required to bless the hearer's ears and then only when preaching of the Word takes first place.

Don't just sit there! Get up and do something. Make a call that will change your life. Get rid of everything that prevents or distracts you from fulfilling your God-given destiny. Write down your decision on paper and secure it somewhere safe so that you can remind yourself of this day and refer to this life-changing moment in history.

Become creative, engage your mind; plan and prepare; research and educate yourself about the thing that you feel so strongly about. **Sell everything that you do not need to finance your plans and dreams**. Live simply with the bare necessities of life and embrace your destiny to serve God with all of your heart and soul and mind. Come over from the 'dark side' and begin to shine for Christ.

'Arise, shine; for thy light is come and the glory of the LORD is risen upon thee.' Isaiah 60:1

'Awake thou that sleepest and arise from the dead and Christ shall give thee light.' Ephesians 5:14

Become a pilgrim and a warrior for the truth. Rise up to the place God wants you to be. Give glory to the name of Jesus Christ and honour him with everything that you possess.

Now is the moment to be 'Redeeming the time, because the days are evil.' Ephesians 5:16

THE LAODICEAN NIGHT CLUB

Chapter Twenty One

The Laodicean Nightclub

It is more likely to be those without money or resources that are actually the same ones who have great desires and inspirations for evangelism and the propagation of the Gospel, whilst those with the vast reservoirs of wealth and income have no honest passion for the work of the Lord, unless it is to get them on the platform somewhere next to some big speaker. Oh, it is true that they show great enthusiasm for 'God's work', but there is always an ulterior motive lying hidden in the secret corridors of their heart. They know that by 'tipping' the visiting rich preacher they will get into his good books and can now use his (or her) name to elevate them to a higher seat in the 'synagogue'. Even in India, the rich Christians would sooner give a gift of land or buildings or money to the American 'revivalist' or visiting 'healer' or tithe-begging 'teacher', than distribute their wealth amongst the poor of their own church people. This is because their wicked hearts are completely deceived into believing that rubbing shoulders with the famous and 'man-exalted' prophets of this age actually means something to God and the multitudes around them.

They curse their own people by clamouring to the greed of man-made 'ministries and 'god-channel' charlatans. Whilst the poor and needy in their own community desperately look for food and water just to survive, these are more interested in sending their cheques to fatten the bank accounts of the greed preachers from the States. They are a curse to their own race and are despised by those who see through their pretence at being righteous.

The God-fearing individual, who earnestly longs to serve God, is constantly working on ideas and creative plans for presenting the Gospel to this lost generation. Quite often though, he or she is a desperate soul who has no money or financial support to be about the Master's business and so cannot fulfil the dream that they have.

They know they could win the world and see multitudes saved, but are constrained by the constant burden of debts and poverty that always seem to be a non-negotiable mountain in front of them. If they had the backing to develop their vision and dreams, then the world might well be turned upside down. What a blessing and profit it would produce if the rich invested in such potential world-changers. It might not bring them any glory in this age, but it would pay dividends in Heaven.

The religious rich, on the other hand are actually either jealous of them, or despise them because of their lowly condition and dismal personal circumstances. Aloof in their egotism, they think surely if they were from God they would not be struggling to pay their bills or even find enough money to buy food this week.

To them, their own financial success and comfortable lifestyle is some sort of 'evidence' that God must be with them and fully approving of them. But actually, they are products of the delusion that has thoroughly infected the 'new-age' church around the world. They are part of the church-gatherings which God speaks to in Revelation chapter 3: 'Because thou sayest, I am rich and increased with goods and have need of nothing; and knowest not that thou art wretched and miserable and poor and blind and naked.'

They are the 'holy (but not so holy) club', which arrogantly believe that the proof of their own righteousness lies in the accumulation of wealth and status. The only reason they get to sit with the televangelist 'stars' on so-called 'Christian' television, is because they have bribed the preacher with their dough.

They are too embroiled in their own self-ambition and wealth-gathering to ever be of any benefit to the true kingdom of God. Oh, yes, they may sit on the same platform as the rich and famous and dine in the finest of restaurants and hotels and walk amongst the fashion-conscious pastors and 'pastoresses', but they have absolutely nothing which is of any value to God.

The rich do not necessarily know the Lord, for they cannot see past their money. The famous do not necessarily know God, for they cannot see past their mirrors.

The self-deceived preacher does not know God, for he cannot see past his own self-acclaimed gifting and abilities to fool the people.

In Nigeria, the ugly and vile greed of the rich pastors and their wives is an utter abomination to God and whilst they sit there smugly bumping off anybody who gets in their way, the poor believers in their own country are being persecuted and killed every day simply for being 'Christian'. However, they despise the less fortunate amongst them, whilst they use their congregations as mindless money-mules to fill their own bank accounts even more. Shame and confusion be upon them! They are an embarrassment and disgrace to the name of Jesus Christ and should be thrown into the most miserable prison in their land for the next thirty years.

Their wealth and assets should be seized and redistributed amongst the poor and needy and their children made to do hard labour in correctional facilities where they might learn to work for their living. That also goes for any deceitful African pastors here in Great Britain and elsewhere in the world where they think that they are above the laws of the country and the law of God.

All their screaming "In the name of Jesus!" means nothing. The more they have to shout at the people, the more they prove that they do not know God themselves. All of the noise and commotion, the suits and the glamour just proves the falseness of a religion that actually has very little to do with God even though they use His name and His Book a lot. The tricksters, fraudsters and 419 scammers should all be seen for what they are and the congregation who behave in the same way need to repent and humble themselves before God quickly, lest judgment falls and it becomes too late to put things right.

Sadly, the silly sheep will keep 'baa-ing' after their leaders, keep on throwing their money into his or her ever-deepening pockets and believe that they, and they only, are the true church upon earth. So let the sheep go to the slaughter, but if any one hears what God says, then run for your life from this wicked Laodicean nightclub.

I remember a fellow telling me about the 'Judas Sheep' at the local abattoir. He told me that amongst the multitudes of dopey sheep, there is occasionally an unusual one that learns how to avoid getting himself or herself killed. When the cattle wagons come in with a fresh batch of live animals, the creatures being transported to their doom have a 'sense' of death apparently, and become reluctant and fearful to leave the lorry and go into the factory. The 'Judas' sheep therefore goes up the ramp into the wagon and convinces the other sheep that all is well and there is nothing to worry about. He then leads them all down the plank and into the yard where they will ignorantly but surely await their destruction. 'Judas' himself of course will also be put to death when another like him comes along.

The money-hungry, wealth-loving, fame-seeking pastors, apostles, evangelists, bishops and all the other sad little names they like to adorn themselves with may well be the 'Judas' sheep leading their congregations down to the slaughterhouse.

Head for the hills from whence cometh your true strength; find the green pastures where the Good Shepherd leadeth His own sheep; learn to read the Bible with the Holy Spirit as your gentlemanly tutor instead of the sweaty high-blood-pressured spluttering preacher telling you that only he knows what God is saying.

Distribute your increase and wealth amongst the poor of God's own family instead of allowing the fat 'prophet' and 'prophetess' to ransack your purse and wallet whenever they choose.

Will any of the sheep hear this? It is most unlikely, because they live in fear of what their pastor might think, or what others may say, or in case the leader puts a curse on them and their families for disobedience to his command. Now if that is not 'slavery', then I wonder what is.

Christ did not come to bring us religion or organizations; he came to set His people free.

You are not meant to be the servant or slave of your pastor. He is meant to be your servant and he can have his daily bread as and when he earns it; and if he is a worthy and humble servant of God, then let him receive of the increase of those to whom he ministers and if he is true, then he will also walk humbly with God and not exalt himself through the adulation of his followers, nor walk around with his head stuck up his nose. He is not meant to be elevated on some pedestal, but is supposed to elevate the people of God for whom he has a responsibility to pray and teach the Scriptures with sound doctrine. He is only worthy of honour if he preaches, teaches and lives the same sound doctrine.

'Moreover as for me, God forbid that I should sin against the LORD in ceasing to pray for you: but I will teach you the good and the right way.' 1Samuel 12:23

He is not a 'king' to be revered and bowed to, but a humble servant of God who refuses the worship of men and seeks only the glory of his Saviour. He should be respected only if he teaches Biblical truth, is not interested in personal wealth, is possessed with a passion for the lost, the poor and the dying, is a man of prayer and is content with such as he has.

If he wants to be a successful businessman then let him go and do that and let another become the pastor. 'Let another take his office.' Psalm 109:8; Acts 1:20

It is a contradiction of terms and a conflict of interests to try and be the minister and be a multi-millionaire businessman. The Levites (the teachers and those responsible for the spiritual welfare of God's people) inherited nothing of this world. God was their inheritance. This maintained their purity of motive and the honest focus of their ministry.

A man who is caught up in all the business and affairs of this life has no place in the pulpit, even though he demands it and looks somewhat impressive on the stage. Money might buy you a platform and a following, but only the real Levites are both destined and called to the ministry and subsequently are devoted to the service of God and the edification of God's people. The unique conditions of the Levite meant that he looked to an eternal future for his rewards, for God was all his inheritance according to the Holy Scriptures.

Just read through the lives of some of the greatest missionaries and pioneers the world has ever known (and I do not mean any single one of the television religious 'stars' of today) and you will see the true heart of a true Levite. (Deuteronomy 18:1-5)

Furthermore, when speaking of the king or ruler of the people, God states the following as conditions for holding such an office:

'He shall not multiply horses [vehicles, properties, assets] to himself, nor cause the people to return to Egypt [indulge in worldly pursuits and avarice], to the end that he should multiply horses [tithed from their increase]: forasmuch as the LORD hath said unto you, Ye shall henceforth return no more that way. Neither shall he multiply wives to himself, that his heart turn not away: neither shall he greatly multiply to himself silver and gold. That his heart be not lifted up above his brethren and that he turn not aside from the commandment, to the right hand or to the left: to the end that he may prolong his days in his kingdom, he and his children, in the midst of Israel.' Deuteronomy 17:15-20

Notice that this was applicable to the office of the king or ruler over the people and even he must keep from indulging himself in personal greed and gain. This is because the king is there for the benefit and blessing of the people and not himself. His heart should be engrossed in the care and welfare of those his subjects. How much more the Levite (the minister)?

'Pure religion and undefiled before God and the Father is this, To visit the fatherless and widows in their affliction and to keep himself unspotted from the world.' James 1:27

'For the love of money is the root of all evil: which while some coveted after, they have erred from the faith and pierced themselves through with many sorrows. **But thou, O man of God, flee these things**; and follow after righteousness, godliness, faith, love, patience, meekness. Fight the good fight of faith, lay hold on eternal life, whereunto thou art also called and hast professed a good profession before many witnesses..' 1Timothy 6:10

Paul, seeing all of the pitfalls and dangers to this young minister Timothy, warns him and instructs him into the right way and not the way of greedy Balaam. (2Peter 2:15)

It is not, nor ever shall be the money-greedy charlatans who are called to God's service, but the Levites who are separated unto the Gospel of Jesus Christ. They may not have much of this world's treasures, but they are rich in Christ and walk with God.

'Paul, a servant of Jesus Christ, called [to be] an apostle, separated unto the gospel of God.' Romans 1:1

Why is it these days that any 'likely lad' or platform 'wannabe' who promotes himself as the mouthpiece of God is accepted and listened to by the heaving crowds of mindless conference-goers? The ignorant audiences would sooner accept the tattooed lout and the laughing fool than listen to the distilled and holy word of God being taught in purity. A clown on the keyboards gets the laughs for his frivolity and pathetic jokes and the woman howling like a dog at the front of the church is seen as some 'manifestation of God', rather than the rampant and contagious disease of delusion and deception.

'It is time for thee, LORD, to work: for they have made void thy law [they have done away with what the Word of God really says].' Ps 119:126

All the shouting, gyrating, sweaty preachers and loudmouthed 'preacheresses' who declare their own goodness and righteousness (Isaiah 42:8), should be seized, stripped of their fraudulent and scammed wealth and cast out of the congregation and made to work in a factory, or mine, or some other such place.

'For they that are such serve not our Lord Jesus Christ, but their own belly [their own selfish and greedy agendas]; and by good words and fair speeches deceive the hearts of the simple.' Romans 16:18

Now, 'If any man teach otherwise and consent not to wholesome words, even the words of our Lord Jesus Christ and to the doctrine which is according to godliness; **he is proud, knowing nothing**, but doting about questions and strifes of words, whereof cometh envy, strife, railings [personal slander), evil surmisings [assumptions], perverse disputings [arguments] of men of corrupt minds and destitute of the truth, supposing that gain is godliness: **from such withdraw thyself**.' 1Timothy 6:3-5

What a significant few words those are to today's fancy-pants ministry game: 'supposing that gain is godliness'. It has become popular these days for people to assume (and of course as taught by most of the religious-tv personalities) that if you are getting richer and gaining wealth, then this is the proof that you are righteous and that God is with you. Ministers seek after all of this world's gadgets and gimmicks, its fashion and fortunes and presume that obtaining such things validates their ministry more.

But it is all a lie and will eventually carry the whole congregation with its leader off to perdition. A people should seek after God, not for what they can gain and barter, but for his righteousness, for his kingdom and for knowing Him in truth.

Here in this country where church-going has declined so much over the last few decades, there is still hope, but that hope will only be revived when God by His Spirit comes in power and grace to this beautiful Isle. It will not be revived through the religious television programming that claims itself to be 'God's mandate' for this end-time generation, neither will it come through the concerts and pretty looks of the performing artists. They may well tickle the 'believers', but they do not impress the world or God.

I personally believe that hundreds of thousands of indigenous white British people have a real faith in God that is both strong and deep, but they never darken the doors of a church because they see through all the veneer of the make-believe prophets and the make-believe congregations. This can be clearly seen during such events such as the Royal British Legion's Festival of Remembrance and the gatherings for Remembrance Sunday every November in Whitehall and all across this country when our people come out in deep reverence and respect.

The Salvation Army, in its early days went into the slums and desperation of poverty and isolation with the good news of the Gospel; and brought love, care, help and support to those lost in the dreadful whirlpool of sin's misery. It preached the truth valiantly that men and women must repent and took the message to the streets, the bars, the dancehalls, the factories and everywhere that people congregated.

The band was not an entertainment feature, but an evangelistic weapon that rallied the troops, sounded an alarm and heralded the Gospel message on the streets throughout Great Britain. The soldiers were fearless men and women who lived only to serve God, forsook the world and its toys and were impassioned with a love from on high to reach every needy and lost soul throughout the kingdom.

Their meeting houses were never intended to become churches where everyone could sit back and enjoy a Sunday service. These mission halls and reclaimed drinking houses were sanctuaries for those needing salvation and help, platforms for preaching and proclaiming the Gospel, training rooms for equipping the soldiers of Christ and wrestling rings where souls were torn from the grip of Satan and brought into the light of God.

Oh, that the Salvation Army might find its roots and Founder's vision once again! Oh, that the passion of the pioneer and death-defying evangelist would come back! That would be the beginning of a beautiful revival.

For then we would surely see, 'Men who have not bowed the knee to the image of Baal [false gods, false teachings, worldly triviality].' Romans 11:4; 'Men that have hazarded [risked, surrendered, put in harm's way] their lives for the name of our Lord Jesus Christ.' Acts 15:26

As I sit here writing, I search in my heart and mind for how to bring like-minded hearts together to begin works of righteousness in this nation. I wonder where the true, passionate, ready, willing and able souls are who would dare to rise up and do something in the world for the glory of God and the salvation of the lost.

There are literally thousands upon thousands of church people who want to sing, or start a band or become a 'worship leader', but where are the soldiers of Christ? Where are the faithful Warriors? Where are the true Guardians?

If you have a house, a flat, even a simple bed-sit, then you have a place to begin the work of God. You can transform it from being a place of worldliness and sin by kicking out the television and cleansing it of all that is an offence to God. You can then start a prayer meeting with just one or two others and get a Bible study going. Then you can dedicate one wall to pinning up a map of your country and listing all of the needs and areas of concern that need someone to stand in the gap. Take cuttings from the newspaper and stick those up and begin to formulate your own personal mission for reaching this nation for Christ.

You may indeed find it hard to get another Christian to join you whose heart is knit with yours, but start yourself and pray and God will bring some good people along to you. Maybe they will not be the regular church-goers, but backsliders and rejects from the church, or even the unconverted who care for this country more than the church at large does.

A young woman was arrested and sentenced recently for shouting 'racial abuse' on a tram somewhere in our capital. I saw the video footage and it appeared that she may have had a few drinks or something, but this defenceless woman was obviously deeply distressed and angry about what she took as a personal issue that affected her, namely, immigration that is completely out of control. Firstly, I might mention that when the Muslims march on our cities with their obnoxious placards declaring war on us, telling our police to go to hell and shouting death and decapitation to our soldiers and all 'unbelievers', they go undisturbed, unchallenged and none of them get arrested for stirring up racial hatred or religious intolerance.

I am not justifying in any way what this young lady did, but I noticed that she kept referring to this country as 'my Britain', 'my lovely Britain' and saying how it is now ruined and rubbished. She obviously has a deep love for her own country and a sense of patriotism that made her so verbal and indeed so crazily brave in that carriage where she was completely outnumbered. So far at least eleven million people have taken the time to watch the footage of her outburst and looking beyond the insult, surely recognise the spirit of the old British bulldog still alive and well, even though it was a politically and socially incorrect way of showing it.

How many Christians in all of the churches here have any love whatsoever for this nation? If so, where is the proof? What are you doing about it? How much time and money are you spending to bring about a change? When did you last cry to God in any seriousness for the restoration of this great land and its people?

Do you actually care? And if not, why do you continue to stay here? You should go somewhere else, quickly. But for those of you who do love this country and love its historic race, begin where you are. Start with what you have in your hand. Do not wait for all the things that you might wish to have, but take the little, the five loaves and two little fishes, the drop of oil in the bottle, the little meal left in that container and begin to pour it out, give it away, pass it on and before long you will see the miracle of God in your home.

As I have said before, the miracle is in your house, even in your hand but it will not show itself until you take that insignificant nothingness and do something with it. The loaves and fishes only multiplied after the disciples began to give them out. The rod of Moses only became a snake when he cast it to the floor. The oil only became a river of blessing when the woman filled her house with empty vessels and started pouring it out. The little cake for Elisha only became a miraculous bread shop after the widow woman gave away all that she had. The world was turned upside down only when the disciples, in all of their human weakness and insufficiency went out and preached the gospel.

THE POWER OF THE ANCIENT WEAPONS

Chapter Twenty Two

The Power Of The Ancient Weapons

An old man stood on the top of a hill overlooking a great valley in which was marshalled two armies preparing for battle. Set against each other, readying for fierce combat, it seemed that the smaller of the two forces was clearly outnumbered and ill-equipped to take on the screaming hoards of the opposition.

The Amalekites were a dark and foreboding people who loved nothing more than to kill, destroy and annihilate any race who they chose to despise. On this occasion they had come from their fortified towns and cities to chase an unusual tribe that were wandering through the desert looking for somewhere to settle. Their singular purpose was to exterminate every single man, woman and child before they could ever find a place they might call 'home'.

So, now they had caught up with them and had drawn the battle line across the burning sand. Their swords and spears sharpened ready for slaughter, they cried in defiance and mockery to the men on the other side to come and try their strength.

The tribe of Israel were a small company with an army of men who were probably disillusioned, discontent and definitely of a rebellious nature. They professed to be followers of the only One true God of the universe and indeed had been witnesses to some of the most outstanding miracles the world had ever seen. Not so long ago they were slaves in Egypt where they were forced into hard labour and lowly conditions and it had been through the most unusual happenings and 'mystical' phenomena that they had gained their freedom. Even after they had fled the country, the wicked pharaoh gathered his battalions of fighters and chariots to go after them and murder every one of them if they refused to come back.

Surrounded and trapped, with the fearsome armies of Egypt behind them and the uncrossable obstacle of the Red Sea in front of them, they had nowhere to go and all hope of freedom and liberty seemed utterly lost.

They were quick to blame their leader for bringing them into such dire distress and told him that they would have been better off staying where they were than to have been brought into this dreadful situation.

Moses already had a rather colourful history from the day of his birth. The Egyptian midwives were under orders to murder as many baby Hebrew boys as they could, but his mother had devised a plan to give her newborn child a living chance to survive and had hidden him in a floating basket amongst the reeds and bulrushes of the river. The pharaoh's daughter had discovered him there one morning and brought him back to the palace to be brought up as her own son.

He became very powerful in Egypt over the course of years and it was through his intervention and appeals to the pharaoh that the Israelite's case was even considered. He had in fact murdered one of the Egyptian taskmasters who was beating one of his own countrymen and hid his body in the sand hoping that nobody had noticed. Unfortunately for him they had and the crime came to Pharaoh's ears. Moses had to run for his life.

It was some while after in the backside of the wilderness that God met with this forlorn and downcast runaway and revealed His power and glory to him through the setting fire to a bush that never actually burnt.

He met with the Living God and fell to his knees before him. In that place he received a charge and instructions from the Lord God that he must go to Pharaoh and command him to let the Israelites go.

He complained saying that the ruler would not listen to him and he himself was quite inadequate to speak on behalf of God. God then asked him what he was holding in his hand and he replied that it was a rod (a stick). He was told to throw it on the ground and when he did so it became a snake. He then had to pick it up by its tail and it became his walking stick once again.

This old stick would become the symbol of God's authority and power in the hand of Moses and would prove to become a mighty weapon and sign of deliverance to all of the Israelites over the coming months and years.

God revealed His name to Moses and told him to go tell the pharaoh that 'I AM' has sent him to give warning to let God's people go.

So Moses set off to the palace in Egypt with the stick in his hand and the name of God as the authority of his recent commissioning to the office of Ambassador of Heaven.

The Bible shows us the extensive use of the rod of Moses (as it became known) and the multitudes of times that it was to bring about amazing victories, miraculous signs and wonders, plagues and diseases, strange darkness and swarms of locusts, millions of frogs invading the homes of the Egyptians, thunder and lightning and hailstones that killed both the cattle and people and smashed down the trees. Rivers turned into blood, food fell from out of the skies and water gushed from a rock in the dry and parched desert. When it was stretched over the Red Sea, the waters parted and made a way for God's people to be delivered and the Egyptian army to be destroyed.

And on this particular occasion we find Moses climbing to the top of a hill overlooking this battleground and holding high the same rod of victory above the armies below. So long as he held the rod out over the landscape, the Israelite army (led by Joshua) advanced and were winning, but as his arms grew tired and heavy and began to fall down, the Amalekites gained the advantage.

So, two other men, Aaron and Hur made Moses to sit down on a rock and they held his arms up with the rod until the setting of the sun and the outright victory of Joshua and his troops over the entire retreating enemy.

Let us look at what Moses was doing. Let us see why he could determine the outcome of such pivotal events, change the course of history for his nation and perform astonishing miracles even in the most unlikely and drastic of circumstances.

God spoke with Moses face to face just as a man speaks to his friend (Exodus 33:11). There is good reason for this. Firstly, **he was utterly sold out to God and the divine commission placed upon his life**.

Secondly, **he had heard God's voice, met with Him** in a life-changing manner and been given a holy calling and task to fulfil whilst on this Earth. And then, **He knew God and God knew him**.

Furthermore, he had learned that all he need do is obey the voice of the Lord, step out in faith and speak the word in authority and power.

The miracle belongs to God, but the 'catalyst' for the miracle is placed in the hands of God's servant. The rod of Moses was to become this catalyst and when lifted up in faith and assurance, the heavens would open, the earth would divide and crack apart, the great waters of the sea be driven asunder, the rock in the wilderness break open and supply refreshment and judgement fall upon the rebellious people who refused to listen to God's voice.

Let us consider the facts:

- Moses was called and appointed by God, despite being a murderer
- He had a divine encounter that transformed his life
- The simple, almost worthless stick in his hands became the symbol of his authority and power
- He knew where to find God and recognised His voice
- He dared to obey in simple faith
- When he said: "Thus saith the LORD", it was because the LORD *really* had spoken

Here was a man born to fulfil an outstanding destiny and yet was still but a man with all of the weakness of the flesh and subject to feelings, moods and passions. Here was a mighty prophet, an outstanding leader, a noble statesman and a stern commander. Yet here was a man who was known as the most meek (humble) man on earth (Numbers 12:3).

He knew who he was in God and walked in the confidence and assurance that He who had called him would also supply his need and be his defence and strength for all that he would encounter.

Let us look a little more at this amazing man. He certainly knew that there was something different about him as he grew up. He was counted as the Pharaoh's relative, lived in the royal palace, ate like a king, yet also understood that he was a Hebrew. He watched in silence for many a year as his own people were crushed and abused by a foreign power and a foreign religion. He without any doubt knew in his heart that one day he would do something about the whole situation and in a moment of deep anguish and anger he smote and killed one of the guards who was beating up yet another Hebrew slave.

He was now a 'wanted' man, on the run and hiding out in the middle of nowhere, tending the sheep. Every day he climbed that mountain checking his flock and perhaps regretting his rash actions, knowing that he had now spoiled any chance of using his powerful office to turn about the fortunes of his own people. In fact, even they did not want him after seeing his uncontrolled rage in killing a man. They suggested that perhaps one of them would be next on his list for an early grave if they stepped out of line.

Maybe he had fallen out with his wife that morning, or perhaps he was just so depressed by all of his own circumstances and seemingly no great future to look forward to anymore, that once again he led the sheep across the desert to the mountainside to be alone with his melancholy thoughts.

No matter how far down into the valley of darkness and despair a man might go, God has a way of getting his attention. A bush caught fire, which may not have been such an amazing thing out there in the dry land under the burning heat of the sun, but as he looked he realized that for all of the flames and the vehemence of the fire, the bush itself was not affected. The leaves were still green and fresh and did not shrivel or curl at the heat. He said to himself that he would turn aside and have a look at this strange sight.

When we are far from God, when our worries and depressions obliterate the sunlight of his face and the word of His encouragement, then God sometimes steps in and grabs our attention so that He might bring us back to Himself. God's purposes will not be frustrated by our failures or inconsistencies.

It was when Moses turned that he heard the voice of the LORD. We do not hear God speak because we never get out into the wilderness to be alone.

We sit in front of computers and televisions night and day and therefore fail to find the plan and purpose of God for our lives. It is when we come away from the world and all of its silly attractions and entertainments that we afford ourselves the chance of meeting with Him and having our lives revived and set on fire.

Moses had an encounter with the holiness of God just as Isaiah did (Isaiah 6) and his life would never be the same again. Talk about being born again!

This was the transition of death into life, of blindness into sight and of hopelessness into the certainty of an amazing future.

Here he received his high calling and instructions about what he should do next, but it was not to be presumed that he might just go and start his ministry any old how. As he set off to begin this amazing journey, the Bible says that God met him and sought to kill him (Exodus 4:24-25).

From the Scripture we may understand that even though we have been called and commissioned, we dare not just go trotting off in our pride and presumption that we are now 'men of God' and strut around as though we are God's gift to His people.

Moses was brought to a grinding halt because he thought he could do God's work whilst leaving things undone in his own life and disobedience remaining in his house.

He should have circumcised his son according to the command of God in Genesis 17:11 on the eighth day after his birth, but had utterly failed to do so. As it was, Moses was rushing off to Egypt knowing that he had broken the covenant of circumcision and perhaps assuming that it did not matter. His wife quite obviously was not in favour of this 'bloody' necessity and perhaps was even the reason that he had not done it in the first place.

However, he could not go to lead God's people until he himself was willing to put right the things that were wrong in his own life and circumstances.

We may see a parallel in Numbers 22 where Balaam presumed to be the mouthpiece of God and with a haughty thought ran off in his pride to elevate himself.

'Those that walk in pride he [God] is able to abase.' Daniel 4:37. Perhaps it was this second encounter with God that caused Moses to become the meekest man on earth.

'By mercy and truth iniquity is purged: and by the fear of the LORD men depart from evil.' Proverbs 16:6

'And now, Israel, what doth the LORD thy God require of thee, but to fear the LORD thy God, to walk in all his ways and to love him and to serve the LORD thy God with all thy heart and with all thy soul.' Deuteronomy 10:12

Men and women today rush onto the platforms and conference stages declaring that they are anointed and have the word of God in their mouths saying: 'Thus saith the Lord this' and 'Thus saith the Lord that.' They prance around in all of their vaunted arrogance and self-conceited pride thinking that they are above everyone else. But God says: 'I have not sent them', 'yet they prophesy a lie in my name; that I might drive you out and that ye might perish, ye and the prophets that prophesy unto you.' Jeremiah 27:15

It is happening all over the place these days and congregations are being seduced by pretenders and self-appointed 'ministers' of the Lord. Moses had the same trouble in his time, but they were all destroyed along with those that followed them (see Numbers 16).

We cannot minister effectively if sin and disobedience remains in our lives and in our homes. We cannot exercise authority when we will not submit to God's will in everything. We cannot wield the weapons of our warfare if our hands and hearts are unclean.

You can scream commands at the top of your voice, push

people over on their backs during the 'ministry time', tell the devil to depart and go to the pit; you can 'prophesy' all sorts of wonderful and amazing things, but all of it is to no avail if there is sin in the house. If I am a deceiver, a liar, a thief, or a trickster, then it is all just show and pomp.

If I hold unforgiveness in my heart toward anyone, especially to those of the household of faith, walk in pride and self-deception, then I am just an old wind-bag with no power, no anointing (even though I might 'feel' anointed) and no 'God is with me' reality.

Moses could walk eye to eye with people because he walked face to face with God (Deuteronomy 34:10).

Most ministers these days would be too scared to let you into their secret lives, their secret habits, their secret bank accounts and their secret thoughts, because they do not let God in there either.

'Woe unto them that seek deep to hide their counsel from the LORD and their works are in the dark and they say, Who seeth us? and who knoweth us?' Isaiah 29:15

"Then said he unto me, Son of man, hast thou seen what the ancients of the house of Israel do in the dark, every man in the chambers of his imagery [the secret imaginations and fantasies of his mind]? for they say, The LORD seeth us not; the LORD hath forsaken the earth.' Ezekiel 8:12

'They say still unto them that despise me, The LORD hath said, Ye shall have peace; and they say unto every one that walketh after the imagination of his own heart, No evil shall come upon you.' Jeremiah 23:17

Moses came to understand 'that God is light and in him is

no darkness at all.'

'If we say that we have fellowship with him, and walk in darkness [ignorance and deceit], we lie and do not the truth: But if we walk in the light, as he is in the light, we have fellowship one with another, and the blood of Jesus Christ his Son cleanseth us from all sin. If we say that we have no sin, we deceive ourselves, and the truth is not in us.' 1John 1:5-8

We need to sort our own lives out before we try to sort out others. We need to clean our own room before we tell others how dirty theirs is.Moses had to put things in order before he could order the house of God.

Most of the well-known televangelists and conferences speakers need so many things to prove that they are called of God. Big cars, designer suits, private jets, expensive houses, businesses and investments, plastic surgery and face-lifts and a group of 'yes' men and women who obey their every command and wish. They tell us that they must have a radio station, a television show, millions in the bank, tithes and offerings, gifts and donations and offices and staff to do all their administration and PR work.

All their followers and attendees are quick to support them in their claims and demands, believing the words of the preacher more than the word of God.

God asked Moses what he had in his hand and Moses looked and said, "a stick, a rod cut from a tree somewhere".

That will do. That was enough. That was good enough for God. With that simple stick God would show His power, qualify His servant Moses and deliver His people.

And that is how it will be yet again if anyone will hear what the Spirit of the Lord is really saying in this generation. 'Not by might, nor by power, but by my Spirit, saith the LORD of Hosts.' Zechariah 4:6

God is not looking for professionalism, technology and gadgets, television shows, or gorgeous clothes and fashion statements. He can do without it all. He is after the heart that will obey Him, trust Him and go in simplicity and purity to the people with His holy and righteous word. God wants to work mightily on behalf of His own, but will not share His glory with a man or woman even if the silly sheep run around all day after them buying their books, DVDs and all the other nonsense that they sell to their congregations.

The rod of Moses was not painted, gold-plated, decorated with jewels and precious stones, nor polished and held aloft as a Prima Dona. It was a stick, remained a stick, but was mighty in the hand of God and Moses.

'But we have this treasure [the knowledge of God] in earthen [clay, lowly, even scarred and broken] vessels, that the excellency of the power may be [clearly seen to be] of God and not of us.' 2Corinthians 4:7

The Welsh revival did not begin or continue on a glorious platform with shiny curtain drapes and gold-painted chairs and flashing coloured lights making the place look homely. It began with one young man on his knees in a cold Sunday School room on bare floorboards.

The excellency of the power is not in the noise and entertainment of the travelling worship band no matter how lovely and emotional they may sound; neither is it in the screaming and perspiration of the silk-suited preacher. The excellency of God's power is exhibited in the life of the meek and humble in spirit who tremble at the word of the Lord. They may not have wonderful clothes, but they have a wonderful heart. They may not drive around in luxury, but they have the luxury of being content with all that God gives them. They may not have a television following, but all of Heaven watches in on them every day. They may not be loved and praised by all the deluded conference goers, but they are loved with an everlasting love and admired by all of the saints already with the Lord.

Only these have the right to exercise the ancient weapons that the saints of old knew more about than all of the 'intercessor and deliverance ministries' know about today.

Only these are entrusted with the excellency of God's power. Only these will work any deliverance in the earth; and only these can change the future and bring hope to our dying communities. There may be ten thousand so-called 'prayer warriors' at the prayer conference, yet only one of these might actually get through to God and have their prayer answered.

The church is full of children playing games with make-believe weapons. I say 'make-believe' because that is exactly what they are. They make themselves believe that they have something that they do not possess. They use all the right words and phrases, but still the doors do not open, the miracles do not happen, the heathen do not submit themselves and nothing really changes.

Sure, some Christians might fall on the floor and shake and all that stuff and strange but doubtful phenomena occur during 'worship' time, but where does that get any of us? What does that do to the powers of darkness and the violent attacks of the devil against our nation?

How does that save the multitudes running to Hell and eternal torment? What lasting good is that to anyone else, or even to the one who gets such unusual feelings and weird 'experiences'. Away with it all and away with all of the insane behaviour of shouting "fire" or "more" or whatever else and seeing people behaving like lunatics screaming and rolling about the floor!

The real weapons that brought salvation and deliverance, that defeated the counsel of ungodly men, that won the battles that seemed impossible and the conflicts which would wipe God's people from off the face of the earth, were entrusted to those who were trustworthy.

They had clean hands and pure hearts and had not lifted their souls to the worthless vanities and fads of this passing world (Psalm 24:3-4). They were men of sound minds and were both rational, intelligent and possessed a good deal of common sense. They cared only for the things that pleased God and sought for a heavenly kingdom and home, declaring themselves as pilgrims and strangers upon earth (Hebrews 11:13-16). They were not absorbed with all the passing fashions and dainties of a corrupt age, but were taken up with God and His kingdom upon earth. They were single-minded, had their hearts fixed on eternal matters and wrought righteousness in the earth (Hebrews 11:33).

For some delusional reason the modern church has its heart set on the wealth and riches of this world and how it can get more and more of it into its bank account. The church has lost itself in the amoral deception that its focus should be on leisure, pleasure, profit and gain.

Do we not realize that time is running out fast and the world and all of its corruption and worthless, time-wasting indulgencies are soon to be burned up?

'The day of the Lord will come as a thief in the night; in the which the heavens shall pass away with a great noise and the elements shall melt with fervent heat, the earth also and the works that are therein shall be burned up. Seeing then that all these things shall be dissolved, what manner [type] of persons ought ye to be in all holy conversation [conduct of living] and godliness, looking for and hasting unto the coming of the day of God.' 2Peter 3:10-13

We can all go round patting each other on the back and telling ourselves how blessed we are and giving one another the title of 'Man of God' (or 'Woman of God', as the case may be), but it is all vanity and poppycock. Anybody who has to publicise themselves as a man or woman of God is no such a person.

We live in troubled times that are soon to become more dramatic than we might imagine. Whilst the church is 'doing its thing', the whole world is spiraling toward chaos and destruction. The clamoring after wealth and success has diverted the people of God from the coming storm which will send trembling through the congregations and consternation in the ministry.

The beast of persecution is raising its ugly and brutal head all over the world and yet we still go on as though it will not come to our door. Would those victims of the recent disgusting and barbaric massacres in Nigeria by the 'peace-loving' Muslims ever have contemplated that their lives would be brought to such a violent end? Would the Christian believers in Egypt and other 'sensitive' areas have been prepared for the violence shown to them by a religion that claims to be tolerant and unprejudiced?

Do America, Europe and Great Britain really believe that the same religious hoards now populating and segregating their cities will not become the same wretched persecutors of our true Christian liberty in days to come? Just look and see, for already the game is afoot and the government and church are either totally ignorant or stupidly foolish in not seeing and addressing the growing threat.

Are we all too scared to speak about these things in case we upset the religious bigots and their demands, whilst some of our young women are raped, beaten and even murdered by despots just because they believe they have the right to do so?

The Church of Jesus Christ needs to rise up with one voice and bring the Word of God to the forefront at every level of society, but it cannot because it is all caught up in 'conference fever' and 'trancing' to the travelling 'worship groups'. It is tongue-tied because it abandoned the 'old paths' and knows not what is truth or what is error anymore. It lay down the Royal Sword and took to dancing and jiving with the rest of the world in its vain frivolities. It is silent in fear because it cannot give a distinct answer, because it does not know what it believes these days. It sacrificed pure doctrine for the worship of false prophets and teachers and listened to the lying voices of the platform performers more than the Word of God.

'For if the trumpet give an uncertain sound, who shall prepare himself to the battle?' 1Corinthians 14:8

I will not spare in telling the truth. Running along to the latest 'Hillsong' concert is not going to change your world.

God did not choose such things to bring the Gospel to the unsaved, neither is it the means of salvation or the way to revival. It is all too often just another 'entertainment' evening to divert believers from the real commission. It may sound sweet and give you warm feelings, but it will not save our young people or deliver our country from evil. If it were possible, then it would have done so by now after all the millions of pounds and dollars spent on it.

One to one evangelism and 'Go ye into all the world and PREACH the gospel' is still the only way of turning the tide and making a difference. Why do Christians think that by standing in a light-flashing, pyro technical, smoke-machine, turbo-driven PA thundering, dancing, leaping, sweating worship concert they will change their nation? It is nonsense to believe such a thing.

It is the ancient weapons of 'All Prayer', Faith, Implicit Obedience and the written and spoken Word that will bring deliverance and restoration. It is the gospel on the streets, in the marketplace, the office and factory that will ultimately bring a spiritual revolution to a people, for it is the gospel that is the power of God unto salvation to all who believe. The worship evening 'do' is often just a means to make the believers feel better, show off the skills and abilities of the performers and their instruments and sell a whole heap of CDs and DVDs.

Pull out the plugs, switch off the power and you will soon discover that the god of the sound system mysteriously vanishes and the showmanship of the band and their 'magical' instruments disappears like a vapour. All that is left is silence and it might just be possible that in that silence some folk might actually seek after God instead of the CD and find Him, even though He be not far from any one of us. (Acts 17:27)

When you get thrown into jail or beaten to death for following Christ, your sweet little worship band will mean very little to you then, but the Word of God in your heart and mouth will be mighty to the pulling down of strongholds and declaring the power of God unto salvation to all who still can hear you. I know the disciples were thrown into prison and whilst singing praises to God the doors were marvellously opened and they were delivered, but these were fearless and courageous preachers of righteousness, not a travelling entertainment troupe.

I love good music and true worship and enjoy writing songs myself and hearing them sung and I believe that worship and praise can move God to 'set ambushments' against the enemy on occasions (2Chronicles 20:22) and bring the 'anointing' down at times (2Kings 3:15). However, these incidents are few and far between in the Scriptures, but the Word is constant and it is the preaching and teaching of the Word that is going to bring change. I spent many years in music academy and am aware of both the power of music as a medium and also its potential deception, especially when the 'entertainment' aspect of it mesmerizes the people more the than hearing of the word of truth.

It will not be 'Hillsong', neither the 'Alpha course' that will save Great Britain, or any other country for that matter; neither will wall-to-wall chorus singing change our cities.

We need to rediscover the original and awesome weapons of God's prophets and apostles. Strumming a guitar like an unconverted rock star in front of the hand-raising congregation is not going to worry the devil or the armies of hell.

You can see the same audience responses at any of the world's concerts where Christ is both hated and despised. The weapons that the Bible describes are not made with human hands, nor dependent on man's creative ingenuity. They are, however, mighty through God to the tearing down of Satan's strongholds. They are to be sought after diligently and should a man discover their whereabouts and the skills to use them, then he truly will become a mighty soldier of God. A single note played on a trumpet, a single word brought from the Lord, a single text flying over a nation when performed and carried by a true warrior will have more effect than ten million songs sung by ten million church-goers.

A solitary man walks out across a field, unseen, unknown. He raises a flag and unfurls it into the wind; he stands defiantly against an invisible tide, an unseen but overwhelming army. Alone, in the ugly shadows of mighty, sinister and dark beasts of evil that ravage his nation, he dares defy them and tell them that 'not by might, nor by power', but in the name of the LORD of Hosts he is come and will drive them into hell itself. Nobody knows he is there and should a stranger pass by and observe him, he might be somewhat astonished at such a sight, for he cannot see or have any comprehension of the vital role this individual is playing on behalf of his people. In the pitch dark of night or the fleeting grey twilight skies, a soldier fights the battles of the Lord, just as David the great king of Israel did. (1Samuel 25:28)

When Heaven sees and acknowledges such a man, then you can be sure that a Warrior has arisen! A Guardian stands in the gap! There is hope for our children and our countrymen.

During the second world war a man named Rees Howell would climb the mountains of South Wales, stand in the gap and intercede before God on behalf of the government, our fighting troops and the future of our nation. It was his life, his calling, his vocation and his duty.

'Then he [the angel] answered and spake unto me, saying: This is the word of the LORD unto Zerubbabel, saying, Not by might, nor by power, but by my spirit, saith the LORD of hosts.' Zechariah 4:6

'Then said David to the [giant] Philistine: Thou comest to me with a sword, and with a spear, and with a shield: but I come to thee in the name of the LORD of hosts, the God of the armies of Israel, whom thou hast defied.' 1Samuel 17:45

Legends of the Kingdom, ARISE!

It is your destiny!

It is your time.

It is not the flashy conference, the 'awesome' worship group, the titillating preacheress, the swooning congregations, the extraordinary buildings, the private jet planes, or the hyperventilating prophet that will make any change in the nation or work any righteousness in the earth. It will be when a few humble souls get to learn how to resurrect and use the ancient weapons as did the prophets of old, that the glory of God will be manifest and the enemy be put to flight.

CAN THESE BONES LIVE?

Chapter Twenty Three

Can These Bones Live?

Throughout this country lie the remains of warriors, God's warriors. In amongst them are many of the Guardians who were destined for this generation, but who fell in the heat of the day when the fight was ferocious against them. Some of them thought the battle to be already lost and in dismay and disillusionment went home to make money instead.

All of these had lived for some time with a purpose and in the dream that one day they might do something exemplary in the kingdom, but alas, they had been carefully targeted by the hatred of the enemy, struck without mercy, thrown down into the mud and trampled all over by the laughing horsemen.

Many of them had no clue as to the importance of their mission, or the great threat that they posed to the enemy just by being alive. They failed to see their vital role and whilst busy helping to protect everyone else, they carelessly forgot to protect themselves. (Song of Solomon 1:6) They had been singled out from the crowd, cornered and then mutilated and humiliated in front of all their acquaintances and fellow-soldiers.

None pitied them or laid any value on their lives, dismissing them as though they were nothing and of even less worth. Laughter roared across the field each time one of them was struck down and the frenzied onlookers jeered and thrust out their fingers in accusation and judgement as they plummeted to the cold ground.

They buried their faces in shame and stole away from the glaring looks of what were once their companions and friends. They never rose again to make a second stand but slid silently into the Forest of Shadows to lesser occupations and ignominy, trying to forget the past and looking to see how best to occupy themselves now that their hopes had died. This forest eclipses all the former glories and victories of these once brave knights of the kingdom. It also hides the awesome light that they once had, in case another generation should rise and dare to be valiant also.

The history of former conquests and victories of a God-honoured nation lies buried likewise beneath these tall, foreboding trees, for should it ever come to light, it might stir up the dormant gift of manhood, courage and indignant boldness that the enemy has subtly suppressed in the young potentials of this wasted age.

But these past heroes are like dead men still living, for the only thing in life that ever gave them life was their joy and delight in serving the King, fighting his battles and championing his cause. Now they dare not raise their heads too high and only speak in whispered tones one to another, lest the sneering and despising beasts of Cynical City should mercilessly strike them down yet again.

But these were the valiant men of war, the champions and officers who were being trained and readied to save the nation and alter the future for coming generations. Some of them were schooled in wisdom and knowledge and could have revolutionised the thinking and hearts of men. Others were outrageous and fearless fighters who would have taken their stand courageously against the bloodthirsty hoards of Hades. Still others among them were skilled in the use of sword and shield and would be training up battalions of junior soldiers by now, had they not failed.

And of the Guardians, were those whose voices would pierce the darkness of evil, shake the ground with their orders and strike terror into all who dared to defy the King's commands. These men, these warrior hearts, these seers and prophets, all now despised and rejected by the crowds of spectators and self-conceited monks, had so much potential, so much extravagance and so much love for their Commander.

Their bones lie here and there, vague reminders of terrible conflicts and malicious gossip that rendered them ineffective and paralyzed their vocal chords.

To look upon them would be to say there is no hope, nay, not even a glimmer that might see them fulfil any useful role within the coming war; for just over the horizon a mighty army, armed to the teeth, is getting itself ready for conquering and savagery. With all the Warriors and Guardians despatched and out of the way, they have stirred themselves up confidently to wipe the ground with their stinking breath and defiantly fly their inglorious flags across this land of redemption.

The 'pretend' religious armies from foreign shores who make a lot of commotion both in singing, screaming, shouting and wailing, believe that they are match enough for this coming host; but all of their noise and clamour and none of their beautiful clothes and gold rings will cast any spell upon the rage of this enemy. Their intoxication with money, riches, success, wealth and scams has left them inebriated with covetousness and pride and quite unable to march to, let alone fight a holy war. They will all run back into their painted castles and hide behind their local captain-pastors and huddle together in fear and confusion, for they know not the art of war, neither the word or commands of the King; and this is not their land and not their fight, so they care less.

Can these bones live? Can these fallen heroes of faith ever rise again and save the day?

O ye dry bones, hear the word of the LORD!

"Behold I will cause breath to enter into you, and ye shall live!"

You who fell in the day; you who fell in the darkness of night; you who passed from life into death and stole away in shame from the field of conflict, hear the word of the LORD. You who were hated, despised and mocked, put to shame and thrust out from the family, there is a word for you yet. "I will lay sinews upon yo,u and will bring up flesh upon you, and cover you with skin, and put breath in you, and ye shall live; and ye shall know that I am the LORD." Ezekiel 37:6

You who once knew the glories of the King, who basked in His presence, who heard His voice, who loved His worship, who sang His praises, who rejoiced in all His goodness, who delighted to do His will, HEAR THE WORD OF THE LORD.

What is impossible to man, impossible to the church, impossible to the half-hearted professors of religion, impossible to the multi-millionaire pastor conmen, im-

possible even to reason, IS POSSIBLE WITH GOD!

Dry bones, hear the word of the LORD!

You may be dry, burnt by the heat of the scorching and parching sun, left dumped in the desert by your 'friends' to be devoured and torn by every wild beast of prey (Ezekiel 34:8), but you are not dead. God speaks to dry bones, not annihilated bones.

Already, right now, as you hear this word, bone is coming to bone. There is a noise and a shaking even as we speak, (Ezekiel 37:7). They may be stiff, they may be dry, they may be half-buried in the fast-sinking sands of time, but they are moving toward each other, looking for the connection, responding to the irresistible word of God. Retirement is over, strength will be imparted and never so much as now for this coming decisive battle.

Shout it from the roof tops! Prophesy it from the hills and mountains! Cry it in the cities, in the country, in the village and preach it throughout the land!

"Dry bones, hear the word of the LORD!

Let the Warriors and Guardians arise from the dust and live, live, live!" Thus saith the Lord GOD; "Come from the four winds, O breath, and breathe upon these slain, that they may live." 'Awake, O north wind; and come, thou south,' blow upon these that sigh in Zion. Come Thou holy wind of God and breath into us the breath of life. (Song of Solomon 4:16; Ezekiel 9:4)

Come Holy Spirit, we need Thee; Come sweet Spirit, I pray;
Come in Thy strength and Thy power;
Come in Thine own special way. *(Author uncertain)*

"Behold [look and wonder], O my people, I will open your graves, and cause you to come up out of your graves and bring you into the land of 'Salvation'.

And ye shall know that I am the LORD, when I have opened your graves, O my people, and brought you up out of your graves, and I shall put my Spirit in you, and ye shall live and I shall place you in your own land: then shall ye know that I the LORD have spoken it, and performed it," saith the LORD." (Ezekiel 37:12-14)

Breathe on me, breath of God,
Fill me with life anew,
That I may love what Thou dost love,
And do what Thou wouldst do.

Breathe on me, breath of God,
Until my heart is pure,
Until with Thee I will one will,
To do and to endure.

Breathe on me, breath of God,
Blend all my soul with Thine,
Until this earthly part of me
Glows with Thy fire divine.

Breathe on me, breath of God,
So shall I never die,
But live with Thee the perfect life
Of Thine eternity.

(Edwin Hatch, 1835-1889. Derby, England)

'**Rejoice not against me, O mine enemy: ....I shall arise**.' Micah 7:8. '**I will arise and go to my Father**.' Luke 15:18. '**The LORD is my light and my salvation; whom shall I fear? the LORD is the strength of my life; of**

whom shall I be afraid?' Psalm 27:1

Come, Warriors! Come, Guardians! Come, mighty army of the LORD.

Prepare for battle, for the Captain of the LORD of Hosts is with us and He it is that goes before us. (Joshua 5:13)

'I will go before thee and make the crooked places straight: I will break in pieces the gates of brass and cut in sunder the bars of iron.' Isaiah 45:2

'For mine Angel shall go before thee and bring thee in unto the Amorites and the Hittites and the Perizzites and the Canaanites, the Hivites and the Jebusites: and I will cut them off. Thou shalt not bow down to their gods, nor serve them, nor do after their works: but thou shalt utterly overthrow them and quite break down their images.' Exodus 23:23-24

'The LORD, he it is that doth go before thee; he will be with thee, he will not fail thee, neither forsake thee: fear not, neither be dismayed.' Deuteronomy 31:8

GLORIOUS MARTYRS OF CHRIST IN ENGLAND

Chapter Twenty Four

Glorious Martyrs Of Christ In England

The Guardians of former generations

Just look at these few brief accounts (taken from Foxes Book of Martyrs with some language revision for easier reading) of those believers who dared to stand for the liberty of the Gospel and the freedom of future generations, in case you ever think that your lot is hard and nobody has it as bad as you do:

Dr. Ridley and Hugh Latimer (former Bishop of Worcester)

They had opposed the corruption of the Roman Catholic priests and denied that the wine and bread became the literal blood and flesh of Jesus Christ during the 'Lord's Supper' (Breaking of Bread). The result was imprisonment and death by being burned alive.

The night before he was to die, Dr. Ridley had his beard washed and his legs; and as he sat at supper, the same night, at Master Irish's, (who was his keeper,) he invited his hostess and the rest at the table, to his 'marriage' (the burning); "for," said he, "tomorrow I must be married" and so showed himself to be as merry as ever he was at any time before. "Though my breakfast shall be somewhat sharp and painful, yet I am sure my supper (with the Lord) shall be more pleasant and sweet."

When they arose from the table, his brother offered to stay all night with him. But he said, "No no, that you shall not. For I wish (God willing) to go to bed and to sleep as quietly tonight, as ever I did in my life."

On the north side of the town, in the ditch over against Balliol college (Cambridge), the place of execution was appointed: and for fear of any opposition that might arise to stop the burning of them, the Lord Williams was commanded, by the queen's letters and the householders of the city, to be there to assist with as many officers as needed. And when every thing was made ready, the prisoners were brought forth by the mayor and the bailiffs.

Dr. Ridley, looking back, saw Master Latimer coming a little way behind, unto whom he said: "Oh, be ye there?"

"Yes," said Master Latimer, "I'm coming as fast as I can follow."

So he, following a distance off, at length they came both to the stake, the one after the other, where first Dr. Ridley entering the place, earnestly holding up both his hands, looked towards heaven.

Then shortly after seeing Master Latimer, with a wondrous cheerful look he ran to him, embraced him; and as they that stood near reported, he comforted him, saying: "Be of good heart, brother, for God will either quench the fury of the flame or else strengthen us to abide it."

With that he went to the stake, kneeled down by it, kissed it and effectually prayed and behind him Master Latimer kneeled, as earnestly calling upon God the same as Ridley. After they arose, they talked with one other a little while. What they said I can learn of no man.

Upon being asked to retract their statements and renounce their beliefs, Dr. Ridley exclaimed, "so long as the breath is in my body, I will never deny my Lord Christ and his known truth: God's will be done in me!"

And with that he rose up and said with a loud voice: "Well then, I commit our cause to Almighty God, who shall without exception judge all."

To this saying, Master Latimer added his voice, "Well! there is nothing hidden but it shall be exposed."

Then the smith took a chain of iron and tied the same about both Dr. Ridley's and Master Latimer's middle: and as he was knocking in a staple, Dr. Ridley took the chain in his hand and shook the same, for it was loose in his belly. Looking at the smith, he said: "Good fellow, knock it in hard, for the flesh will not hold it."

Then his brother did bring him gunpowder in a bag and would have tied the same about his neck. Master Ridley asked what it was. His brother said, "Gunpowder." "Then," said he, "I will take it to be sent of God; therefore I will receive it as sent of him. And have you any for my brother;" meaning Master Latimer. "Yes, sir, that I have," said his brother. "Then give it unto him now, in case you come back too late." So his brother went and fastened the same gunpowder unto Master Latimer.

Then they brought a bundle of sticks, aflame with fire and set the fire going at Dr. Ridley's feet. To whom Master Latimer spake in this manner: "Be of good comfort, Master Ridley and play the man. *We shall this day light such a candle, by God's grace, in England as I trust shall never be put out.*"

And so the fire was brought unto them. When Dr. Ridley saw the fire flaming up towards him. he cried with a wonderful loud voice: "Lord, Lord, receive my spirit;"

Master Latimer crying as vehemently on the other side: "O Father of heaven, receive my soul!" who received the flame as it were embracing of it. After that he had stroked his face with his hands and as it were bathed them a little in the fire, he soon died (as it appeared) with very little pain or none.

And thus ended the life of this old and blessed servant of God, Master Latimer, for whose laborious ministry, fruitful life and precious martyrdom, the whole realm of England hath great cause to give thanks to Almighty God.

But Master Ridley, by reason of the evil nature of the fire on his side, because the wooden bundles were laid on top of gorse and stacked too high, the fire burned first beneath, being kept down by the wood; which when he felt it, he desired them for Christ's sake to let the fire come unto him. Which when his brother-in-law heard, but did not really understand and so, intending to rid him out of his pain, he heaped even more wood upon him, so that he almost covered him.

This made the fire even more vicious beneath, that it burned clean all his lower body parts, before it once touched the upper; and that made him leap up and down under the wood and often desire them to let the fire come unto him, saying, "I cannot burn."

For, after his legs were consumed, because of his struggling through the pain, (whereof he had no release, but only his pleading to God,) he showed one side toward us clean, shirt and all untouched with flame.

Yet in all this torment he forgot not to call unto God still, speaking the words: "Lord, have mercy upon me," intermingling his cry: "Let the fire come unto me, I cannot burn." In such agony he laboured till one of those standing by with his hook pulled off the wood bundles above and where he saw the fire flame up, Ridley twisted himself unto that side. And when the flame touched the gunpowder, he was seen to stir no more, but burned on the other side, falling down at Master Latimer's feet.

It moved hundreds to tears in seeing the dreadful sight; for I think there was none without some humanity and mercy, who would not have lamented to see the fury of the fire raging upon their bodies.

But whoever considered their occupations in time past, the places of honour that they held in this commonwealth, the favour they were in with their princes and the opinion of learning they had in the university where they studied, could not help but weep, to see so great dignity, honour and estimation, such worthy men, so many godly virtues, the study of so many years, such excellent learning, to be put into the fire and consumed in one moment.

Well! dead they are and the reward of this world they have already. What reward remaineth for them in heaven, only the day of the Lord's glory, when he cometh with his saints, shall reveal.

"I beseech Thee, Lord God, take mercy upon this realm of England and deliver the same from all her enemies."

Prayer of Dr. Ridley before his murder in 1555.

Robert Lawson

'Robert Lawson was a single man of the age of thirty years and by vocation a linen-weaver, who was arrested in the night by one Robert Kereth, at the commandment of Sir John Tyrrel of Gipping-hall in Suffolk and so was immediately carried to Eye dungeon in Suffolk, where he remained a certain time and after was led to Bury, Lancashire.

The reason for his arrest was, that he would not go to church to hear mass and receive their popish idol (the sacrament, which states that they are drinking the real blood and eating the real flesh of Jesus).

There were three martyrs who were carried to their deaths that day, Roger Bernard, Adam Foster and this Robert Lawson. After they had made their prayer, being at the stake (a wooden stake to which they were chained and then burned alive) and their 'tormentors' stoking the fire, they most triumphantly ended their lives, in such a happy and blessed condition, showing their outstanding constancy and joyful end, to the great praise of God and their commendation in him and also to the encouragement of others in the same faith to do the same.

The Lord of strength fortify us to stand as his true soldiers in what standing soever he shall think it good to place us. Amen.'

John Careless

'He was a godly and humble man and made this confession of faith before going to the stake to die for Christ sake at the hand of those religious bigots. Look at his testimony as he was marched off to be burned alive:

Who ever saw such a thing? God became man and was crucified for me, that, by his death, I might live. Alas! that ever I should become so wicked a wretch and so unkind a, creature, to displease so loving, kind and merciful a God and Father.

Oh, forgive me! Forgive me for thy great mercy's sake, for thy truth and promise' sake and I will never trespass again against thy divine Majesty any more, but will gladly serve thee in true holiness and righteousness all the days of my life, by the grace and assistance of thy true and Holy Spirit: the which I beseech thee to give me also, that he may govern me and guide my heart in thy true faith, fear and love; that in all my works, words and thoughts, I may glorify thy holy name, who livest and reignest one God and three persons, to whom be all honour, glory, praise, thanks, power, rule and dominion, for ever and ever, Amen."

As he spake this, a servant of one of the bailiffs threw a bundle of sticks at his face, that the blood gushed out in many places: for the which fact the sheriff reviled him, calling him a cruel tormentor and with his walking-staff brake his head, that the blood likewise ran about his ears.'

Julius Palmer, John Gwin and Thomas Askin

'When the fire was kindled and began to take hold upon their bodies, they lifted up their hands towards heaven and quietly and cheerily, as though they had felt no pain, they cried: "Lord Jesus, strengthen us, Lord Jesus, assist us, Lord Jesus, receive our souls!"

And so they continued without any struggling, holding up their hands and knocking their hearts and calling upon

Jesus until they had ended their mortal lives. Among other things this is also to be noted, that after their three heads, by force of the raging and devouring flames of fire, were fallen together in a lump or cluster, which was marvellous to behold and that they all were judged already to have died, suddenly Julius Palmer, as a man waked out of sleep, moved his tongue and jaws and was heard to pronounce this word, "Jesus!"

So, being turned into ashes, he yielded to God as joyful a soul, (confirmed with the sweet promises of Christ) as any one that ever was called to suffer for his blessed name.

God grant us all to be moved with the like spirit, working in our hearts constantly to stand in defence and confession of Christ's holy gospel. Amen.'

Katharine Cawches, Guillemine Gilbert, Perotine Massey and an infant, the son of Massey

The time then being come, when these three good servants and holy saints of God, the innocent mother with her two daughters, should suffer, in the place where they should consummate their martyrdom were three stakes set up.

At the middle post was the mother, the eldest daughter on the right hand the youngest on the left. They were first strangled, but the rope brake before they were dead and so the poor women fell in the fire.

Perotine, who was then heavily pregnant, did fall on her side, where happened a dreadful sight, not only to the eyes of all that stood there watching, but also to the ears of all true-hearted Christians that shall ever read this history.

For as the belly of the woman burst asunder by the vehemence of the flame, the infant, being a fair man-child, fell into the fire and soon after being taken out of the fire by one W. House, was laid upon the grass.

Then the child was taken to the church official and from him to the bailiff, who gave orders that it should be carried back again and cast into the fire.

And so the infant, baptized in his own blood, to fill up the number of God's innocent saints, was both born and died a martyr, leaving behind to the world, which it never saw, a spectacle wherein the whole world may see the gross cruelty of this merciless mutation of catholic tormentors.

Near about the same time that these three women with the infant were burnt at Guernsey, three others suffered likewise at Grinstead in Sussex, two men and one woman; the names of whom were **Thomas Dungate,** John Foreman and **Mother Tree,** who for righteousness' sake gave themselves to death and torments of the fire, patiently abiding what the furious rage of man could say or work against them; at the said town of Grinstead ending their lives.

The burning and martyrdom of **Thomas Moor**, a simple innocent, in the town of Leicester.

As the bloody rage of this catholic persecution spared neither man, woman, nor child, wife nor maid, lame, blind, nor cripple; and so through all men and women, as there was no difference either of sex or age considered, so neither was there any condition or quality respected of any person.

Whosoever they were, that would not acknowledge the pope to be Christ's vicar and the 'sacrament of the altar', whether he were intellectual or unlearned, wise or simple innocent, all went to the fire, as may appear by this simple poor creature and innocent soul, named Thomas Moor.

He was retained as a servant to a man's house in the town of Leicester, about the age of twenty-four and who, for speaking certain words, declaring that his Maker was in heaven and not in the idols and church altar, was arrested in the country, whilst with his friends; who coming before his local priest, was first asked whether he believed his Maker (God) was there in front of him (pointing at the high altar): to which he said 'No', (the altar is not God, neither does He dwell there).He was therefore taken off and burned alive at the stake, but he giving thanks unto God.

The martyrdom of **Edward Sharp** at Bristol.

About the beginning of the next month following, which was September, a certain godly, aged, devout person and zealous of the Lord's glory, born in Wiltshire, named Edward Sharp, of the age of forty years or thereabout, was condemned at Bristol to the same martyrdom, where he, constantly and manfully persisting in the just quarrel of Christ's gospel, for disliking and renouncing the ordinances of the Roman Catholic church, was tried as pure gold and made a lively sacrifice in the fire: in whose death, as in the death of all his other saints, the Lord be glorified and thanked for his great grace of constancy; to whom be praise for ever, Amen.

Four who suffered at Mayfield, in Sussex.

Next after the martyrdom of Edward Sharp, above, followed four, which suffered at Mayfield, in Sussex, the twenty-fourth day of September, 1556; of whose names, two we find recorded and the other two we do not know and therefore, according to our register, the two names we know are John Hart, Thomas Ravensdale, a shoemaker and a leather worker. These four brave soldiers of Christ, being at the place where they should suffer, after they had made their prayer and were at the stake ready to abide the force of the fire, they constantly and joyfully yielded their lives for the testimony of the glorious gospel of Jesus Christ, unto whom be praise for ever and ever. Amen.

The day after the martyrdom of thcse four at Mayfield, which was the twenty-fifth of September, was a young man (which by trade was a carpenter, whose name we have not) put to death, for the same testimony of Jesus Christ, at Bristol, where he, yielding himself to the torments of the fire, gave up his life into the hands of the Lord, with such joyful constancy and triumph, as all the church of Christ have just cause to praise God for him.

The martyrdom of **John Horn and a woman, at Wootton-under-Edge**, in Gloucestershire.

Now not long after the death of the said young man at Bristol, in the same month were two more godly martyrs consumed by fire at Wootton-under-Edge, in Gloucestershire, whose names are above specified, which died very gloriously in a constant faith, to the terror of the wicked and comfort of the godly. So gloriously did the Lord work in them, that death unto them was life.

The burning of **Simon Miller** and **Elizabeth Cooper**, at Norwich.

This good woman being condemned and at the stake with Simon Miller, to be burnt, when the fire came unto her, she shrank a little at the pain, with a voice crying, "Hah!" Simon Miller heard her and put his hand behind him toward her and willed her to be strong and of good cheer: "for, good sister," said he, "we shall have a joyful and a sweet supper today (with Christ)": then she, being as it seemed thereby strengthened, stood as still and as quiet as one most glad to finish that good work which before most happily she had begun. So, in fact, she ended her life with her companion joyfully, committing her soul into the hands of Almighty God.

Rose Allin and her maid.

Rose, being imprisoned and tortured for her faith, her young maid had come with some ointment to treat her wounds.

'Then the cruel Roman Catholic Mr. Tyrrel, taking the candle from Rose Allin's maid, held Roses' wrist and the burning candle under her hand burning cross-wise over the back so long, till the very sinews cracked asunder.

During the time of his torturing, Mr. Tyrrell said often to her: "Why, whore! wilt thou not cry? Thou young whore! wilt thou not cry?" Unto which always she answered, that she had no reason, she thanked God, but would rather rejoice. He had, (she said), more cause to weep than her mistress, if he really thought about it.

In the end, when the sinews (as I said) brake, that all the

house heard them, he then thrust her from him violently and said: “Ah! strong whore; thou shameless beast! thou beastly whore!”, with such-like vile words. But she, quietly suffering his rage for the time, at the last said: “Sir, have you done all you will do?” And he said: “Yes and if thou think it be not good, then mend it.”

“Mend it?” said Rose: “nay, the Lord mend you and give you repentance, if it be his will. And now, if you think it so good, begin at the feet and burn to my head also. For he that inspired you to do this (the devil), shall pay you your wages one day, I warrant you.” And so her maid went and carried her mistress some drink, as she was commanded.

And this Rose Allin being prisoner, told a friend of hers this crucl act of Mr. Tyrrel; and showing him what happened she said: “While my one hand was a burning, I had a pot in my other hand and could easily have laid him on the face with it if I had wished; for no man held my hand to restrain me in the matter.”

Also being asked of another, how she could abide the painful burning of her hand she said, at first it was some grief to her, but afterward, the longer she burned, the less she felt, or well near none at all.

And because Mr. Tyrrel was not the only one who acted with such cruelty, you shall hear another similar example of a blind man's hand burnt by Bishop Bonner, as is proved by another testimony, who was a gentleman to the said bishop, who declared before credible witnesses what follows. Bishop Bonner, having this blind man before him, spake thus unto him: that such blind lowlifes which follow heretical preachers (referring to the true believers), when they come to the feeling of the fire, will be the first that will fly from it.

The blind man replied, that if every joint of him were burnt, yet he trusted in the Lord not to run away.

Then Bonner, signifying privately to certain of his men about him what they should do, they brought to him a burning coal; which coal being put into the poor man's hand they closed it fast again and so was his hand dreadfully burnt.

Seven more beautiful souls martyred

The second day of August, 1557, between six and seven o'clock in the morning, William Bongeor, William Purcas, Thomas Benold, Agnes Silverside, Smith, Helen Ewring and Elizabeth Folkes, were brought from Mote hall unto a piece of ground hard by the town-wall of Colchester, on the outward side.

They being there and all things prepared for their martyrdom, at the last these faithful martyrs kneeled down and made their humble prayers to God; but not in such a way as they would, for the cruel tyrants would not allow them; especially one Master Clere, among the rest, (who once had been an evangelist), showed himself very violent unto them all: the Lord give him repentance, if it be his good will and grace to be a better man!

When they had made their prayers, they rose and made them ready for the fire. And Elizabeth Folkes, when she had plucked off her petticoat, would have given it to her mother, (who came and kissed her at the stake and exhorted her to be strong in the Lord,) but the wicked persecutors would not suffer her to give it. Therefore, taking the said petticoat in her hand she threw it away from her, saying: "Farewell, all the world! farewell faith! farewell hope!" and so taking the stake in her hand said, "Welcome love!".

Now she, being at the stake and one of the officers nailing the chain about her, in the striking of the staple he missed the place and struck her with a great stroke of the hammer on the shoulder-bone; at which she suddenly turned her head, lifting up her eyes to the Lord and prayed, smilingly and gave herself to encouraging the people again to trust God.

When all the six were also nailed likewise at their stakes and the fire was started about them, they clapped their hands for joy in the flames, so much so, that the standers-by, which were, by estimation, thousands, virtually all cried out: "The Lord strengthen them; the Lord comfort them; the Lord pour his mercies upon them," with suchlike words as was wonderful to hear.

And so they yielded up their souls and bodies into the Lord's hands, for the true testimony of his truth.

The Lord grant we may imitate the same under the same or similar circumstances, (if he so vouch us worthy,) for his mercy's sake. Amen.

Ten more souls murdered by the Romish priests

On one day, were brought forth into the castle-yard, to a place appointed for burning, William Mount, John Johnson, Alice Mount and Rose Allin (mentioned before): which godly constant persons, after they had made their prayers and were joyfully tied to the stakes, calling upon the name of God and exhorting the people earnestly to flee from idolatry, suffered their martyrdom with such triumph and joy, that the people looking did shout when they saw it.

That day ten souls glorious were burned, their happy lives released unto the Lord, whose ages all did grow to the sum of four hundred and six years, or thereabouts.

The Lord grant we may well spend our years and days, likewise, to his glory. Amen.

George Eagles

George Eagles was hanged for his faith, but after he had hanged a small time, having a great check with the halter (rope), immediately one of the bailiffs cut the halter asunder and he fell to the ground being still alive, although much amazed with the check he had off the ladder.

Then one man, William Swallow of Chelmsford, a bailiff, did draw him off to the sled that he was dragged on originally and laid his neck thereon and with a cleaver (such as is occupied in many men's kitchens and blunt) did hackle off his head and sometimes hit his neck and sometimes his chin and did foully mangle him and so opened him up.

Nevertheless, this blessed martyr of Christ abode constant in the very midst of his torments, till such time as this tormentor William Swallow did rip the heart out of his body.

The body being divided in four parts and his bowels burnt, was brought later to William Swallow's door and there laid upon the fish-stalls before his door, till they had made ready a horse to carry his quarters, one to Colchester and the rest to Harwich, Chelmsford and St. Osyth's. His head was set up at Chelmsford on the market-cross, on a long pole and there stood, till the wind did blow it down; and lying certain days in the street tumbled about, until some-one caused it to be buried in the church-yard in the night.

Cicely Ormes

Cicely Ormes was a very simple woman, but yet zealous in the Lord's cause, being born in East Dereham and was there the daughter of one Thomas Haund, a tailor.

Hear her stand for Christ and the gospel: "Good people! I believe in God the Father, God the Son and God the Holy Ghost, three persons and one God. But I recant utterly from the bottom of my heart the doings of the pope of Rome and all his popish priests and servants. I utterly refuse and never will have to do with them again, by God's grace. And good people! I would you should not think of me that I believe to be saved in that I offer myself here unto the death for the Lord's cause, but I believe to be saved by the death and passion of Christ; and this my death is and shall be a witness of my faith unto you all here present. Good people! as many of you as believe as I believe, pray for me."

Then she came to the stake and laid her hand on it and said: "Welcome the cross of Christ." Which being done, she, looking on her hand and seeing it blacked with the stake, wiped it upon her smock; for she was burnt at the same stake that Simon Miller and Elizabeth Cooper was burnt at. Then, after she had touched it with her hand she came and kissed it and said: "Welcome the sweet cross of Christ;" and so gave herself to be bound ready.

After the tormentors had kindled the fire to her, she

said:"My soul doth magnify the Lord and my spirit rejoiceth in God my Saviour." And in so saying, she set her hands together right against her breast, casting her eyes and head upward; and so stood, heaving up her hands by little and little, till the very sinews of her arms did break asunder and then they fell. But she yielded her life unto the Lord as quietly as if she had been in a slumber, or as one feeling no pain; so wonderfully did the Lord work with her: His name therefore be praised for evermore. Amen!

Young Will Fetty, eight years old and his father

John Fetty had lain in the prison by the space of fifteen days, hanging in the stocks, sometimes by the one leg, or the one arm, sometimes by the other and other times by both, it happened that one of his children, (a boy of the age of eight or nine years,) came unto the bishop's house, to see if he could get leave to speak with his father.

At his calling, one of the bishop's chaplains met with him and asked him what he wanted and whom he would see. The child answered, that he came to see his father. The chaplain asked again, who was his father. The boy then told him and pointing towards Lollards' Tower, showed him that his father was there in prison. "Why," said the priest, "your father is a heretic."

The child, being of a bold and quick spirit and also godly brought up and instructed by his father in the knowledge of God, answered and said: "My father is no heretic; for you have Balaam's mark."

With that the priest took the child by the hand and carried him into the bishop's house, (whether to the bishop or not,

I know not, but quite likely he did) and there, amongst them, they did most shamefully and without any pity so whip and scourge, being naked, this tender child, that he was all in a gore-blood (like mincemeat).

Then, in mockery and bragging of their catholic tyranny, they caused Cluney (the bishop's servant), having his coat upon his arm, to carry the child in his shirt unto his father being in prison, the blood running down by his heels.

At his coming unto his father the child fell down upon his knees and asked his blessing. The poor man then beholding his son and seeing him so cruelly beaten and wounded, cried out for sorrow and said: "Alas, Will! who has done this to you?" The boy answered, that as he was seeking how to come to see his father, a priest with Balaam's mark took him into the bishop's house and there was he so handled.

Cluney then violently plucked the child away out of his father's hands and carried him back again into the bishop's house, where they kept him a further three days. After fourteen days the child died.

John Whitman of RYE, Sussex

Whilst on a trip to Ostend, he challenged the priest over idol worship and dared to contradict him.

The next day, being Tuesday, he was brought out again before the judges into the same place. And being examined as before, he refused to retract his beliefs, but increased in his affirmation: and so sentence was given upon him to have his hand cut off and his body scorched to death and after to be hanged up.

So the day following, being Wednesday, he was brought out of prison to the town-hall, standing in the market-place, all things belonging to execution being made ready there; which when they were all set, the hangman went into the hall and with a cord tied the hands of Whitman and came out leading him with it.

So as soon as Whitman was out of the house, he made such haste and as it were, ran to the place of execution, so that he dragged the hangman after him.

There was a post set up with spars from the top of it, a slope down to the ground, like a tent, to the end that he should be only slowly scorched to death and not burned quickly.

When he was come to the place, the hangman commanded him to lay down his right hand upon a block, which he immediately with a hatchet smote off.

The good man still continuing in prayer faithfully, the hangman stepped behind him and bid him put out his tongue, which he did, as far as he could out of his mouth, through the which he thrust a long instrument like a pack-needle and so left it there.

Then the judges, standing by in the common-hall, read again his charge and sentence. But he could make no answer, his tongue hanging out of his head: so he was stripped out of his cassock, his clothes being put off in prison and put inside the tent and made secure with two chains; and fire was put round about, which broiled and scorched his body most miserably, all black, he not being seen, but heard to make a noise within the tent.

When he was dead, he was carried out to be hanged upon

a gibbet beside the town. He is in the presence of God and his blood still cries from the ground to heaven above.

I have listed but a small and glorious roll-call of names from the multitudes of Christian believers who suffered and died at the hands of the Roman Catholic Church just here from this precious English soil (let alone elsewhere in Scotland, Wales, Ireland and Europe).

These truly were among the Guardians of the faith in previous centuries that made the ultimate sacrifice for God and for the certainty of future generations in this nation and throughout the world.

Their blood was the seed of the church that would birth a harvest of souls across every continent upon earth. You can slaughter one and ten will rise in his or her place. Nay, a thousand. Yea, even one hundred thousand shall be birthed from such noble blood.

You and I have the truth today because of these wonderful servants of God.

It is time for the Guardians in this generation to rise. Our country faces just as great, if not greater evils than did they in their day.

I vow to thee, my country - all earthly things above
Entire and whole and perfect, the service of my love;
The love that asks no question, the love that stands the test,
That lays upon the altar the dearest and the best;
The love that never falters, the love that pays the price,
The love that makes undaunted the final sacrifice.

And there's another country, I've heard of long ago
Most dear to them that love her, most great to them that know;
We may not count her armles, we may not see her King;
Her fortress is a faithful heart, her pride is suffering;
And soul by soul and silently her shining bounds increase,
And her ways are ways of gentleness and all her paths are peace.

By Cecil Arthur Spring-Rice (1859-1918)
British Chargé d'Affaires in Tehran in 1900

THE CROWN FLAG

Chapter Twenty Five

The Crown Flag

I have spoken of the 'Crown Flag' in this book and I shall just mention how it came about and how we first used it.

There were five ministers from various backgrounds meeting with some others at a special Bible study every Monday and Friday evening. We just opened the Scriptures and searched out the truth and God revealed and opened up astonishing insight to us.

A powerful move of God graciously took place during those times, resulting in awesome encounters in the holy Presence. At the end of what sometimes would be a two-to-three hour study, we would begin to wait on God.

"Often we would be standing in honour and awe of His majestic Person for periods that seemed to be timeless. It was as though we had been summoned to appear at the counsel of witnesses as spoken of in Hebrews 12.

We had come to Mount Zion, the City of the Living God, the General Assembly and Church of the Firstborn, to an innumerable number of angels and the Counsel Chambers of God. It was in this holy place that we saw a great many seats as if set out around the chamber of the Kings court. Each seat was set apart for those who were called and it was required that we appear before this great King to receive instructions and give our progress reports each one.

Our names were placed in front of our seats and it seemed that each time we met, if one on us were absent, there was a demand as to why we had not appeared.

This is where we were to receive our commission and charges. This is where they return from the battle-field to report their accomplishments and hear the King's strategy for the next advance.

It did not matter in the least whether anyone else in the whole world knew who we were or what our commission. We only knew that this is where the mysteries of the work of the Kingdom are truly carried out, for this Kingdom cometh not with observation, but worketh mightily in the realms of the Spirit. For we wrestle not against flesh and blood, for our warfare is with those powers and principalities that cannot be fought with intellect or muscle, but only in the power of the Holy Spirit and in the Name of the God of Jacob." ('The LORD hear thee in the day of trouble; the name of the God of Jacob defend thee.' Psalm 20:1)

'Unto you it is given to know the mysteries of the kingdom of God: but to others in parables; that seeing they might not see and hearing they might not understand.' Luke 8:10

'Let a man so account of us, as of the ministers of Christ and stewards of the mysteries of God.' 1Corinthians 4:1

'We speak the wisdom of God in a mystery, even the hidden wisdom, which God ordained before the world unto our glory.' 1Corinthians 2:7

"Our names were not important 'out there', for we serve the King of kings and we work without explanation and do what we do because He tells us to. Our answer is to Him alone and it is of no consequence what others may think of our hopes and joys.

The King enters the great chamber and we rise to stand and give Him honour and glory, wisdom and might, majesty and praise.

We stand our heads bowed, the court now hushed to a silence, our breath taken away at the sheer honour of being permitted, nay, I say, personally invited to this most reverent place. We dare not move, in fact we wish not to move, but are held rooted in godly fear and a dreadful desire to just drink and drink of this glorious moment.

And time stands still. And we have no words to speak and even if we did, no words could ever express the incomprehensible sight our eyes behold."

No wonder David cried, "My soul LONGETH, yea, even fainteth for the courts of the Lord," (Ps. 84 v 2)

"It was in this hallowed place that God first gave the vision of the church rising up across the world with the Crown Flag standard. This is where the flag was revealed and birthed. This flag was all about honour and wherever His servants stand with this banner they give Jesus honour and praise. They declare the excellence of our mighty warrior King and His soon return and herald the majesty and power of His kingdom.

The vision of the flag and its purpose was first imparted and drawn out at the table where we sat to study. One Friday night as we were waiting on God, the vision was given to one of the ministers at the table. And it was from this very place that we would so often walk out to carry that royal standard to some place where God's Spirit would direct us and then stand in the authority of the King and give honour to Christ. It seemed that just standing with the flag was sufficient to draw the smile of approval from heaven and bring fear and terror to the camp of the enemy. Wherever we stood with the flag it brought immediate attention and curiosity. People seemed drawn to the flag unexplainably. Vehicles would slow down and stop with the drivers or passengers asking what the flag was. Christians would run over to tell us that they knew what this flag was about, commenting on how awesome it was!"

"We could not explain the effect the flag was having apart from the fact that God was the imparter of the vision for it and He himself was honouring our raising of this ensign for His glory. We thought very much about that verse in Isaiah 62 v10, where the prophet says, 'Go through, go through the gates: prepare ye the way of the people: ....lift up a standard (flag) for the people.' In fact, just a few weeks later a senior pastor in Coventry was shown the Crown Flag. He looked at it and said, "I have already seen that." This did not make any sense, as the only people who knew about it were this small group of ministers!

On being asked how he could possibly know anything about it he told us that just three weeks earlier he had been in a minister's conference waiting on God. During that anointed session God had given him a vision of the church rising across the world with a great banner! He said that the Crown Flag was the very flag which he had seen!'

It was in this same place where they were meeting that God imparted the plan to secure their town with the authority of His kingdom.

"We were to place certain scriptures (the Crown Flag Declaration, sealed in a waterproof packet) around the base of 6 feet long wooden stakes and hammer them into the ground at the side of each road that enters and exits the perimeter of the town."

So early one Sunday morning around the time of the sun arising, the five of us took 9 stakes, some blue cord and a huge sledgehammer and buried those stakes into the ground, leaving three feet of the wood exposed. We then tied a three-fold blue nylon cord to the top of the stake and stretched it back away from the town anchoring it to the ground with a smaller wooden stake. This, to us, symbolised the stretching of a canopy over the town as in Isaiah 54:2 and 'lengthening our cords and strengthening our stakes'. The three strand blue cord symbolised a three-fold cord which 'cannot be easily broken'.

After doing each one we declared aloud the Crown Flag Declaration at each place which we now call a 'Prayer Gate'.

The Crown Flag Declaration

A sound of battle is in the land!

The time is fulfilled and the kingdom of God is at hand.

Repent and believe the gospel.

All this assembly shall know that the Lord saves not with sword and spear: for the battle is the Lord's and He will give you into our hands.

Lift up your heads, O ye gates; and be ye lift up, ye everlasting doors; and the King of Glory shall come in.

Who is this king of glory?

The Lord strong and mighty, the Lord mighty in battle.

Lift up your heads, O ye gates; even lift them up, ye everlasting doors; and the king of Glory shall come in.

Who is this King of Glory?

The Lord of hosts, He is the King of Glory.

This is the generation of them that seek Him, that seek thy face, O Jacob.

Open the gates that the righteous nation, which keeps the truth, may enter in.

LET THY KINGDOM COME, LET THY WILL BE DONE,

IN MY LIFE, IN MY FAMILY,

IN THIS TOWN,

IN THIS NATION,

in all the earth, as it is done in Heaven.

We encircled the entire town and declared that the Kingdom of God was at hand.

Every day for the next eighteen months each one of us would go to pray at least once a day at our designated gates. Sometimes we would as individuals, or together prayer-walk the whole circumference of the map which we had marked out with boundaries and key prayer points (see back cover). This map we all carried and used extensively. A visiting minister from America who was overjoyed and amazed at seeing the flag, asked us why this town? We said we did not know really, but just that this is where God had placed us at that time.

We would target key places for special prayer and mark places where teenagers gathered, for extra prayer. We placed the same Scriptures in the school grounds of seven teaching establishments and even took the Declaration and buried it in the cemetery where many youngsters would hang out in the dark of night amongst the dead, drinking and smoking because they had nothing better to do!

It was like sowing the seed, the word of truth for the present generation and generations yet to come. Nothing we did was done 'lightly', but everything was born and nurtured in prayer.

We launched a special evangelism campaign throughout the area and delivered the Gospel to every one of the 10,000 homes in the town.

Over the period of eighteen months of praying round the town, we saw crime reduced by 50% (government statistics), drug dealers captured, no serious vehicle accidents, nightclubs and drinking houses lose half of their clientele and the Gospel impact the entire area with outstanding results.

We walked in the authority of the kingdom and began to realize something of who we were in Christ and why one day this world will see and acknowledge the true sons of God and the influence they exerted whilst they walked this earth.

This flag flies in different places around the world right now and perhaps it will be raised in your hometown before long either doing battle secretly over the fields, or flying as a witness and testimony on the streets.

'So shall they fear the name of the LORD from the west and his glory from the rising of the sun. When the enemy shall come in like a flood, the Spirit of the LORD **shall lift up a standard [a flag, an ensign] against him.**' Isaiah 59:19.

'Go through, go through the gates; prepare ye the way of the people; cast up, cast up the highway; gather out the stones; **lift up a standard [a flag, an ensign] for the people**.' Isaiah 62:10

WHERE WERE YOU?

Chapter Twenty Six

Where Were You?

Mr. Justice Ouseley (a High Court judge) ruled today that councils throughout England do not need to say prayers before their official meetings in future. He went even further in saying that it was unlawful to allow prayers to be said before such meetings, despite the fact that this has been the practice since Elizabethan times.

This came about through the insistence and 'jerkish' agitations of a local councillor in Bideford, North Devon. He, Clive Bone, is an atheist and felt somewhat intimidated having to sit in at 'prayer-time' before proceeding with the day's agendas. He joined with the National Secular Society (another organization who are terrified of Christians) to oppose the practise. It seemed to upset him that people cared enough to apply to God for wisdom and help in the matters of running the local government. He obviously felt that he was more than adequate to run everything himself without divine assistance. Perhaps that is why he is no longer a councillor!

'The fool hath said in his heart there is no God.' And only a hell-bent half-wit would seek to prevent people from praying, especially when our nation faces so much social and economic turmoil. He must indeed be quite the fool, and judging by the number of comments from around the populace, many people consider him a bitter and twisted man who seems to be on the side of all those who wish to demolish everything that once made this nation great.

Who was it that failed to stand in the gap when this wretched heathen marched against our heritage with his soul-damning demands? Evil can only march in where the warriors have vacated their positions.

Where were you and where was I when this attack on our liberties and Christian freedoms took place? What was it that kept us back from the battlefield, from making up the breach in our defences?

What exactly were we doing when the devil came to trample over another piece of our Christian heritage and future blessedness?

Why were we not out across the fields, walking down the streets, up on the roof interceding for, and protecting this land? We do not always need to know everything that is going on in order to be effective in our prayer. We just have to be in the right place and stand there with the sword of God's deliverance raised defiantly in our hands.

Was sin and temptation at your door, enticing you with all her wares? Were you so preoccupied with the mundane and trivial things of this world, that you forgot the need to take time and stand in the gap to defend your people?

Was it the television, the DVD, the internet or some other tool of Satan that kept you away from the fight?

Did the lust of the flesh, the cravings of your body and mind drug you sufficiently to surrender your promise to God to pray for your country daily?

I tell you, we are where we are as a nation because the Warriors and Guardians of the truth are lazy, indifferent, unconcerned, and simply criminal in the abandoning of their posts.

God forgive us!

Our children and future generations are being intoxicated and murdered by the devil himself whilst we play with his vices and time-absorbing sidetracks.

The battle rages day and night and your presence on the field really can make a difference.

You wonder why so much evil besets us and why the antagonists and anti-Christ protestors gain the upper hand? It is because we do not take the welfare of our people to heart and do not believe that our national security and freedoms depend on us doing our duty and obeying the Lord. Of course, if we have no care for our nation or our heritage, then nothing will inspire us to fight. If we do not love the people in front of our eyes then we will not move ourselves an effectual inch to pray for them.

If we do not believe that God can and will do something when we step out and obey him, especially when we do not feel like it, then we shall die in our apathy; and our nation will die along with us.

But be sure of this, there is a day of accounting coming when you and I will explain to God why it was we sat at home rotting in fool's comfort and laziness instead of going out and tearing down the enemy's citadels of rebellion.

The judge and the atheist could not have had any success in the matter mentioned earlier if it were not for the fact that a Warrior or a Guardian were absent from their post. The security and welfare of this nation, along with all of its populace, is dependant upon the faithfulness, diligence, persevering prayer and concern of such servants of God.

'Love not the world, neither the things that are in the world. If any man love the world, the love of the Father is not in him. For all that is in the world, the lust of the flesh, and the lust of the eyes, and the pride of life, is not of the Father, but is of the world. And the world passeth away, and the lust thereof: but he that doeth the will of God abideth for ever.' 1John 2:15-17

It is time for us to get serious about who we are in Christ and the authority and influence that we can exercise here in this world. They may indeed have stopped some councils from praying, but this should just cause an army of warriors to rise up and pray in the fields and in the streets of all our towns and cities. Let the corrupt local officials come under the searching light of God and have their wicked lives and secret practices revealed before all.

They are only scared of Christianity because it carries the very light that will expose all of the corruption, greed and deceit within our town halls and government.

If they will not allow prayers inside the council chambers, then let a Warrior stand outside the building and call upon the name of God to bring down the citadels of secularism and avarice, and purge out these hostile enemies who lord it over the people.

God will give our enemies into our hands, and all the community will see and acknowledge that the Lord delivers not with sword or spear, and He will give them what they deserve. (1Samuel 17:47)

It is time to arise and take the land back which has been stolen from us. It is time to cast down the imaginations that are set against God's own people. It is time to pull down the plans that evil men make to rid our land of the Gospel of Jesus Christ.

So, make a choice today; come to a solid decision:

Stay as you are - and die. Or get up, stir yourself and do something amazing for God, and for your country!

'And I sought for a man among them,
that should make up the hedge,
and stand in the gap before me for the land
that I should not destroy it....'
Ezekiel 22:30

EXPOSITION of Psalm 106:23 - SPURGEON (revised)

'They forgat God their saviour, which had done great things in Egypt; ....therefore he said that he would destroy them, had not Moses his chosen stood before him in the breach, to turn away his wrath, lest he should destroy them.' Psalm 106:23

God's people had defiantly continued in their sin. Therefore God said that he would destroy them (the Israelites). The threats of judgment and destruction came at last. For their first sin in the wilderness he chastened them, sending leanness [hardship] into their soul; for the second he weeded out the offenders, the flame burned up the wicked; for the third he threatened to destroy them; for the fourth he lifted up his hand and almost came to blows (Psalm 106:26); for the fifth he actually smote them, 'and the plague brake in among them'; and **so the punishment increased with their perpetuation in sin**. This is worth noting, and it should serve as a warning to the man who carries on in his iniquities. God sends words and warnings before he comes to blows, 'he said that he would destroy them': but his words are not to be trifled with, for he means what he says, and he has power to bring them to pass.

'Had not Moses his chosen stood before him in the breach.' **Like a bold warrior who defends the wall when there is an opening for the adversary, and destruction is rushing in upon the city, Moses stopped the way of avenging justice with his prayers**. Moses had great power with God. He was an eminent type of our Lord, who is called, as Moses here is styled, 'mine elect, in whom my soul delighteth.' As the Elect Redeemer Christ Jesus interposed between the Lord and a sinful world, so did Moses stand between the Lord and his offending and sinning people. The story as told by Moses himself is full of interest and instruction, and greatly magnifies the goodness of the Lord, who graciously turned from the fierceness of his anger.

With disinterested affection, and generous renunciation of privileges offered to himself and his family, the great Lawgiver (Moses) interceded with the Lord to turn away his wrath, lest God should destroy them. See here the power of a righteous man's intercession. **Mighty as was the sin of Israel to provoke God's vengeance, prayer was mightier in turning it away**. How diligently should we plead with the Lord for this guilty world, and especially for his own backsliding people!

Who would not employ so powerful an agency for so gracious an outcome? The Lord still listens to the voice of a man. Shall not our voices be often exercised in praying for a guilty people?

EXPLANATORY NOTES AND QUAINT SAYINGS.

Psalm 106:23: Moses his chosen stood before him in the breach. Moses stood in the gap, and diverted the wrath of God. The hedge of religion and worship was broken down by a golden calf, and he repaired it.

Numbers 16:41-42: the people murmured, rose up against Moses and Aaron, trod down the hedge of authority, and therefore the plague brake in upon them; then Aaron steps into the gap, makes up the hedge, and stops the plague (Numbers 16:47-48).

That which they these two did was honourable; and they were repairers of breaches (Isaiah 58:12). We, through infinite mercy, have had from time to time some Guardians like Moses and Aaron, to make up our hedges, raise up our foundations, and stop some gaps; **but all our gaps are not yet stopped**.

Are there not gaps in the hedge of doctrine? If it were not so, how come there are such false, blasphemous, and disgraceful teachings in the churches? Are there not gaps in the hedges of civil and governmental authority? Do not multitudes trample upon our laws and ministry, all authorities, both human and divine? Are there not gaps in the worship of God? Do not so very many tread down all Christianity, all good practises, yea, the very Scriptures also? Are there not gaps in the hedge of justice, through which the criminals, terrorists, and scammers enter, which oppress the poor, and crush the needy? Amos 4:1

Are there not gaps in the hedge of love; is not that bond of perfection completely broken down throughout our society? Are there not bitter envyings and strife amongst us; do we not bite and devour one another? Are there not gaps in the hedge of conscience? Is not the peace broken between God and your souls? Does not Satan come in far too often at the gap, and disturb you? Are there not gaps also in your personal relationships, whereby he gets advantage? Surely, if we have eyes in our heads, we may see gaps enough. — (William Greenhill)

'The breach.' This is a metaphor taken from a city which is besieged, and in the walls of which the enemy having made a 'breach' is just entering in, to destroy it, unless he is driven back by some valiant warrior. Moses stood, as it were 'in the breach,' and averted the wrath of God, when he was just going to destroy the Israelites. See Exodus 32:1-35. — (Thomas Fenton)

If Christians could be brought to understand the value and power of intercessory prayer, surely it would abound on every side. It is a terrible reproof against the lying prophets of Ezekiel's time: 'Ye have not gone up into the gaps, neither made up the hedge for the house of Israel to stand in the battle in the day of the Lord.' (Ezekiel 13:5). Compare Exodus 32:9-14. — (William S. Plumer)

And it is a terrible reproof on the lying prophets and false teachers of today who only talk of wealth and prosperity, and make the gaps of destruction wider through their pride and arrogance, infuriating God even more.

It is time to return to God, get serious about prayer, and stand in the gap for our loved ones, our people and our nation.

'And they that shall be of thee shall build the old waste places: thou shalt raise up the foundations of many generations; and thou shalt be called, The repairer of the breach,

The restorer of paths to dwell in. If thou turn away thy foot from the sabbath, from doing thy pleasure on my holy day; and call the sabbath a delight, the holy of the LORD, honourable; and shalt honour him, not doing thine own ways, nor finding thine own pleasure, nor speaking thine own words.' Isaiah 58:12-13

'Behold, the LORD'S hand is not shortened, that it cannot save; neither his ear heavy, that it cannot hear: But your iniquities have separated between you and your God, and your sins have hid his face from you, that he **will not** hear.' Isaiah 59:1

Suggested reading for anyone who sincerely wants to learn sound doctrine and inspire themselves with the pioneering spirit of the missionaries.

Teaching:

King James Authorised Version Bible

Strong's Exhaustive Concordance: (KJV) This amazing and huge volume gives the Hebrew or Greek meaning for every single word in the Bible. A powerful piece of equipment for every minister of truth and really leaves no excuse for not being able to understand the KJV Bible. It lists every single word in the entire KJV Bible.

Dr. James Strong took 45 years to compile and write this phenomenal tool with the help of over 100 colleagues. It continues to be one of the most useful Bible helps available.

Confession of Faith: by A A Hodge (Banner of Truth)
The doctrine of the church of Jesus Christ. This is a must for all serious Bible students. Do not worry too much about the section on Infant Baptism, although I think that there may still be great merit in this practise within the Church of England insomuch as it brings a sense of accountability upon parents and at least an acknowledgement of God and His ways, particularly among those outside of the kingdom who do not even attend church regularly. Who knows, but this particular 'celebration' of a child might be the means of drawing the whole family to Christ in days to come. At the very least it establishes the Christian principals and the name of Jesus Christ amongst the inhabitants of this now utterly godless nation. I do not say that it makes the child a Christian. In independent churches and all other Protestant denominations, the act of 'Dedication' should be offered to all in their local community as being a way to build bridges and share the Gospel with the unsaved. It also helps to bring the national and historical faith of this nation back into focus and back into the mindset of the population. In these tricky times it might well serve to create a sense of cultural and historical identity especially for the younger generation and our children, before we lose all sight of who we really are as a people.

Old Paths: J C Ryle

Holiness: J C Ryle

Expository thoughts on the Gospels: J C Ryle

Psalms: (The Throne of David), Spurgeon. A concise paperback is available, or the full uncondensed set of volumes as the original work.

Matthew Henry: Full Commentary (Spurgeon would tell his young men that if they did not have a copy, to go sell their coat and get one). You can buy the single concise volume, or better yet, get the full set which contains far more commentary along with the Scripture text.
Online: http://www.ccel.org/ccel/henry/mhc.i.html

Foxes Book of Martyrs

(All these books are available from Metropolitan Tabernacle Bookshop, London, UK)

Inspirational books:

The Flaming Tongue. Edwin Orr

Rees Howell – Intercessor. Norman Grubb

Search for biographies of:

Hudson Taylor

C T Studd

William Carey

David Livingstone

Henry Martin

George Muller

William Cameron Townsend

John Williams

William Booth

John and Charles Wesley

William Carey

George Whitfield

Mary Slessor